GOLD IN THE SUN

Volume Five of a Series
on the Historic Birthplace of California

THE HISTORY OF SAN DIEGO

IN THE SUN

Written by
RICHARD F. POURADE

EDITOR EMERITUS, THE SAN DIEGO UNION

Commissioned by
JAMES S. COPLEY

CHAIRMAN OF THE CORPORATION, THE COPLEY PRESS, INC.

Published By The Union-Tribune Publishing Company

PREVIOUS BOOKS

"The Explorers," published 1960
"Time of the Bells," published 1961
"The Silver Dons," published 1963
"The Glory Years," published 1964

CONTENTS

MAJOR ILLUSTRATIONS

DEDICATION

Although rich in historical past, the Southwestern corner of the United States of America and the northern areas of Mexico's Baja California could only be considered to be in swaddling clothes at the dawn of the 20th century.

The areas centering on San Francisco and Los Angeles had prospered through transportation, commerce and communications while the first scenes of discovery were geographically isolated as history's pages turned to 1900.

Then came improved highways to the north and to the east, rapid communications, diversion of the Colorado River water to create an agricultural empire in the Imperial Valleys of California and Mexico, the automobile, aviation, the United States Navy and an awakening interest in the ideal climate of the territory.

And so it came about, in the span of the 20 years of reporting in this, the fifth volume in a series of histories, that a new discovery was made in the potentials of a vast geographical area in which San Diego shines as the "Harbor of the Sun."

JAMES S. COPLEY

TOM GOULD

Southern California was a land different from the rest of the United States and from 1900 on an argument raged as to whether smokestacks or geraniums should come first, or if it could have both and still have the way of life sought by so many in the great westward migrations.

AN INTRODUCTION

The imagination of people of the Sixteenth Century was captivated by an account of a fictional island lying at the right hand of the Indies and very close to the terrestial Paradise, and it took such a hold that even Cortez thought he might have found it when he landed on the peninsula of Baja California.

The captains and missionaries who succeeded Cortez in the explorations of the Pacific Coast may have forgotten the story, even if they had ever heard of it, but all of them who reached the coastal area of what is now Southern California were aware they were looking upon a favored land.

The first to come, Juan Rodríguez Cabrillo, noted the abundance of grass and game and saw that the natives went about wearing very little clothing to protect them from the weather. More than 200 years later the engineer Miguel Costansó, with the Royal Spanish Expedition sent to settle California, wrote of the sweet-smelling plants, the rosemary and sage, and the profusion of wild grapes and the pretty little pale-pink roses which reminded him so much of Old Castile.

Father Junípero Serra himself, after his arduous journey up through Baja California to San Diego, found "it is beautiful to behold and does not belie its reputation."

The traders and ranchers who followed the soldiers and the missionaries established a pastoral life possible only in a land kind to the indolent and beguiling to the innocent. Before they knew it, they were citizens of the United States, by force of arms or apprehensive acquiescence.

It wasn't long before millions of persons were made aware of the benevolent climate and waiting soil of Southern California and the rush was under way.

Their experiences have been related in previous volumes of a historical series centered on the birthplace of Western civilization on the Pacific Coast. The previous books have been THE EXPLORERS, on the period of settlement; TIME OF THE BELLS, the story of mission and presidio life; THE SILVER DONS, the era of the great ranchos; and THE GLORY YEARS, the booms and busts of the first wave of immigration and speculation.

By 1900, it was time to ask what all these new people were doing with the land they had taken over with such eagerness.

Were the values which drew them to Southern California in the first place in danger of being lost in the rush of population and the crush of expansion? Was the Southern California of sunshine and orange trees, which had been publicized so alluringly, likely to become no more real than the mythical island lying close to the terrestial Paradise?

This book is a close look at the period from the Turn of the Century to the Roaring Twenties, and how one town met the challenge of change and growth. What happened to San Diego may not be typical of what happened to all other cities and towns of Southern California, but the differences only illuminate the issues over which the people argued, whether they wanted smokestacks or geraniums, or, as it were, could they have their cake and eat it too? Let's begin and see how it all came out.

Richard F. Pourade
Rancho Santa Fe, California

One

The Town that Wanted to Grow Up and Be Something

The story of the arid West is the story of water. In this sketch made by the French artist Carl Eytel in the early 1900's, the Colorado River flows silently but powerfully through the canyon above Yuma. What the river did and how best to use its water shaped the development of millions of acres and scores of towns.

CHAPTER I

In the late afternoon of September 6, 1901, in Buffalo, New York, an anarchist by the name of Leon Czolgosz shot and fatally wounded William McKinley, the twenty-fifth President of the United States. The assassin said he had been incited by the speeches and writings of the radical Emma Goldman.

The death of President McKinley eight days later brought to an end an era of placid transition characterized by general prosperity, stability and public trust, and through which the United States had emerged as a world power. Theodore Roosevelt succeeded to the presidency and the Twentieth Century opened. Great physical and economic expansion and a flood of immigration were followed by social and political upheavals.

In the East cities reached skyward and there was a surge of enthusiasm for new forms of architecture, for beautification and parks and for civic planning. In the West empires of arid lands were opened to irrigation and settlement by a new generation of pioneers. On the Pacific slope rough towns became cities and the manner in which they were to grow presented exciting challenges to break with the mistakes of a congested East.

Within a short time after he assumed the presidency, Roosevelt encouraged a revolution in Central America by which Panama became an independent state and granted to the United States in perpetuity a right to finally construct and operate the long-sought canal across the isthmus to connect the Atlantic and Pacific oceans and shorten the sea route to California by 8000 miles.

The promise of the canal was to have a profound influence on events in California. The booms and busts of the period of the building of the transcontinental railroads had left San Diego at the end of a branch line, a small town at the southwestern-most tip of the United States, while its rival, Los Angeles, 125 miles to the north, with its two great rail terminals, was reaching the proportions of a major city with a population of more than 100,000.

At the turn of the century the population of San Diego County was only about 37,000, almost equally divided between the city and county. For an area of more than 8500 square miles, or 5,440,000 acres, stretching seventy miles along the coast and 150 miles eastward to the Colorado River, it was thinly settled and its resources barely touched. To the south was the Mexican border, to the east the high, steep mountains and the Colorado Desert. To the north, Los Angeles was moving swiftly to consolidate its position as the metropolis of Southern California and to acquire

It was a tranquil land, with a warm bay and protecting mountains, which welcomed the Twentieth Century. When this scene of San Diego Bay as seen from Point Loma was painted by C. A. Fries, Southern California had not decided in which direction its future lay.

a harbor for the commerce that everyone expected would develop with the building of a canal across the isthmus and the opening to trade of the ports of the Far East.

In its annual review edition of January 1, 1901, THE SAN DIEGO UNION optimistically stated that, standing on the threshold of the Twentieth Century, San Diego could look backward with pride at her growth and achievements and forward to an unusually promising future. But, in an editorial, THE SAN DIEGO UNION commented:

The LOS ANGELES TIMES *has just issued a special edition designed to show the resources and development of the county in which it is published. The work as a whole is commendable. Unfortunately, the proprietor of that paper was unable to restrain his chronic hatred of San Diego. So in the map which he publishes, showing the field of Pacific commerce, San Diego is carefully eliminated, and Los Angeles, a city twenty miles in the interior, is moved down to the coast and made to appear a port of Southern California, the deception being heightened by various devices representing purely imaginary steamer lines from that fictitious entrepot of commerce.*

Not to be outdone, San Diego's State Board of Harbor Commissioners, in a report on proposed improvements prepared in cooperation with the Chamber of Commerce, sketched a bay containing 174 imaginary piers of varying lengths and all connected to marginal rail lines, and a map of sea lanes of the Pacific Ocean converging at the port of San Diego.

(Next page) Before the opening of the Panama Canal, steamship lines of the Pacific converged on San Francisco. Los Angeles was a mere geographic spot on maps of Pacific sea lanes and San Diego as a port did not exist. Nobody bothered to show where it was. Yet, the canal precipitated a competitive race for trade which vitally influenced the entire Pacific Coast.

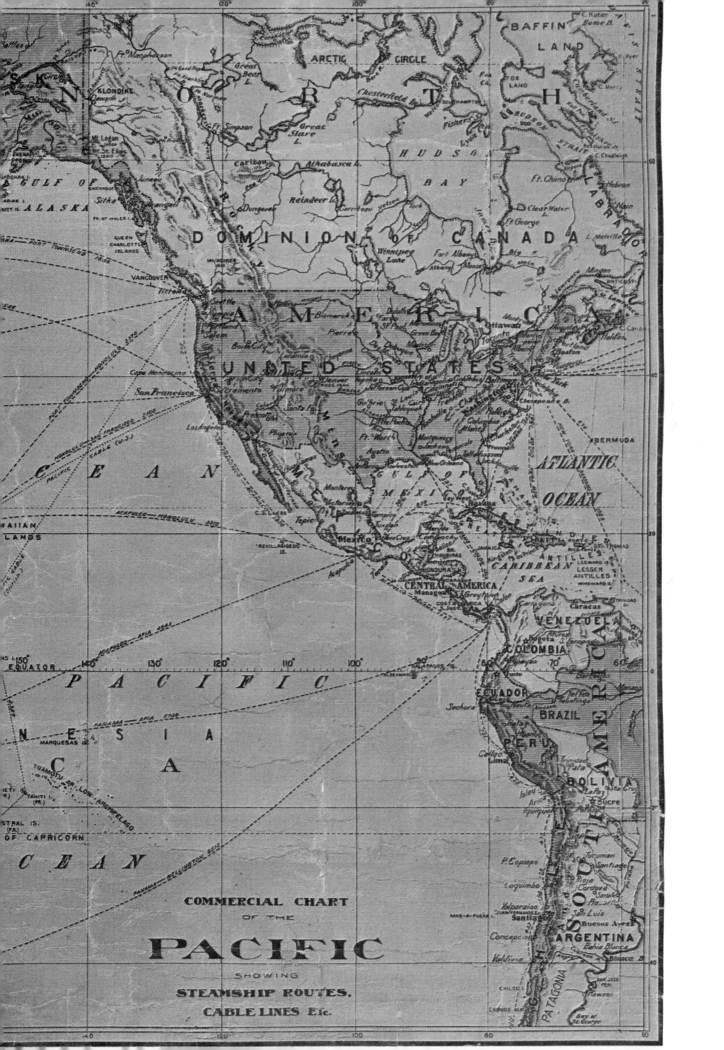

COMMERCIAL CHART

OF THE

PACIFIC

SHOWING

STEAMSHIP ROUTES,

CABLE LINES Etc.

Another map showed the mountain passes through which San Diegans still hoped would come a direct transcontinental railroad line to supply the out-going cargoes to move across the piers and into the holds of the ships of the world. This dream had never died, and San Diegans who had been buffeted by disappointment after disappointment now vowed again that if they had to do so they would see to it themselves that the road was built.

The town's only link with the rest of the country was by the Santa Fe's "Surf Line" running south from Los Angeles, and it was all that remained of the high promises that San Diego was to become its principal western terminus.

The San Diego-Eastern Railway Committee was not without influence, including among its incorporators George W. Marston, the pioneer merchant; U. S. Grant Jr., son of the former President of the United States; and E. S. Babcock, one of the original partners in the erection of the famed Hotel del Coronado who was associated in other local enterprises with John D. and Adolph B. Spreckels of the wealthy sugar family of San Francisco.

By public subscription a sum of $40,000 was raised to finance engineering studies for a line running from San Diego to Yuma on the Colorado River and then eastward through southern Arizona to connect with the terminus of the El Paso and Southwestern Railroad, a total distance of 500 miles.

An elaborate prospectus describing "the neglected opportunity

Regardless of the high mountain barrier to the east, or what Los Angeles might believe, San Diegans were convinced all railroads into Southern California could find a natural terminus at San Diego.

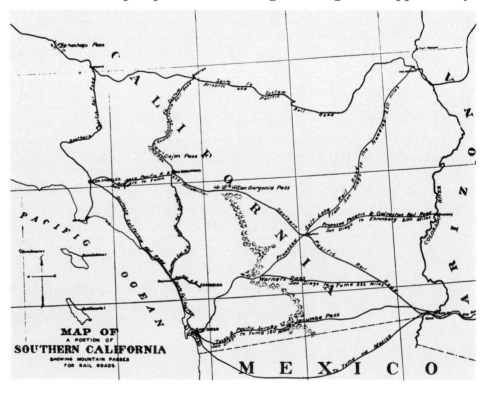

8

of railroad builders" contended that despite adverse United States government reports a railroad could be built up through the mountains roughly paralleling the international border, with easy curves and a maximum grade of 2.8 percent, and descending through rugged Carrizo Gorge, either at a grade of 3.4 or 1.4 percent, depending on the choice of routes and costs.

These grades were compared favorably with those of the transcontinental lines of the Santa Fe, with a maximum grade listed as 3.5 percent, and the Southern Pacific, as 2.2 percent, both of which went directly into Los Angeles. It was optimistically estimated that by using the least expensive descent to the desert the line from San Diego Bay to Yuma could be constructed at an average cost of $21,780 per mile, or for a total cost of $4,573,850. The prospectus stated:

This magnificent port is located upon the shortest route between our great manufacturing and mercantile centers and the Orient. And when the San Diego-Eastern Railway is completed, with proper connection between Yuma and El Paso, the all-rail distance by the new route to the Pacific and the Orient will be shorter by from 200 to 600 miles than by existing routes.

As far as the local newspapers were concerned, San Diego was "the capital of the Southwest":

It claims as its true backcountry the entire Southwestern region, from the summit of the Rocky Mountains to the shore of the Pacific Ocean. In this vast district there is not a railroad or a mine, there is not a community, an irrigated farm or a lonely stock ranch which must not, in time, pay tribute to San Diego. This must be so in response to natural economic laws which are operative elsewhere in the United States and throughout the world...exactly the same forces which made Boston the commercial capital of New England; New York and Philadelphia of the Atlantic seaboard; Savannah and New Orleans, the South; Chicago, the Middlewest; Seattle and Tacoma, the Pacific Northwest; and San Francisco, northern and middle California, will decree that San Diego shall be the commercial capital of the Southwest.

It was no minor skirmish that San Diego chose to fight. The political power in California was held by the Southern Pacific Railroad and it was Charles Crocker, one of the original "Big Four" of the California railroad empire, who had stated that they had "their foot on the neck of San Diego and intended to keep it there."

But all of the "Big Four" were now dead, Collis P. Huntington being the last to die, in 1900. And in the East, Edward Henry Harriman, a stock broker who had rescued the Union Pacific from bankruptcy, was acquiring control of the mighty Southern Pacific with its 8000 miles of rails on the Pacific Coast and east to Ogden, Utah, and to New Orleans in the South, an act that soon would bring down upon him and other industrial giants the wrath of President Roosevelt and the "Trust Busters."

San Diego went ahead with its plans. In Los Angeles another group challenged both the Southern Pacific and the Santa Fe and proposed the construction of a rail line from Los Angeles to Salt Lake City. Then, in Salt Lake City, Harriman allowed information to be made public that the Union Pacific would construct its own line from Utah to San Diego and thus place his tracks into the three major points of California—San Francisco, Los Angeles and San Diego.

The DAILY STATESMAN of Boise, Idaho, commented:

It is apparent that the latest development in this field is the plan of the Harriman road to open up closer communication with San Diego and establish a fleet of steamers plying from that port to all Pacific points...these steamers will equal those on the Atlantic in their arrangement for the comfort of passengers and they will be equally swift.

San Diegans were unimpressed. They had heard it all before, for almost a half century, on and off, and they had become skeptical of beguiling railroad promises. Merchants and land owners wanted a direct line east, not to anywhere else. Marston and other members of the committee visited Tucson and other sympathetic Arizona towns, El Paso in Texas and the financial centers of the East. Financiers listened but were noncommittal.

Whatever the future might or might not bring to San Diego's growth and prosperity, in the number of the smokestacks of industrial expansion, and in the transshipment of the products of the Midwest and the South, developments closer to home held a promise unmatched in American agriculture.

The coastal range divided San Diego County of 1900 into two starkly contrasting regions. The western slopes of the mountains slide off rather gently toward the sea coast, and are often green and in some places wooded; the eastern side of the range drops steeply, and grimly, to the floor of the hot Colorado Desert and the Salton Sink.

For more than a half century it had been known that the sink could be irrigated by a gravity flow of water from the Colorado River. The sink lies somewhat east of the base of the coastal mountains and west of a higher East Mesa and the Chocolate Mountains and reaches a low point of 273.5 feet below sea level. In some

Edward Henry Harriman

10

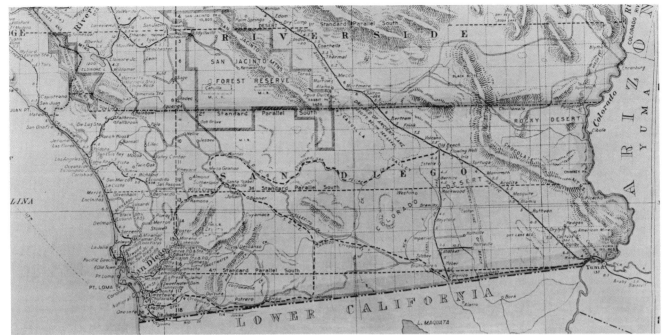

places silt more than 12,000 feet thick, deposited over the ages by the floods of the Colorado, overlies the bed of an ancient sea.

A Spanish trail from Mexico to California had crossed this lonely desert and in later years gold seekers and immigrants following the Southern Trail traversed it to reach the coast at San Diego or Los Angeles, sometimes with terrible suffering.

In the closing years of the Nineteenth Century, there were few persons to appreciate the desert's beauty and brave its terror. The Southern Pacific had breached the desert when it laid its tracks from Los Angeles down San Gorgonio Pass and through the deepest part of the basin and up and across a Colorado River bridge to Yuma, on the route to New Orleans. Cattlemen ventured into the sink, to winter their herds on the pepper grass around the seven lakes formed by occasional overflows of the river.

One of them was Anderson B. Derrick, who drove lean stock down the mountains for fattening through the winter and then back up the mountain trails to market in the Spring. There were endless vigils without communication of any kind except for occasional horsemen or an immigrant wagon. When he married, he took his bride into the desert with him, for their honeymoon, and and they knew that a life could be made in the land which the Spanish called "The Hollow of God's Hand." As the lakes dried there was salt to be mined in the deepest basin of the sea bed.

Others had come to die. Hall Hanlon was ill with tuberculosis when he went into the desert but lived to raise cattle on a large section of land at the point where a rocky escarpment diverted the

At the beginning of the Twentieth Century, San Diego County extended all the way to the Colorado River, an immense area of mild coastal mesas, high mountains and blistering deserts—a country within a country.

Pilot Knob

Colorado River to the south and into Mexico. It was known as Pilot Knob and was a landmark for the old river steamboats. It was Hanlon who showed how the Colorado's water could be sent into the Salton basin.

There was rich soil and perpetual sunshine, and now man would create his own rainfall, to be turned on and off as desired, and in just the proper amounts, through a series of canals fed from the waters of the Colorado.

In May of 1901 the California Development Company succeeded in bringing water into the valley by way of Mexico, which was necessary to avoid the seemingly impenetrable sand dunes which stretched thirty miles in length along the edge of the East Mesa, from a point within the United States to just below the border.

Water was diverted from the river by a head-gate a mile above the border at Hanlon's ranch, and sent through a deep, man-made trench named the Imperial Canal for four miles paralleling the river southward and then cut into an old overflow channel known as the Alamo.

The channel meanders for forty miles through the arid delta of the Colorado in Baja California, and eventually crosses into the United States. For centuries the Alamo and another channel known as the New River had carried overflow water from Colorado River floods and wasted it into the Salton Sink, leaving small lakes that appeared and disappeared with the passing seasons. To earlier immigrants the unexpected appearance of a flowing river had been a "miracle of the desert."

The development company, under the driving enthusiasm of George M. Chaffey, an engineer of wide experience, cleaned the Alamo channel of its undergrowth and at Sharp's Heading on the border regulated the flow of water into distribution canals to serve the farms of homesteaders and the ambitions of land promoters.

For the privilege and necessity of using a canal running through Baja California the company agreed to share the water with a Mexican company for development of delta lands below the border.

Settler's home in the desert

Chaffey and L. M. Holt, editor of a Riverside newspaper, prepared a promotional campaign for the sale of land and changed the name of the Salton Sink to the Imperial Valley. Stock of the California Development Company was sold all over the United States, and settlers flocked into the desert and joined in organizing mutual companies to purchase and reallocate the water. By the next Spring 400 miles of irrigating ditches had been dug and water was available for more than 100,000 acres.

The pioneers who were staking out homestead claims in the

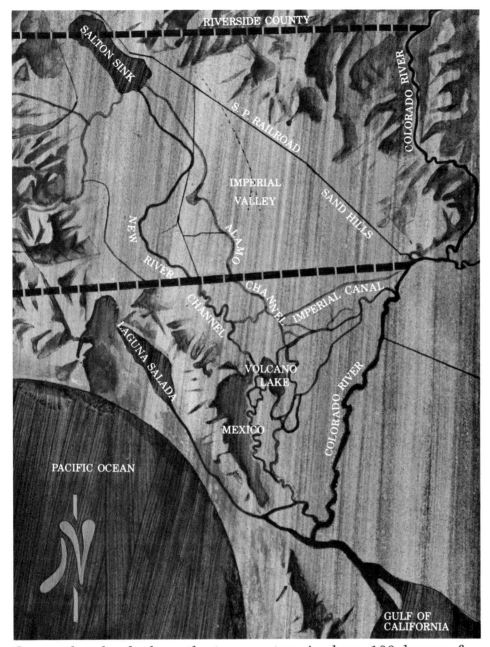

Labels on the map:
RIVERSIDE COUNTY
SALTON SINK
S. P. RAILROAD
COLORADO RIVER
IMPERIAL VALLEY
SAND HILLS
NEW RIVER
ALAMO CHANNEL
CHANNEL
IMPERIAL CANAL
LAGUNA SALADA
VOLCANO LAKE
COLORADO RIVER
MEXICO
PACIFIC OCEAN
GULF OF CALIFORNIA

This relief map shows the geographical formation of the Imperial Valley and the Colorado River Delta, at the time of the first settlements. There were no levees to contain the river and the Salton Sea area was a sink watered from time to time by river overflow carried by thin and rambling channels.

flat treeless land where the temperature is above 100 degrees for almost a third of the year, had little concern over the fact that the Colorado River flowed high above the floor of the basin which they were farming, in a bed it had built 150 feet above sea level with its own silt long before any human eye, that of the Indian or anyone else, had seen the power of its springtime rages.

Towns rose out of the sand, first Imperial City, and then the settlements of Calexico and Mexicali, one on each side of the border near where the water entered the valley; and then Brawley and Holtville and finally El Centro. Some of the settlers came only with loaded wagons and with little or no money, to stake out

Even signposts were lonely

homesteading claims. Many of them managed to survive through help that came from developers such as W. F. Holt and his brother Leroy Holt, who bought up state and railroad tracts and staked them to their start in a new land.

Others gave up when their women-folk could not adjust to a country with colors that were so pale compared with the dark greens and the golds and reds of changing seasons of their home-lands. Here the land was flat and sandy, and faded pink and blue hills often seemed to vanish in a haze that magnified the distances and the loneliness.

The epic struggle of the settlers was related a few years later by Harold Bell Wright in the novel, THE WINNING OF BARBARA WORTH, which in its time had as great an impact on the country as had Helen Hunt Jackson's RAMONA of the 1880's. He wrote:

In the fierce winds that rushed through the mountain passes and swept across the hot plains like a torrid furnace blast; in the blinding, stinging, choking, smothering dust that moved in golden clouds from rim to rim of the Basin; in the blazing, scorching strength of the sun; in the hard, hot sky, without shred or raveling of cloud; in the creeping, silent, poison life of insect and reptile; in the maddening dryness of the thirsty vegetation; in the weird, beautiful falseness of the ever-changing mirage, the spirit of the Desert issued its silent challenge.

Agitators soon were to follow to tell the settlers they shouldn't have to pay for what had been government land or reward a private company for water that nature itself had so thoughtfully provided in the Colorado River.

But nature was not always bountiful, as so many had learned on the other side of the mountains, where rainfall was more frequent but could alternate floods with droughts to erase the efforts of years.

How pioneers crossed the desert

Though the rain had been light in the past season, as it had been for several years, 10,189,213 pounds of lemons and 2,535,119 pounds of oranges had been handled by cars of the National City & Otay Railroad serving settlements and agricultural areas along the southerly end of the bay, National City, Chula Vista, Otay, Sweetwater River Valley, Nestor and Tia Juana River Valley. The San Diego, Cuyamaca and Eastern line running to Foster's Station at the northeast corner of El Cajon Valley at the foot of the mountains, had carried 5,516,000 pounds of fruit, much of it in raisins; 6,720,000 pounds of hay; and 155,000 pounds of honey.

Pioneer wagon of 1900

In four years the shipments of San Diego County lemons to the ever-widening markets of the country had increased from 228 cars, by rail and water, to 592, and the growers were proud to learn that their fruit was being compared most favorably with the lemons imported from Sicily in the Mediterranean.

There was not, of course, any immediate need for the 174 piers suggested in the San Diego Board of Harbor Commissioners' projection for the bay, but the Rivers and Harbors Committee of the House of Representatives agreed with the Corps of Engineers on a $268,000 project to dredge and eliminate shoaling. Jetties at the bay entrance were under construction. San Diegans also felt that the Navy should complete the coaling station, started in 1898 on the lee shore of Point Loma but never finished, because of the frequent fleet exercises off the Southern California coast and the new obligations of the United States in the Pacific as a result of the war with Spain. The fort on Point Loma, so hurriedly started during war with Spain, had been allowed to languish, with only a few guns guarding the seaway into the harbor.

With the turn of the Century, though, the fourth emplacement for the ten-inch gun batteries was completed on Ballast Point, as well as emplacements for two- and three-inch guns, the construction of frame barracks undertaken, and, a year later, the 115th Company of Coast Artillery was organized at the old San Diego barracks and transferred to the fort which in 1899 had been named in honor of Gen. William S. Rosecrans. A Civil War general, Rosecrans had resigned to interest himself in various railroad promotional schemes and eventually had been elected to Congress from California.

As for the town, for more than a decade time had stood still. However, John D. Spreckels, who resided in San Francisco, remained firm in his belief that San Diego someday would be a second San Francisco, and the money earned by the family in sugar and shipping was to be poured by the millions of dollars into a town the Spreckels name would dominate for more than twenty years.

He already owned the street car system, two of the town's three newspapers, most of Coronado and North Island which comprised the wide sandy peninsula enclosing the bay to the south, and Hotel del Coronado, already known around the world as a resort hotel. With E. S. Babcock, he controlled the Southern California Mountain Water Company, which was supplying a large area, but not as yet the city of San Diego, with water, and was engaged in mercantile operations.

San Diego had seven miles of paved and forty-five miles of graded streets; fifteen miles of electric railway and twenty-two

John D. Spreckels

15

miles of motor railway; sixteen miles of cement sidewalks; twenty-five churches; fourteen schools; a $100,000 opera house; and, above all, a 1400-acre park as yet mostly undeveloped and unused. Home owners grew geraniums and were content. The climate was a lure to those who could afford to escape both the cold and heat of the East and the Midwest. When he was Chief Signal Officer of the Army, and thus head of the United States Weather Service, Gen. A. E. Greeley wrote:

The American public is familiar on all sides with elaborate and detailed statements of the weather at a thousand and one resorts. If we may believe all we read in such reports, the temperature never reaches the eighties, the sky is flecked with just enough of cloud to perfect the landscape, the breezes are always balmy, and the nights ever cool.

As far as many of the early settlers were concerned, Southern California was no place for factories and developers and this appealing area south of the City of San Diego was known as Paradise Valley.

There is possibly one place in the United States where such conditions obtain — a bit of country about forty miles square, at the extreme southwestern part of the United States, in which San Diego, California, is located.

That it should capitalize on its climate was advice offered to San Diego back in the 1870's by a Swiss professor named Louis Agassiz, who visited the harbor as a member of a scientific expedition. San Diego, he told a meeting of its citizens, was situated on the 32nd parallel and was thus beyond the reach of severe winters, and "this is your capital, and it is worth millions to you."

But railroads and smokestacks were still very much in the people's minds, even though Mayor Edwin M. Capps in his report to the Common Council in 1901 suggested that San Diego concentrate on promoting the tourist business. He stated:

One of the greatest natural resources that this city is possessed of is her matchless climate. This one factor alone, coupled with a slight effort on the part of her citizens, is sufficient to place San Diego in the foremost rank as a tourist resort.

We should cater to the entertainment of the tourist, make it pleasant and congenial, have public places of resort in the nature of beautiful parks, fine boulevards, roads and drives...I do not think it at all visionary to say, with the proper development of attractive resorts...that this city would become the winter residence of no less than five or six thousand of these most desirable citizens, each of them spending from $200 to $1000 for the season.

The Chamber of Commerce did some promotional advertising, though it largely was confined to advertisements in the local newspapers and directed to visitors already in San Diego or in adjoining areas:

In looking for a new home, either temporary or permanent, your first thought is, what are the health conditions. San Diego, California, is the healthiest city in the United States...There are no marshes or pools in the vicinity to breed mosquitoes and malaria; the diseases prevalent among children elsewhere are practically unknown, while youth and middle age can enjoy life to the full, and those who have grown old and rheumatic in other less favored climes here regain their strength and vigor. The span of life is no longer complete at three score and ten. Men of eighty and ninety walk the streets with vigorous step, and why should it be otherwise amid such perfect surroundings, in a climate where you may be out-of-doors every day and at every hour of the day during the entire year?

San Diego was known for its beautiful and unusual cloud formations but a French-born engineer by the name of Octave Chanute was attracted to the area by the low wind velocities, in order to carry out his studies in the science of flight. He and his assistants photographed the flight of pelicans and remarked that he believed they held the secret of air navigation.

A dozen years before John Montgomery, a student with a scientific turn of mind who had studied the flight characteristics of seagulls, had successfully flown a glider, in man's first controlled flight, on the Otay Mesa. The future not only of aviation but of San Diego rose with the constant breezes that flecked across a sunlit bay.

The winter and summer tourists filled the hotels and at Hotel del Coronado Spreckels in 1900 erected tents below the hotel

Tent cities were common in the early days of Southern California but none was more famous or more inviting than Coronado Tent City on a narrow sliver of land known as the Silver Strand.

on the Silver Strand. Here the early settlers of the interior and particularly of Imperial Valley found relief from the heat in the temperate air and the inviting surf. "Tent cities" were common vacation resorts in those days. To the striped canvas tents were added palm-thatched huts. There was rowing on the bay and band concerts in the evening.

The religious groups and cults which were to give Southern California a unique and sometimes bizarre flavor were organizing and building, and the most ambitious of them all were the Theosophists, who had selected Point Loma for their version of the Acropolis of America.

A three-story hotel and sanitarium had been erected by one of the Theosophists, Dr. Lorin Wood, and when their first international convention rolled around, the hotel as well as an adjoining tent city were filled with hundreds of delegates who arrived by train and a special steamship bearing the Universal Brotherhood's flag of purple and gold. Seven trumpet blasts heralded the opening of the pageant, with delegates chanting "Truth, light and liberation," and fifty miles away atop towering Mount Palomar, a fire was lighted that was visible in the night to the faithful on the windy ridge of the southwestern-most point in the United States.

Subsequently, Madame Katherine Tingley, the Purple Mother of the Theosophists, took over the hotel-sanitarium; over its inner patio was erected a huge dome of aquamarine glass, and next to this structure there arose a temple, round and topped with another dome of glass of amethyst color. The domes in turn were surmounted by spires representing flaming hearts and their burning lights could be seen far at sea.

All in all, it promised to be quite a century.

Two

Here Come the Cultists and the Health Seekers

*Domes of colored glass lent mysticism to
the temples of the Theosophical Society
on Point Loma in the early 1900's, when
so many similar groups were lured to
Southern California by climate and the
promise of a new way of life.*

CHAPTER II

The Theosophists on Point Loma had no more lighted their lamps
for the misguided, and the settlers of Imperial Valley had barely
produced their first crops, when adversity struck, and from unexpected directions.

The federal government had not looked with pleasure upon the
private development of Imperial Valley. The Reclamation Act
creating a Reclamation Service was on its way through Congress
with the support of President Roosevelt, who believed that irrigation works to reclaim and settle the vast arid public domain of the
West should be built by the government.

In October of 1901 the Agricultural Department sent a soil expert, J. Garnett Holmes, to the Imperial Valley to examine and report upon the alkaline conditions of the soils, and a little later he
was joined by Thomas H. Means. Both of them were young in years
and experience. The early seed already was producing crops more
abundant than farmers ever before had seen. Thousands of acres
were lush with sorghum, maize, wheat, barley, alfalfa and even

fresh vegetables. They completed their work and reported to Washington.

After many rumors had spread, their report was made public by Milton Whitney, Chief of the Bureau of Soils, on January 10, 1902. It held that sixty-two percent of the land was heavily impregnated with alkali. It concluded:

One hundred and twenty-five thousand acres of this land have already been taken up by prospective settlers, many of whom talk of planting crops which it will be absolutely impossible to grow. They must early find that it is useless to attempt their growth...

No doubt the best thing to do is to raise crops like the sugar beet, sorghum, and the date palm (if the climate will permit), that are suited to such alkaline conditions, and abandon as worthless that which contains too much alkali to grow those crops.

No man knew for sure whether his land was included. Credit was withdrawn from the valley and business came to a standstill. The Southern Pacific halted work on the laying of its branch line to valley towns. Several thousand farmers were on the verge of ruin.

The panic subsided somewhat when some of the prominent developers of the valley took other government officials and business men into the fields where they had to grope their way through heavy crops of barley to find the stakes marking the very areas where the soil experts once had made tests proving such crops could not be grown.

In San Diego, where so much faith had been placed in the future of Imperial Valley, W. W. Bowers, who formerly had represented

the area in the Congress, wrote a letter to the SAN DIEGO SUN commenting:

As I looked upon the great luxuriant fields that challenge all California to equal, I was reminded of the government agricultural experts (God save the mark, experts?) who, after private individuals had risked their all and demonstrated to the government and an equally great and uninformed people that the "desert could be made to blossom as the rose"—these experts reported that their tests of the soil showed that it was "so heavily impregnated with alkali as to unfit the most of it for growing crops." In all my ride I did not see any alkali land, nor one foot that would not grow crops if watered and planted. Indeed I have not seen any fertile section of land in California so entirely free from alkali. So much for government experts.

In time, the Department of Agriculture reconsidered and modified its report, and confidence was restored, but the valley learned it had an opponent whose power would be a greater threat to their private domain than the river which they so confidently thought they could easily keep under control.

But the experts were not entirely wrong. For millions of years the Colorado River had carried salts of sodium and calcium into the basin and covered them with silt. The experts only miscalculated in the time they estimated it would take for salts to rise to the surface and whiten the earth.

The restoration of confidence in the valley attracted the interest of Los Angeles merchants. A warning that San Diego had better look to its future relations with the people of Imperial was given

There was little to relieve the barren landscape in Imperial Valley, as shown in this view from the Holtville Hotel in 1904, and the early settlers built what they needed and turned a desert into an empire.

by the county surveyor S. L. Ward upon his return from a trip to the New River country, as it was often referred to. He said that unless a better wagon road was constructed the trade of the prospering valley would go to Los Angeles.

A Chamber of Commerce committee which included George White Marston, M. F. Heller and Col. S. W. Fergusson, general manager of the Imperial Land Company, appeared before the County Board of Supervisors and urged improvement of the Mountain Springs road, and Marston said that "now after these men have spent so much money and done so much work, San Diego sits by without doing a thing."

The Supervisors suggested that as money from one road district could not be spent in another, and the cost of the project would be considerable, the financial help of the business community would be necessary. Cheered by the news that the county seat at last was paying some attention to its distant stepchild, Henry C. Reed, the valley's first editor, published an editorial in the IMPERIAL PRESS which stated:

The business man of San Diego...is coming to realize that rich rewards lie hidden in the wonderfully fertile soil of this mis-called desert region...which he heretofore...thought of only as a place where men lost their lives for want of water and are buried in the stomachs of hungered coyotes.

Henry C. Reed

Action was slow in coming, and there were other distractions. The national government as well as the state government began to take an interest in what was happening on Point Loma, with the importation of children from Cuba and a series of sensational articles in the LOS ANGELES TIMES which accused the Theosophists of many irregularities of conduct.

Though the Theosophists had received a friendly welcome in San Diego, their teaching of reincarnation finally aroused the ministry, and a dozen pastors from San Diego and five from neighboring towns signed a document with appeared in THE SAN DIEGO UNION of August 21, 1901. It stated in part:

We, whose names are undersigned, are impelled to state publicly our convictions as regards Theosophy and the teaching emanating from the Point Loma Homestead...the circumstances attending the modern revival of Theosophy...are not such as commend themselves to our reason or moral sense; while its ancient sway in the Orient has blighted countless lives and has left India a moral and spiritual desert.

The teachings of Theosophy are diametrically opposed to the Gospel of Christ as it is presented in the New Testament and taught

Katherine Tingley dominated the Theosophi-cal Society on Point Loma for two decades of alternate periods of peace and storm.

by the Christian Church.

An answer in the same newspaper was followed by a personal defense by Madame Tingley in the Fisher Opera House, which she purchased and renamed the Isis Theater to foreclose its use by her opponents.

The attack by the LOS ANGELES TIMES in October of 1901 was based on a report that a woman had been rescued from what was described as the "spookery" on Point Loma, and that she had been forced to labor in the fields, and was locked up in a cell at night; that another woman had been forcibly separated from her husband; that children were forbidden to speak to anyone and were kept on the verge of starvation; that midnight pilgrimages were made by both sexes "in their night robes." This was vivid reading, for San Diego as well as most of California.

Madame Tingley's troubles mounted when a leader of the cult in San Francisco, Dr. Jerome Anderson, cried out in protest at the ceremonial trend Theosophy had taken at Point Loma. In the SAN FRANCISCO CHRONICLE of March 25, 1902, he stated, in part:

I have seen men and women of wealth, education and high social

*Theosophical children
in Cuba*

position humble themselves before her in a way that sensible people can hardly conceive of. I stood it myself for a while. I wore long gowns and ridiculous hats in her presence and tried to take part in the foolish ceremonies, with some belief that they might have a meaning. But I knew it meant that pretty soon we should have to crawl into Mrs. Tingley's presence on all fours...

New York was next to be heard. Mrs. Tingley had been interested in Cuba as a fertile ground for her evangelism, and she imported children from there to be educated and indoctrinated at Point Loma. In October of 1902 eleven children, nine boys and two girls between the ages of five and ten, were detained at Ellis Island by the United States Immigration Service after it was reported there had been a demonstration in Cuba against their being sent to San Diego. It soon became apparent that other forces were at work. The New York Society for the Prevention of Cruelty to Children intervened on the grounds that the atmosphere at the Theosophical center was not suitable for children.

Mrs. Tingley, however, had powerful supporters in her behalf, including among her influential believers Albert G. Spalding, the sporting goods manufacturer, whose children had been placed in the school at Point Loma. Mr. and Mrs. Spalding were drawn to San Diego and became active in all its affairs.

Two official investigations were begun. Gov. Henry T. Gage of California sent representatives of the State Board of Health and Board of Examiners to Point Loma, and they were followed by Frank P. Sargent, U.S. Commissioner General of Immigration, who was accompanied by the district's congressman, M. J. Daniels of Riverside.

D. C. Reed

Mayor Emilio Bacardí of Santiago de Cuba had notified United States authorities in New York that he had not been aware of any demonstrations against the removal of the children, but as a result of the furor he suddenly turned up in San Diego to conduct an investigation of his own. A member of a famous family, Bacardí had befriended Madame Tingley on her visit to Cuba and had aided in the selection of a site for a Theosophical temple and in the selection of children to be sent to San Diego for education.

Even though they had been entranced by the developments, and ministers had denied the teachings of Theosophy, San Diegans were well acquainted with many of the leading personages at the White City and could not believe the reports of the abuse of children and the suggestion of immorality.

San Diegans organized their own investigation by forming a chapter of the Society for the Prevention of Cruelty to Children.

Two members of the investigating committee were Hugh J. Baldwin, superintendent of county schools, and D. C. Reed, a former mayor of the city.

The state's investigators departed without formal comment but indicated they also did not believe the charges of cruelty and immorality. On November 23, Sargent returned to San Diego from the Point and told THE SAN DIEGO UNION:

I have seen many institutions of the kind, carried on by all sorts of sects and all sorts of religions, but I have never seen a place as cleanly and as well appointed as the institution at Point Loma.

The report to San Diego by Baldwin on behalf of the trustees of the Society for the Prevention of Cruelty to Children, was even more enthusiastic:

The rooms of every building were found well lighted and ventilated and were neatly furnished...Intense patriotism exists among these children, and all the children show great devotion to our country and its flag which flies above their heads in the breeze...In conclusion, we the trustees of the San Diego Society for the Prevention of Cruelty to Children, after a close and thorough examination of the buildings and surroundings of the corporation known as the Point Loma Homestead...find it in excellent condition, of the highest morals.

The Cuban children were released from Ellis Island. To avoid their being taken into custody at the insistence of the New York Society for the Prevention of Cruelty to Children, Reed, the former mayor, who had been sent to New York, took possession of the children as an agent of the mayor of Santiago de Cuba. Spalding chartered a boat and picked them up at Ellis Island. During a fog the boat changed the announced course and landed them at Jersey City, where each of the children was given an escort of a burly athlete from Spalding's Athletic Club, and spirited aboard a train.

A few days later the weary and bewildered children were taken off a train at Old Town and transported by carriages to Point Loma. The following day, a Sunday, there was a civic welcome, with the City Guard Band leading a parade up D Street, or Broadway, from the Santa Fe depot, to Fourth Street and the Isis Theater, between B and C Streets, which was completely filled for the occasion. Judge E. W. Hendrick expressed the hope that the children's education at Point Loma would help toward the end of stabilizing Latin America politically and that they would become patriots to world mankind.

Mrs. Tingley sued the LOS ANGELES TIMES for libel, asking

Isis Theater

27

Samuel Shortridge

Julius Wangenheim

$50,000 in damages, and when the case came to trial the newspaper's manager, Harrison Gray Otis, complained that he could not receive a fair trial in San Diego because of the existence of strong feelings against his newspaper. The bearded, tobacco-chewing Superior Court judge, E. S. Torrance, denied the motion for a change of venue, on the grounds that the ill feeling against the defendant was not on account of the libelous article written against Mrs. Tingley but simply because the defendant had consistently belittled San Diego.

Chief counsel for Otis was Samuel Shortridge, who was to become a United States senator. They were unable to produce any evidence supporting the charges in the articles in the TIMES, or, in fact, to produce the persons with whom the information was supposed to have originated, and they knew the case was lost when Mrs. Tingley, who had been injured in a fall, entered the courtroom with the aid of a crutch. She was dressed in black, spoke softly and told of the mental suffering she had experienced at the hands of the TIMES.

The judge held that libel had been committed and that the jury's sole duty was to determine the amount of damages. The jurors awarded her $7500. Otis appealed to the Supreme Court and lost. Mrs. Tingley had been completely vindicated. The institution on Point Loma, which expanded to cover more than 500 acres and had the first Greek Theater in America, became a part of the life of the community.

The Theosophical headquarters as well as the climate were attracting visitors and settlers and the population of the town had risen gently by several thousand by 1902.

With its two bays, rolling hills and the sea, San Diego more than most towns of the West had seen the advantages of open spaces and had protected from land speculators the 1400 acres of former pueblo lands that had been laid aside for a public park, and some tree planting had been done along its edges.

But as a result of the general awakening of interest in city planning that arose with the advent of the Twentieth Century, and the interest in attracting tourists that went back to the advice of former Mayor Capps, a park improvement committee was organized by the Chamber of Commerce at the suggestion of the merchant and banker Julius Wangenheim. In his memoirs, Wangenheim wrote:

It happened that on a spring Sunday morning in…1902, I was walking with my daughter Alice through a portion of the undeveloped park…In the course of the walk I met a good friend, Chauncey

Hammond, and an English acquaintance of his. The Englishman expressed surprise that with such lovely scenic and horticultural opportunities, we had done nothing in the way of park development. The remark got under my skin, and I resolved to do something about it.

A sum of $11,000 was soon publicly subscribed, and it was decided to follow the procedure of the development of the Golden Gate Park in San Francisco, and to start work in one corner and proceed progressively during subsequent years. The work was begun at the corner of the park at Date Street, and then, when Marston donated $10,000 for roads through the park, a decision was reached to hire and bring to San Diego a nationally-known landscape architect to outline a comprehensive plan. The man selected was Samuel Parsons Jr., president of the American Society of Landscape Architects and consulting architect for the park system of greater New York, and Marston induced him to come to San Diego.

Samuel Parsons Jr.

He arrived in December of 1902, and after making a preliminary study, told the Chamber of Commerce that the park was unique among American city parks, both in terrain and flora, and every effort should be made to preserve the panorama, from the mountains in the east and the south to the seascape of Point Loma and the Coronado Islands. He said:

My strongest impression as to the treatment of the park itself, after this first examination, is to preserve the beauty that now exists ...the broad free, natural lines of the San Diego park call for simplicity of treatment...Considering the fact, or perhaps because of the fact, that this park has this wonderful mesa and canyon effect, it seems to me that I have never seen...a park where so little change of surface is necessary...Cuts and fills, which constitute one of the chief causes of the great cost of most parks, seem necessarily almost eliminated from the scheme of the San Diego park.

He suggested that the first development be in the southwest section and that different kinds of trees should be planted at each of the entrances; that roads should run along the rims of the canyons, so as to leave as many broad mesas as possible; that plantings be done primarily with a view of harmony with existing flora, and that high trees such as eucalyptus should not be scattered over the high mesas, but that "many portions of hillsides, where the land is tolerably flat and elevated, can be beautified by broad plantations of pepper, acacia, and even some varieties of eucalyptus where the outlook toward the mountains and the sea would not be injured."

(Next page) This was San Diego just after the turn of the Century. It was Circus Day and all the people were there, as shown by this view of Fifth Street looking south from below D Street, or Broadway.

29

KODAK FINISHING.

In July, Parsons' partner, George Cooke, arrived to begin the work. Beauty, however, already had taken root. He found two sections of the park set out with cypress, pine and oak trees, and with rare plants from Africa and Australia which were thriving in the kind but semi-arid climate. These were the results of the endeavors of Kate Sessions, a school teacher with a degree in the science of agriculture from the University of California who had been granted the right to establish a nursery in the park in return for planting trees and making others available for use throughout the town. Her nursery was near Sixth and Upas Streets, in the northwest section, though she also set out trees near Sixth and Date Streets.

In 1903 she accompanied a botanist to Cape San Lucas at the tip of Baja California where she obtained the seed of an unusual palm tree distinguished for its long and slender trunk, sometimes rising to a height of eighty feet, and topped with a beautiful head of fan-shaped leaves, and planted them in a canyon in the park. Though continuing a close association with Parsons and Cooke and the park, Miss Sessions moved her nursery to the area that became Mission Hills, and again began planting there, particularly palm trees, as she had done in the park.

New life was stirring through the town that had been laid out only thirty-five years before by Alonzo Horton. But not all San Diegans agreed that the town's future lay with its climate and scenery, and the many empty buildings left from the population boom of the Eighties were silent reminders of a lack of sources of income. National City and much of the South Bay area in particular had been hard hit by the withdrawal of the shops of the Santa Fe railroad when it abandoned San Diego as its proposed major tidewater terminal.

In his memoirs, Oscar W. Cotton, who arrived as a young man, to engage in the realty business, wrote:

When I arrived in San Diego, the consensus...in Los Angeles was that San Diego was a "City of Blighted Hopes." It was just a little dried-up town on the Mexican border, with no capital assets but "Bay and Climate"—a town that took itself seriously but could never amount to anything because it was too far from Los Angeles—five hours by either of the two...half-empty trains per day.

Cotton invested his savings in land in Pacific Beach, where lots could be purchased for $7.50 each. To sell them, he believed more persons would have to be urged to come to San Diego to make their homes. Los Angeles was becoming the best-advertised city in the country. Its Chamber of Commerce had sent an exhibition

Oscar W. Cotton

train called "California on Wheels" to every important city in the South and Midwest and by 1903 winter tourists in Southern California had risen to more than 45,000. The Spreckels companies in turn, before the opening of each summer season, began sending the Tent City Band on a tour of the Southern California and Arizona "hot belts" and were successful in attracting many temporary visitors.

But in the view of Cotton, as well as of Capps, there were a great many in the United States who could afford to live where they chose, and would come to San Diego and build a city, if they only knew about it, and the problem was how to let them know. M. F. Heller, a merchant, disagreed. According to Cotton, he argued:

Cotton, it's not a good idea to advertise for more people to come to San Diego until we have factories here. There is nothing for them to do. No way they can make a living. The town right now has all the people it can support.

But Cotton and his partners were not to be deterred and finding themselves in possession of several thousand lots in Pacific Beach and Morena, and 900 acres in what later became the southern portion of Clairemont, began proclaiming the advantages of San Diego's "Bay and Climate" in Los Angeles and placing expensive advertisements in eastern newspapers and magazines. In his memoirs Cotton wrote:

After the first thirty days I could see we were sunk financially, but then it took another thirty days to stop the advertising campaign. By that time, $10,000 in advertising space had been contracted for...fortunately, our Los Angeles office was producing a steady flow of business.

By the end of 1904 the population of the town had risen to

Life was still leisurely in 1900 and as with so many towns of Spanish and Mexican heritages San Diego's downtown Plaza had its bandstand.

21,000, or 3000 more than at the turn of the century.

It did seem that industrial and commercial development was as far away as ever. Though Congress had passed the Spooner Act authorizing President Roosevelt to proceed with the Panama Canal, progress in getting started seemed agonizingly slow due to physical and diplomatic problems. The projected railroad to the east had been stalled. The Spreckels interests were biding their time and while San Diegans were interested they were not particularly excited by the news that the Wright Brothers had made the first powered, heavier-than-air flight at Kitty Hawk way off in North Carolina. The Wright Brothers had drawn on the experiments of Octave Chanute, who had studied the flights of pelicans over San Diego Bay.

In his little book on the climate of San Diego published by the San Diego Chamber of Commerce in 1913, Ford A. Carpenter, United States weather forecaster at San Diego, wrote:

During the now historic experiments of Orville Wright...it was very gratifying to be able to renew acquaintance with Octave Chanute, and to hear him quickly revert to his early experiments on San Diego Bay. With characteristic impulsiveness he pointed to the soaring Wright biplane as resembling his old friend, the San Diego pelican.

But the significance of the flight for San Diego was not a matter of speculation.

The same climatic conditions that attracted tourists, the Theosophists and other religious groups to Southern California, also drew social idealists, and reformers of one kind or another, as well as Socialists and anarchists, and San Diego felt their influence very early in the century.

Many Socialist meetings were conducted in San Diego and Socialist candidates were seeking public office, though the town was firmly in the control of the Republican organization. Frank P. Frary, the stage coach line operator, had succeeded Capps as Republican mayor, on a platform of parks, beautification and roads. The congressman representing the Eighth District, of which San Diego County was a part, also was a Republican. He was M. J. Daniels, a banker of Riverside County.

Throughout the state the dominant Republican Party was considered the creature of the Southern Pacific Railroad, with E. H. Harriman as powerful as Huntington ever was, and in San Diego party influence was exerted through Spreckels and the local-level political "boss," Charles S. Hardy, a meat processor and distributor.

Though as yet he was the only one to have made substantial

Charles S. Hardy

Satin Gown Trimmed with Rich Embroideries Veiled with Chiffon. Empire Waist Outlined with Silken...

A Stunning Toilette for the Tea Hour

The tea hour and not the cocktail hour was the social time in the towns at the turn of the Century and this fashion sketch from THE SAN DIEGO UNION *showed the proper way to dress for it.*

investments in San Diego in more than a decade, there was resentment against John D. Spreckels and it appeared in the campaign for Congress in 1902. One of the candidates was William E. Smythe, a Democrat.

The son of a wealthy shoe manufacturer of Worcester, Massachusetts, Smythe had failed as a book publisher in Boston and eventually became editor of the OMAHA BEE, where in the great plains drought of 1890 he witnessed the terrible suffering of the farmers. He became interested in irrigation, founded the magazine IRRIGATION AGE, and wrote a book, THE CONQUEST OF ARID AMERICA, which ran to several editions. He arrived in San Diego in 1902 and sought to enter public life.

He campaigned against the Spreckels interests and claimed that San Diego was monopoly-ridden, with a water monopoly, a land monopoly and a railroad monopoly, but made the mistake in other agricultural counties of coming out in favor of placing all water development under state control, although he tried vainly to convince his hearers that he didn't really mean to disturb any individual riparian rights to water.

To THE SAN DIEGO UNION, owned by Spreckels, Smythe was "Windy Willie." To the RIVERSIDE ENTERPRISE, Smythe's ideas on water were socialistic theories offered as substitutes for "the law of riparian rights which is as eternal as time itself and as immut-

William E. Smythe

Frank A. Salmons

able as the snow-capped mountains that furnish our bountiful water supply."

As for Smythe's charges of monopoly, W. W. Bowers, the former congressman, answered:

I know that all of us were very glad to get the railroad, and with all its extortions we had rather do with it than without. I had rather have water with monopoly than no water and no monopoly.

In the election returns of the Eighth District, which comprised nine southern counties, Daniels won by a majority of 2250. In San Diego County, however, Smythe led by 250 votes.

Water, even more than tourists or a railroad, or for that matter the gold mines and the gem deposits in the mountains, concerned San Diegans. In the coastal area, where most of the people lived, the rainfall averaged only ten inches a year; in the upper mountains, forty inches a year. Bringing the rain of the mountains to the fields of the lower areas, and into the water mains of the towns and settlements was a matter of existence.

The Spreckels interests in partnership with Babcock owned the Otay River system, with its Lower and Upper Otay dams, by which part of the South Bay area and Coronado received water, but their Southern California Mountain Water Company was encountering difficulties in constructing Morena Dam and in developing the Cottonwood Creek system by which they hoped to supply the town of San Diego.

In 1901 the people had voted bonds to purchase their water distribution system. For $500,000 the city obtained the water rights and San Diego River wells of the San Diego Water Company and purchased for $100,000 the distribution system owned by the Southern California Mountain Water Company.

The town was largely dependent on the privately-owned thirty-mile long flume which reached into the mountains for the water stored behind the Cuyamaca reservoir. But the drought that began in 1895-96 persisted. The wells were considered inadequate and the supply from the flume was undependable and often slimy with algae.

There were many to see that who controlled the water controlled San Diego. Ed Fletcher, a young produce merchant, while quail hunting with a friend, Frank Salmons, in the upper San Luis Rey Valley on the old Spanish grant known as the Pauma Ranch, about fifty miles north of San Diego, heard the rush of water. He wrote in his autobiography:

I found myself looking from a slight rise down into a stream possibly a foot deep and ten feet wide. Never was I more surprised.

How welcome that water was—cool and refreshing, coming as it did from a narrow gorge nearby and soon to sink in the gravels below.

Salmons told him the stream was Pauma Creek and came from springs in Doane Valley on Palomar Mountain, nine miles above where they were standing. It was a normal flow though there had been no rain for six months. Fletcher wrote:

I there saw the immediate possibilities of water development both for power and irrigation. Doane Valley is over 5000 feet in elevation. Where we were then standing the elevation could not have exceeded 1500 feet. The water could easily be diverted at that point on the Pauma Ranch by gravity for irrigation of 6000 acres of splendid land, practically frostless, after power had been developed.

The watersheds of the county were to become properties beyond value in a semi-arid land whose people in time would have to span the mountains for water to save their cities and towns. In the early 1900's, water still too often belonged to those who seized it.

Ed Fletcher

Mayor Frary successfully ran for re-election in 1903 on a platform supporting the national policies of President Roosevelt and the state program of Gov. George C. Pardee, but was accused by the Democrats of having done nothing to solve pressing local problems, particularly the water supply.

Hopes for Eastern financial support for the railroad project were slowly dying with the passing years, and it was becoming abundantly clear that Harriman had no intention of running a line from Salt Lake City to San Diego as part of the Union Pacific system, but would instead connect with the line being built out of Los Angeles, to provide a third transcontinental terminal for San Diego's one-time rival for the supremacy of Southern California.

But as the automobile had not fully captured the imagination of the people, transportation generally was still thought of in terms of railroads and roads for wagons. In October of 1904 a mass meeting of interested citizens was called for the Isis Theater and pledges were asked for a fund to begin some construction work on their own. Those attending were informed that farmers in the Imperial Valley, who were objecting to the rates set by the Southern Pacific, were willing to sign pledges of $100 or more and were offering to furnish horses and fodder. Will Holcomb, who presided, told the packed house:

If you are not convinced of the need for a railroad, read a bit about the Imperial Valley, a portion of our own county, to reach which we have to travel 150 miles out of our way through three other counties in order to get into our own again.

RAIL ROAD MASS MEETING

A MASS MEETING TO CONSIDER A PLAN FOR THE BUILDING OF A

IS HEREBY CALLED FOR

Thursday Evening

AT 7:30 O'CLOCK

People's Railroad

At the **Isis Theater**

A preliminary meeting of some of the most prominent business men of this city now have the proposition under consideration. It is the purpose to build, equip and own this railroad by the people of San Diego County. Over one million dollars is already assured. The proposition has been presented to and accepted by Imperial Valley.

Make your arrangements to attend this meeting. It is a meeting of all the people of San Diego, irrespective of race, creed or color. A proposition which has met the approval of the financial and legal interests of the county is certainly of interest to you, and especially since the plan proposed assures a solution of the great railroad question along absolutely independent lines.

Good speakers will be present both from Imperial Valley and the City and County of San Diego. Admission free.

By the PEOPLE'S RAILROAD COMMITTEE.

Per—

W. R. ROGERS
Cashier Merchants National Bank

F. W. STEARNS
Attorney

JUDGE A. HAINES

H. G. CROWE

M. W. FOLSOM

PHILIP MORSE

F. M. ELLIOTT

The new transcontinental railroad lines passed San Diego by but the people would not surrender the future they had envisioned. They would build their own railroad to open the port to the markets of the East.

F. M. Elliott recalled a statement popularly attributed to Collis P. Huntington of the Southern Pacific that grass would grow in the streets of San Diego, and while he said this had not come to pass San Diegans still continued as "hewers of wood and drawers of water for the Santa Fe."

It was decided to organize a People's Railroad Committee, to succeed the San Diego-Eastern, and to sell stock and bonds. After considerable effort had been spent, the Master Builders Committee had produced pledges of $1500. The People's Railroad faded from the news. The San Diego-Eastern Company continued in existence. Though Spreckels had aided the campaign financially he was curiously unresponsive to appeals to intervene more directly.

Three

Who Could Have Guessed these Stones Were Gems?

*The richness of gems found in San Diego
County is evident in the collection of
Mrs. Myrtle Mullineaux, daughter of the
pioneer jeweler J. W. Ware. With them
are typical mining implements. From the
top and clockwise, in natural and cut
stones, are smoky quartz; blue topaz;
kunzite; yellow beryl and (below) blue
beryl; pink morganite beryl and (below)
green beryl; and a group of tourmaline
including bi-color, green, rose, rubelite
and emeralite. In the center, hessonite
garnet.*

CHAPTER III

In many cities all over the United States there was a rising resentment of political "rings" deriving in part from Lincoln Steffens' book THE SHAME OF CITIES and numerous investigations into state and municipal corruption.

Theodore Roosevelt's campaigns against the "trusts" and concentrated political and economic power found popular favor in San Diego County and he received 2382 votes for re-election in 1904. Eugene V. Debbs, the Socialist candidate, however, received 768 votes compared to only 666 for the conservative Democrat candidate for President.

In San Francisco, Rudolph Spreckels, another of the Spreckels brothers, joined in efforts to overthrow a municipal government dominated by a corrupt, labor-backed political machine, while at the same time John D. and Adolph Spreckels were under attack in San Diego.

In 1905 the revolt against the so-called "boss rule" in San Diego resulted in the adoption of a new city charter which reduced

John L. Sehon

the City Council from twenty-seven members to nine, and provided for the initiative, referendum and recall, the first in California, over the opposition of THE SAN DIEGO UNION and the Spreckels interests. THE SAN DIEGO UNION described the charter provisions as populist and socialistic and fought the reduction in the membership of the Council because it believed that twenty-seven men were harder to corrupt than nine.

For the election of a new mayor in the same year, Capt. John L. Sehon, a retired Army officer and a member of the Council, was nominated by the Independents and won the support of Democrats and many Republicans who later were to become identified as Progressives. He supported a proposal to buy lands in El Cajon Valley to acquire additional pumping rights, which conflicted with the plans of the Spreckels companies to provide the town with its future water supply.

The SAN DIEGO SUN supported Sehon. It was owned at the time by E. W. Scripps, the Eastern newspaper magnate who had established himself at Miramar Ranch in San Diego County. Wherever he published a newspaper Scripps was challenging vested interests and defending the "little man," presumably on the premise that there were more poor readers than rich readers. THE SAN DIEGO UNION was contemptuous of its opposition:

According to Capt. Sehon's organ, it is a high crime for two San Francisco gentlemen who have millions invested in San Diego and vicinity, to own newspaper property in this city. According to the same organ, it is quite right and proper for Mr. Scripps, who has only modest investments here, to own a newspaper — or an apology for one.

In a letter to the SAN DIEGO SUN, which stirred up considerable controversy, a writer identifying himself as D. K. Adams argued that there must be some logical reason why San Diego, so favored by nature, should have remained comparatively dormant while all other Southern California cities had forged ahead at an unprecedented pace.

THE SAN DIEGO UNION sprang to the defense of the city, to deny it had not shared in regional growth and that it was being oppressed by corporations and political bosses, and, describing the opposition as a collection of knockers and soreheads, asked, "...Mr. D. K. Adams, are you not in some way related to a Mr. Daniel K. Adams, who, according to the City Directory, is employed by Mr. Ed Fletcher, the Cyclonic Reformer of Golden Hill?"

Sehon and the SAN DIEGO SUN carried the day. Though the voters approved the proposal to develop water in El Cajon Valley, the necessary bonds failed to pass. It developed that Scripps owned the lands, though he said that a group of citizens representing the Chamber of Commerce had persuaded him to buy them, which he did through a San Francisco agent, to hold them for the city and circumvent the speculators. The lands remained with the Scripps family as the Fanita Ranch.

The Republican machine had suffered a serious defeat but was not ready to surrender. A suit was filed questioning the right of a retired military officer and pensioner to serve in public office. Sehon evaded the filing of legal papers and at 2 o'clock in the dark morning of the day he was to assume the mayoralty, he and an accomplice forced open the swinging doors of the City Hall, at Fifth and G Streets, and then broke a glass in the door of the mayor's office and entered and took possession of the official chair. Dawn found him firmly in command of the city.

It was later claimed his accomplice was his attorney, Edgar A. Luce, son of a San Diego pioneer. Sehon defied his opponents on the grounds that possession was nine-tenths of the law, and though the case was taken all the way to the State Supreme Court, he remained at his desk, conducted the city's business, and won out legally as well as politically. A turning point in the fortunes of the little town at the end of a branch line had arrived.

At the age of ninety-one, Alonzo E. Horton, who was known to everybody in town as the Father of San Diego, was the guest of honor at a little ceremony in front of the Horton House in conjunc-

The Horton House, once one of Southern California's fine hotels, had seen better days when this picture was taken in 1905. Soon afterward it came down, to make way for the U. S. Grant Hotel.

Alonzo E. Horton

U. S. Grant Jr.

tion with a civic celebration across the street in the town Plaza. It was on the evening of one of the regular band concerts and took place between the opening musical selection and the beginning of a fireworks display for which several thousand people had assembled.

The ceremony marked the start of the destruction of the hotel which Horton had completed in 1870, three years after purchasing 960 acres at a public auction and laying out the subdivision which became the heart of New San Diego. He had left Old Town, five miles to the north, to fade along with its historic memories that went back almost 100 years to the founding of the first White settlement in California by the Spanish expedition of Gaspar de Portolá and Father Junípero Serra.

The country was experiencing a boom, the long drought in Southern California was over, and a new tide of settlers was moving westward. Work at last had been started on the Panama Canal, and San Diego, as the first port of call for the Pacific Coast states, foresaw the end of its long isolation. The town's population which had been increasing at an average of about 1000 a year would spurt ahead at a rate of about 3000.

The date was July 12, 1905. With Horton in front of the Horton House were the aging Ephraim W. Morse, who had been his partner in much of the development of New San Diego, and W. W. Bowers, the former congressman and state senator who had assisted Horton in completing the hotel in a time of temporary financial stress.

Once one of the celebrated hotels of Southern California, the thirty-five-year-old building was coming down to make way for a hotel that would cover a whole block and would be built as a monument to President Ulysses S. Grant by his son, U. S. Grant Jr., who had come to San Diego in 1893 for his wife's health. Associated with Grant were Louis J. Wilde, who had arrived from Los Angeles in 1903 to become president of one bank and to establish another one, and a capitalist from Cambridge, Massachusetts, by the name of Horace G. Low. How many other persons were involved in the financing is not clear. In his autobiography Julius Wangenheim says it was his bank which advanced Grant $100,000 to start the million dollar hotel.

At the ceremony in front of the Horton House, Bowers was the principal speaker, and commented:

It is such men as Horton and Morse and Grant and Wilde that build cities. Natural advantages, or beauty of situation, never built a city. Men build cities despite...nature and in defiance of it.

44

The memory of the builder lives on and on, while that of the mere accumulator, the hoarder, the mere absorbant dies with his carcass.

At one time one of the wealthiest men in the southland, Horton had lost everything in the economic collapse of the 1870's and now was living out his days on the money he received from the city by its purchase from him of the Plaza. He held no bitterness though he estimated that he had given away land worth a million dollars. Only a week before he had attended an auction of the furnishings of the hotel from which he once commanded the growth of a town, and was happy to be able to buy a hair sofa, two rocking chairs and a writing table.

He told his friends of a generation and the strangers who normally brushed by him on the street that he rejoiced more in the name of "Father" Horton than he would in the title of President of the United States. He symbolically removed a block from the old structure to give to Wilde "that it may have a place in the principal wall of the new structure." Cheers were given for Father Horton and again for the Horton House, according to the report in THE SAN DIEGO UNION, after which the crowd turned its attention to the principal celebration of the evening.

A fifty-gun salute was fired to observe San Diego's "Day of Emancipation" from the monopoly of the Pacific Mail Steamship Company. The United States had taken over management of the Panama Railroad and canceled its exclusive contract with the Pacific Mail line. A special commissioner had upheld the claims of the San Diego Chamber of Commerce that the port had been deliberately neglected and henceforth the Panama Railroad was to carry the freight of all steamships serving Pacific Coast ports. Ships of other lines carrying cargo for San Diego would not have to make the long journey around Cape Horn, and congratulations came from as far away as Phoenix, El Paso and New Orleans.

San Diego no longer was to be looked upon as a "city of blighted hopes" and special Santa Fe trains were bringing a thousand excursionists at a time from Los Angeles. Among those who had their eyes on San Diego County were Henry E. Huntington, the nephew of the railroad builder, who had sold his interests in the Southern Pacific to Harriman and was creating a network of electric streetcar lines in Los Angeles, and Walter L. Vail and C. W. Gates, who owned the historic 47,000-acre Warner's Ranch fifty miles northeast of San Diego on the old Southern Trail to the California gold fields.

The young produce merchant, Ed Fletcher, who was branching out into water and land development, was well acquainted with

Vail and Gates and informed them on a visit to Los Angeles that water filings had been made on the San Luis Rey River on government land below their ranch by an agent of the Pacific Light and Power Company and thought it might not be in their best interests. This was in the same watershed which had so impressed Fletcher a few years before.

Warner's Ranch

The information was received with astonishment. Vail and Gates had been in secret negotiations with the Pacific Light and Power Company, and other parties, involving the extension of Huntington's Pacific Electric Railway to San Diego. A dam was to be built at Warner's Ranch to convey water to a power drop on the San Luis Rey River, to supply the necessary power.

As they had known nothing of the power company's moves to acquire water rights under separate filings, and suspecting treachery, they asked Fletcher to watch the situation and promised to include him in whatever developed. When the power company neglected to renew the appropriations as and when required by law, Fletcher quickly began a series of filings in the names of friends and relatives, until word came from Los Angeles that Vail, Gates and Huntington had reached an understanding with the Pacific Light and Power Company.

The Pacific Electric Railway already had contributed greatly to the rapid expansion of Los Angeles County, with service to new developments in Beverly Hills and on the coast at Redondo Beach and Venice. Its extension southward was expected to open up all of the north coast of San Diego County. The promoters organized the South Coast Land Company, and with Fletcher and his friend Frank Salmons as their agents, quietly bought up lands and existing water rights along the San Luis Rey River, and then obtained all of the original settlement of Del Mar, more than 800 acres in and around Leucadia, 1400 acres of the Agua Hedionda Ranch from the Kelly Brothers, nearly all of Carlsbad, and large holdings in Oceanside.

Pool Spring at Warner's

In time, Huntington also envisioned the extending of his coast line to San Francisco, and in the south eastward through San Diego County to Warner's Ranch and then down San Felipe Valley, along the route of the first transcontinental Butterfield stages, to Imperial Valley. The plans of the Pacific Electric suggested serious competition for both the Santa Fe and Southern Pacific railroads. Rumors of Huntington's plans soon spread throughout the town and contributed to a general economic and speculative boom.

The Spreckels interests did not look with enthusiasm upon the rise of competing commercial enterprises and water developments, and rivalries that were to last a lifetime were beginning. John D. Spreckels also fell out with E. S. Babcock, his San Diego partner in numerous ventures. Babcock went to court and accused Spreckels of having maneuvered his removal as a director of the Southern California Mountain Water Company even though he owned nearly one half of the stock.

E. S. Babcock

It was essentially a fight over water and the value it could give to land. Babcock charged a conspiracy on the part of Spreckels and the San Diego Land & Town Company. In his suit Babcock contended that the water being developed by the company for expected sale to the town of San Diego was being diverted to enrich lands owned by Spreckels in Coronado and those of the San Diego Land & Town Company in the South Bay area.

These latter lands were part of the 10,000 acres which officers of the Santa Fe railroad had induced the Kimball brothers to deed to a holding company in return for making National City the terminus of its transcontinental line. However, National City never became more than a small repair yard, and even this was taken from it, but the Kimballs never were able to regain their extensive holdings.

The San Diego Land & Town Company, according to Babcock, was to have conveyed certain lands to the water company in return for delivery of water to the rest of its holdings. This was not done, however, and with Babcock's removal the water company planned to buy them instead.

In a deposition taken in San Francisco Spreckels acknowledged that he was thinking of acquiring control of the San Diego Land & Town Company from B. P. Cheney of Boston, but insisted that if he did so, he had every intention of delivering the land promised to the water company. Cheney was the same financier who had shown some interest in helping to finance the projected San Diego & Eastern Railway. After some legal maneuvering, Spreckels purchased all Babcock's interest in their joint ventures and the suit was dismissed.

The year saw many developments. The Zuniga Jetty protecting the harbor entrance was completed and the channel dredged to a width of 500 feet and a depth of twenty-four feet at mean low tide. The jetty had been under construction for eleven years, and a few months after its completion, a March storm partially destroyed more than a thousand feet of its 7500-foot length. Another Army fort was built on North Island, opposite Ballast Point, and named Fort Pico in honor of the last Mexican governor of California. A group of Russians of the Molokanye sect founded a new colony on communal lands near Guadalupe in Baja California.

In La Jolla, Ellen Browning Scripps, who had followed her brother, the publisher, to California and built a home in La Jolla, induced Dr. William E. Ritter of the University of California to establish his projected institution for biological research at La Jolla. Ellen as well as E. W. Scripps had been intensely interested in the marine studies he had been carrying on for several summers in Glorietta Bay, off Coronado. With the Scripps' and community help, Dr. Ritter and his university staff began research work in a building of the Marine Biological Association of San Diego, situated near the La Jolla cove, in June of 1905.

Ellen Browning Scripps

San Diegans, however, were more interested in smokestacks, in the possibilities of the silk industry and in drilling for oil, mostly in stock-selling schemes, than they were in gems and pearls and abalone, and for that matter, in gold. Oil drilling would go on for years, and nothing would ever develop, and the prospect of silk from cooperative worms would tantalize investors for two generations.

Louis Wilde went so far as to import thread-making machinery from New Jersey to manufacture silk wear from the 20,000 worms which his manager, Herman Fascher, had housed in the old Victoria Hotel, where he was feeding them on mulberry leaves grown in orchards in Coronado. They were planning to install the machinery in National City and find more suitable quarters for the worms, probably somewhere in Coronado near the source of their food.

Dr. William E. Ritter

In the rich mountain country gold mining had come to a virtual end and been replaced by the production of semi-precious gems. The price of gold had fallen and the cost of trying to keep the mines in the Julian area free of water from underground springs had become prohibitive. Even the extensive Stonewall mine near Cuyamaca Lake, once owned by a governor of California, had been closed down permanently after its new owners had spent $125,000 on its rehabilitation. When the water had been removed, an examination showed that it could not be operated profitably.

For years gem mining had been a secretive and little-known industry, even though a number of San Diegans had staked out claims and were shipping gem material for export around the world. The mountains also held their secrets well. The early geologists who had studied minerals in San Diego County made no mention of gems though their presence certainly was noted before 1872. In that year Prof. W. A. Goodyear made a reconnaissance of the mountain country and his report, though not published by

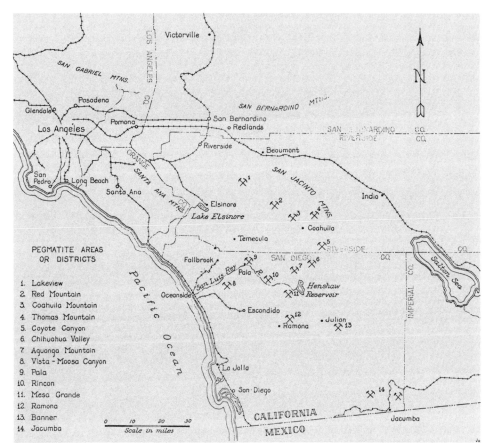

This map by an agency of the State of California shows the location of the principal gem mining areas in San Diego and Riverside Counties.

the State Mining Bureau until 1888, described it as follows:

...the whole country just back of San Diego...to the western edge of the desert is like an angry ocean of knobby peaks, more or less isolated, with short ridges running in every possible direction, and inclosing between and among them numerous small and irregular valleys. As a general rule, the higher peaks and ridges rise from 1000 to 2500 feet above the little valleys and canyons around their immediate bases. But in going eastward from the coast, each successive little valley is higher than the one...preceding, and the dominant peaks also rise higher and higher...until we reach the irregular line of the main summit crest, or water-divide...when the mountains break suddenly off and fall within a very few miles from 4000 to 5000 feet or more, with an abrupt and precipitous front to the east, to the western edge of the desert.

He had noted the presence of black tourmalines but not of colored ones. In that same year Henry Hamilton recognized colored tourmaline on a slope of Thomas Mountain at an altitude of 6500 feet in the San Jacinto Range in Riverside County. Some mining was done and it came to the attention of Dr. George F. Kunz, a special agent for the U.S. Geological Survey and gem expert for Tiffany & Company of New York. It is due to Dr. Kunz' great in-

49

terest in the San Diego gems that the various stories of how the mines were discovered and developed have been preserved.

In one of them it is told how Indian children playing in the Mesa Grande area in the high north central part of San Diego County picked up an oddly-shaped stone, six-sided like a quartz crystal, about three inches long and a little thicker than a lead pencil, and upon cleaning and polishing it, found it to be of a beautiful blue color, bright and partially clear, almost like a sapphire. It was shown to White cattle men and prospectors but held little meaning for them. It was not gold nor was it a diamond. Subsequently other similar stones were found, some blue, others green or red.

Soon after, William Irelan, Jr., state mineralogist, reported the finding of red tourmaline, though not of gem quality, in Pala. The Pala deposits long had been known to Indians and gem stones have been found in ancient graves. F. M. Sickler, who was raised

Fred Sickler was one of those who pioneered gem mining in San Diego County and gathered from Indians the story of the finding of tourmaline.

in the vicinity, later related a story of how an Indian deer hunter by the name of Vensuelada had found pieces of beautiful pink crystals and shown them to a prospector, Henry Magee, who mistook them for cinnabar and located the spot as a quicksilver mine. When it failed to produce mercury, he sent the stones to various chemists who were unable to identify them.

Later the same mine was worked by Tomas Alvarado, a Mexican land owner who thought the stones were a peculiar variety of marble. A few years later a German chemist saw in a New York collection a sample which had the same transparent pink crystals and after an analysis determined they were tourmaline traces in as rich a lepidolite as any found in the world.

It was in 1890 that the first important discovery was made in San Diego County, by Charles Russell Orcutt, an amateur botanist and one of San Diego's early scientists. He was born in Hartland, Vermont, and arrived in San Diego in 1879, to remain the rest of his life. In 1884 he began publishing a little magazine which he called THE WEST AMERICAN SCIENTIST and primarily devoted to the flora of Baja California.

Charles Russell Orcutt

While gathering plant life in regions of San Diego County he collected mineral specimens and sent them to Dr. Kunz in New York, who recognized them as tourmaline and announced the discovery of the rich lepidolite deposits at Pala. No rush similar to that of the gold hills of Julian and Banner in the 1870's developed. The gems were not widely known, especially in California, and stones shown to jewelers in San Diego attracted interest but not excitement.

Though it was also known that colored stones had been found on the huge mountain mass known as Mesa Grande, twenty miles southeast of Pala, prospecting was done only in a desultory way until an agent of J. L. Tannenbaum of New York, whose Himalaya Mining Company operated turquoise mines in San Bernardino County, saw the locality and also recognized the stones as tourmaline.

The Pala district is forty-five miles north of San Diego and about three miles south of the boundary between San Diego and Riverside Counties and comprises about thirteen square miles, mainly the Tourmaline Queen, Pala Chief and Hiriart Mountains. Hiriart Mountain appears on many maps as Heriot Mountain. The gem-rich hills, 1500 to 1900 feet in elevation, rise above the bed of the San Luis Rey River and the little Indian village of Pala and its small Franciscan mission which originally was an extension of the imposing San Luis Rey Mission farther down the river.

Dr. George F. Kunz, the international gem expert who first drew attention to the rich mineral deposits of Southern California, is shown in front of one of the portals of the Pala Chief Mine.

A decade after the discovery of tourmaline at Pala, Fred Sickler while working the Katerina mine also found a mineral which he showed to jewelers and collectors in San Diego and Los Angeles and none of them recognized it. He sent it to Dr. Kunz in New York where it attracted the excited attention of mineralogists. It was in various shades of pink and lilac and was named "kunzite," in honor of Dr. Kunz, and became known as "California's own gem stone."

The Pala Chief mine, located in 1903 by Frank A. Salmons and John Giddens, with the aid of two Basque French prospectors, Bernardo Hiriart and Pedro Peiletch, became the foremost source of kunzite in the world. Salmons, who became county clerk in 1905, and Fred Sickler, were to develop many mines.

Discoveries then came swiftly. Gems—principally tourmaline, kunzite, beryl, topaz and quartz—were found in a broad belt running from the northern end of the county through Pala, Ramona, Julian and to Jacumba near the international border.

The Mesa Grande mines are within a small area of slightly more than two miles square in the upland country to the west of Lake Henshaw, not far from the Julian-Banner gold country. Mesa Grande, at its southwest edge drops off into a deep rock gorge which runs into Black Canyon, through some of the most spectacular scenery in the county, and at its northeast edge rises to a peak that stands 1000 feet above the great Warner's valley.

One of the ridges of this mountain mass is known as Gem Hill at an elevation of 4000 feet, one of those "knobs" which Prof. Goodyear described as rising above the upland valleys of mountain areas. In 1965, a short distance before reaching Gem Hill, there was a little Indian chapel and cemetery which served the Indians who were still living in the area as they had been at the time of the discovery of tourmaline.

The richest mine of them all was the Himalaya in the Mesa Grande district, which was by far the most productive gem-bearing area of California. The Himalaya, opened in 1898 by Gail Lewis of San Diego and later sold to Tannenbaum, yielded more tourmaline than all the other mines together. A mile and a quarter west of the Himalaya was the Esmeralda, acquired and developed in 1904 by H. E. Dougherty of Mesa Grande, and besides tourmaline it yielded the highest quality of golden and white and pink beryl.

Indian Chapel at Mesa Grande

Pink tourmaline was highly prized in China, where it was associated with superstitions, and the green portions of gems mined in San Diego County were cut away and discarded, and the pink shipped to the wealthy of China, mainly through the American

The richest of all the gem mines in San Diego County was the Himalaya in the Mesa Grande district. Its pink tourmaline was highly prized in China.

Gem and Pearl Company of New York. Later evidence indicated this company was controlled by Chinese. From 1902 to 1910 about 125 tons of tourmaline material valued at $800,000 were taken from Mesa Grande mines, nearly ninety tons of it from the Himalaya.

The first discovery in the Ramona district was made by H. W. Robb, of Escondido, in partnership with Dan McIntosh, of Ramona. The Ramona pegmatites were restricted to a hilly area of less than one square mile about four to five miles northeast of Ramona at about 2000-foot elevation. Individual gem-bearing pegmatites were found north of Warner Springs; south of Banner, on the desert side of the mountains below the gold town of Julian; and northwest of Jacumba. The first topaz was found in 1903 by James W. Booth and John D. Farley in the same vicinity in the Ramona area where D. C. Collier, a San Diego real estate developer, had found garnets.

Approximately ninety percent of the gem and near-gem material from Southern California came from only five mines, the Himalaya and San Diego in the Mesa Grande districts, and the Pala Chief, Tourmaline Queen and Katerina in the Pala district. A San Diego County Department of Natural Resources report states that all but a very small part of the rest was taken from ten other mines, the San Pedro, Tourmaline King and Vanderberg in the Pala district; the Esmeralda and Mesa Grande in the Mesa Grande district; the A.B.C. and Little Three mines near Ramona; the Mountain Lily on Aguanga Mountain five miles south of Oak Grove; the Anita near Red Mountain between Fallbrook and Pala; and the Fano on Coahuila Mountain in Riverside County. About thirty-five small and widely scattered additional mines also yielded gem material, and two or three times as many more deposits were seriously prospected.

But Californians remained unimpressed. Dr. Kunz visited the mines and wrote a report, GEMS, JEWELERS' MATERIALS, AND ORNAMENTAL STONES OF CALIFORNIA, which was published in 1905 by the California State Mining Bureau. In his report he stated:

The tourmaline, spodumene, rock-crystals, and other gems—as familiar now to experts and collectors as gold itself—have been better known to residents of Russia, Spain, or Germany than to the inhabitants of the Golden State whence they came. It is a singular fact that these gems are better represented in the American Museum of Natural History in New York, the United States National Museum of Washington, the British Museum in London, the Musée d'Histoire Naturelle of Paris, and other great institutions in the East and abroad, than they are in the State Mining Bureau of California or the State University at Berkeley.

The value of the gems taken from the county reached at least $2,000,000, equal to half of that of all the gold mined at Julian and Banner. As major producers the mines had a short life. The Chinese people's revolt in 1911 which overthrew the Manchu Dynasty and established a republic shut off the major market for tourmaline, and this along with development of mines in other areas of the United States and the world brought about a decline in demand for San Diego stones.

In the Gulf of California, which divides Baja California from the Mexican mainland, except for the Colorado delta country, pearls were still being brought up after 300 years, though the accessible oyster beds were always being fished out. Other beds were too deep for profitable competitive exploitation. Kunz reported that the black pearls found in the waters of La Paz had become so fashionable that their value had increased tenfold, one weighing fifty grains selling for $8000.

Abalone shell was being taken along the Pacific Coast for use for buttons and ornaments. The meat was exported to China. Twenty years before the shell had been considered worthless but an Englishman in San Francisco had seen its possibilities and begun using it in jewelry. Prices in New York and Liverpool rose to $150 to $175 a ton. Kunz said that before the value of the shell was realized, there was a heap south of San Diego which contained over 100 tons of shells.

Abalone fishing and drying mostly was done by Chinese. Kunz reported:

When caught, the abalones are thrown on the beach, and the fish is pulled from the shell with a flat, sharp stick, and stripped of its curtain, boiled, salted, and strung on long rods to dry in the air. This process is very disagreeable, and that of stripping and cleaning so offensive that none but the Chinese will undertake it. The abalones must be as hard as sole-leather when properly dried, and they are then packed in sacks, and sent to China.

The Chinese began the fishing industry at San Diego and later thousands of them were brought down from central and northern California for work on the California Southern Railroad which became the Santa Fe line to Los Angeles. Many of them remained to replace Indians in menial housekeeping tasks, to do laundering, to conduct the familiar gambling games and to raise vegetables in neat gardens in Mission Valley. The city directory for 1905 did not list Chinese residents but did list twenty-eight places of business which they operated. The United States census of five years later reported there were 516 persons of alien extraction, Chinese, Indian and Japanese descent, "and all others."

The number of Indians who had survived the advance of civilization was difficult to determine, though probably there were not more than a thousand still living west of the desert. Once they had numbered more than 5000. Even at that the Indian population of San Diego County was one of the largest in California. The Treaty of Guadalupe Hidalgo was held to have transferred title to all land from Mexico to the United States government, and as Indians had no rights to ownership they were driven onto reservations, of which there were eleven in San Diego County, at the pleasure of the government. Many Indians resisted and preferred to hold out in isolated mountainous areas where their existence drew the sympathy of many people concerned with their fate.

Four

The River that Proved It Was Lord of the Desert

CHAPTER IV

The Colorado River had been peaceful enough. That it flowed past them almost 400 feet above the low points of the valley they were farming was considered a blessing of nature by the settlers.

The river drains an area of 250,000 square miles, reaching into seven states and from the southern end of Yellowstone National Park to the Gulf of California. A decade later, when much more was known about the river and its sudden rages, a United States Geological Survey Report of 1916 gave this description:

When the snows melt in the Rocky and Wind River Mountains, a million cascade brooks unite to form a thousand torrent creeks; a thousand torrent creeks unite to form a half a hundred rivers beset with cataracts; half a hundred roaring rivers unite to form the Colorado, which flows, a mad, turbid stream, into the Gulf of California.

The Imperial Valley once was part of the Gulf of California when it extended as far as the San Jacinto Mountains and San Gorgonio Pass, 150 miles northwest of Yuma. In time the Colo-

High sugar cane in Imperial Valley

Canal drop in irrigation system

Main irrigation channel and typical ranch

rado River, transporting hundreds of thousands of tons of silt each day on its 1800-mile journey, slowly built a broad delta out from its mouth. As ages wore on the silt was deposited in deep layers for hundreds of miles southerly into the Gulf of California and westerly and northerly through the Mexicali Valley and into the Imperial Valley. The gulf was cut in two. In later years, M. J. Dowd, an engineer in the forefront of the effort to control the river, stated:

One has but to stand on the brink of the Grand Canyon of the Colorado in Arizona and look at that great chasm to get some appreciation of the tremendous quantity of material that has been eroded during the past ages by the river and spread over its delta.

The dividing ridge of the delta is about fifty feet above sea level. One side slopes toward the Gulf of California and the other toward the interior valleys where, at the point of the present international border, it reaches sea level and then drops off to the bottom of the Salton basin.

An inland salt water sea was left to evaporate or to be expelled by the frequent flooding of the Colorado River as it lashed back and forth across the delta it had built. Then the basin time and again was filled and refilled with fresh water.

This lake, which has been given the name of Lake Cahuilla, was about 150 miles in length and an average of thirty miles in width, and had a maximum depth of more than 300 feet. The old shore line is clearly visible as a great scar along the sides of the dry eastern mountains and can be traced on the western side of the valley floor by deposits of fresh-water shells.

A remnant of the last historic re-creation of the sea is believed to have existed at the time of the first visits by Spaniards to the Pacific Coast. The average settlers in the Imperial Valley had little or no knowledge of that. While they had become aware that the river had periodically overflowed its banks and watered the valley, even as they themselves had caused it to do with their canals, as far as they were concerned the valley had always been just a desert.

They were more concerned with the serious internal and financial problems of the California Development Company, and an unexpected and alarming low flow of water through the canal and into the valley. Chaffey had resigned and been succeeded by Anthony H. Heber, while Charles R. Rockwood, whose imagination fired much of the original work, had returned as chief engineer. As the Reclamation Service was determined to take over the Imperial Valley and add it to a federal project being developed on the other side of the river in Arizona, the government proclaimed the Colorado a navigable river and held that all filings made under state law were invalid. To add to the dissension, William E. Smythe, the unsuccessful candidate for Congress, moved among the farmers and told them water was the natural possession of the people and the California Development Company had no right to appropriate it and charge them for it.

Smythe won considerable support from members of the Valley Water Users' Association who believed they should own the canal system. He told them that speculation in private irrigation schemes in the arid West had resulted "in the sorriest failures in the annals of American financing," and the government would be glad to assist them in obtaining control of their own water. Both he and the Reclamation Service contended that despite all the arguments to the contrary, a canal could be dug through the yellow sand hills lying west of the river and water brought to the valley entirely through United States territory. Smythe told the people:

The first thing our settlers should understand is that Uncle Sam is not trying to find someone to devour...he will only come to private lands when the owners of such lands are in trouble. Another generation may deliver the people from the bondage of private monopoly because private monopoly is wrong.

Panic again enveloped the valley. Some farmers refused to pay their water bills. Others sued the company for lack of water. Still others were willing to agree to sell out to the government.

But the fiction that the Colorado was navigable was exposed by the introduction of prior federal reports on the precarious experiences of flat-bottom steamboats and the Reclamation Service's own proposals to construct dams across the river.

Legislation was introduced in Congress to legalize the prior diversion and appropriation of water from the Colorado, but Smythe intervened as a witness to demand government ownership of the Imperial system, as the nucleus of a much more extensive system in the Lower Colorado basin. Heber, however, warned:

It is my earnest desire to worship at our own altar and to receive the blessing from the shrine of our government, but if such permission is not given, we shall be compelled to worship elsewhere.

That the company survived, and the Imperial Valley remained a domain of private enterprise, was due to the sagacity and determination of Heber. But in accomplishing this he made a decision which almost destroyed the valley.

The low state of the river had exposed a silting up of the man-

(Next page) Imperial Valley once held a great inland sea and the earliest explorers saw the old water line etched along the sides of the basin. This sketch was made by the staff artist of the government railroad surveys in 1853. That the sea could reappear never troubled the pioneers who settled a valley which sank below the course of the Colorado River.

61

made Imperial Canal, from its heading above the border to where it entered the Alamo channel, which was reducing the vital flow on which thousands of farmers were now dependent. As the water through the channel continued to subside, more and more fields began to dry up and crops to wither under the sun, and the harrassed company was confronted with a long and costly task of dredging out four miles of channel choked with heavy material.

Congress failed to act on affirming the valley's water right, though at the same time rejecting federal intervention partly because no one could see how the federal government could take over a canal system in Mexico, and more studies were recommended. Heber, however, thought he saw the solution to the problem of

Quickly made canals were gouged out of dirt and sand to carry water from the Colorado River around the desert sand hills to connect with a natural overflow channel that led back into the Imperial Valley.

the silted channel as well as to the government claims to control of the water: He would divert the water in Mexico instead of the United States.

This required the permission of the Mexican government, and upon assurances from the company's representative in Mexico City that it would be forthcoming, Heber ordered Rockwood to make the cut immediately. For Rockwood, to make the cut and allow it to remain open, while waiting official authority to install the necessary controls, was a responsibility difficult to accept. But the growers who were losing their crops also insisted that it be done.

In late September of 1904 a cut sixty feet wide was made in the bank of the river at a point four miles below the border. A new channel 3300 feet long was dredged through soft material to reach the lower end of the original Imperial Canal just above where it joined the Alamo channel.

The work was completed in three weeks and life-giving water again flowed richly into the fields of Imperial Valley. But the anticipated permission from Mexico City for the installation of the head-gate did not arrive. The river was its own master.

There seemed no reason for alarm, however, as Rockwood wrote in his own version of the events of the next few years:

We had before us at the time the history of the river as shown by the rod-readings kept at Yuma for a period of twenty-seven years. In the twenty-seven years there had been but three winter floods. In no winter of the twenty-seven had there been two winter floods.

In January Rockwood took a boat down the river on a hunting expedition into the delta where old and dry channels cut everywhere through stunted undergrowth. He left his boat tied to a tree, and when he returned he could see it far out in the river channel. At first he thought it had worked loose, but saw that it was still tied to a tree. Then came a chilling realization: The river was in a flood stage. His boat beyond reach, the apprehensive Rockwood struggled up the lonely delta for three days to reach the cut he had made in the river. Nothing much had happened, as yet. The flood had not enlarged the intake but had caused silting that required dredging to maintain an even flow of water to Imperial Valley. A second flood came soon after, but again did no damage except in silting.

Charles Robinson Rockwood

A third flood came in March of 1905 and at last it was realized that they were facing an unprecedented situation. It was decided that as the river was at a high level the old intake above the border could be used again and the new cut closed. A dam of piles, brush and sandbags was thrown across it. Another flood came down the river and washed it away. A second dam met the same fate. By summer the river had widened the intake from sixty to 160 feet and 90,000 cubic feet of water each second was rushing through the Alamo Canal and down the steep incline of the delta and accumulating in the Salton basin. A new sea was being born.

Now the problem was a serious one and the California Development Company had no money and few friends. The federal government was their enemy and the people of San Diego, the county seat, were indifferent even though they hoped to benefit from the valley's growth. But San Diegans had their own troubles and even their own disasters with which to contend. One of them, while not significant, was to be remembered by San Diegans for the rest of their lives. It occurred on July 21, 1905.

The morning fog had lifted and the white-hulled U.S.S. BENNING-TON lay at anchor in San Diego Bay just to the west of the ferry landing and the Santa Fe wharf at the foot of H Street. The BEN-NINGTON was classed as a gunboat and was 230 feet in length and thirty-six feet in width. With a crew of sixteen officers and 181 men, she had arrived from Honolulu en route to Port Harford in San Luis Obispo County to tow the monitor WYOMING, disabled with a broken propeller, to the Mare Island navy yard. Steam was up and she was awaiting the return of Capt. Lucien Young, who had gone ashore, before sailing.

At 10:33 two of her four boilers exploded in rapid succession. A

Light forces of the United States Pacific Fleet were frequent visitors to San Diego Harbor in the early years of 1900. They were forerunners of the ships that carried this country through several great wars at sea.

citizen was standing on the nearby Commercial wharf when he heard a muffled explosion and saw a large column of black smoke rise high above the masts and then envelop the ship completely. Various objects and debris were driven even higher into the air. The black smoke was succeeded by clouds of steam, through which he could see running figures in various stages of undress, leaping into the water to escape the scalding vapor. There were cries of pain and sharp commands.

The ranking officer on board was Lieut. Alexander Fred Hammon Yates and he was seated in a cabin near the stern when the explosion occurred. He rushed out of the cabin and was almost driven back by clouds of steam. Reaching the deck he called for volunteers to go back below deck, but there were only twelve men left, the rest having succumbed or been badly burned or had gone over the ship's sides. He managed to halt the flow over the sides and with volunteers quickly flooded the powder magazines to prevent another explosion.

The launch MCKINLEY was at a wharf, the tug SANTA FE at the Commercial pier, the government launch DE RUSSEY was on her way across the bay from Fort Rosecrans, and the Coronado ferry RAMONA was on her way to the San Diego terminal. All turned and went to the scene and began picking wounded out of the water. Some of their crewmen and passengers went on board the BENNINGTON to assist Lieut. Yates.

On the deck they found Lieut. Newman K. Perry. He had been standing almost directly over the spot on the starboard side where the explosion took place. Eye-witnesses said he was literally cooked alive, and in his frenzy had torn off all of his clothing.

Torn inside and listing from taking on water, the gunboat BENNINGTON *is shown after her boilers exploded and brought death to sixty men.*

67

Yet, before he died, according to the report in THE SAN DIEGO UNION:

In face of all this suffering, he dictated a telegram to his wife, telling her to be brave and keep a stiff upper lip; that he would come out all right.

THE SAN DIEGO UNION's report continued:

Everything on board was blackened and begrimed by the smoke and soot of the explosion, and this was particularly true of the portion between decks whence the bodies of the dead and injured had been taken...seven bodies were in the fire room, of which three were pinned under a shattered boiler, and four were behind a steel bulkhead which had to be cut away to get at them.

Dr. W. L. Kneedler, the army surgeon of Fort Rosecrans, witnessed the rescue work of the surviving crewmen. THE SAN DIEGO UNION reported:

He found it almost unbearably hot below the main deck, and the water on the floor was almost scalding, nearly burning through his shoes. Furthermore the lower deck was strewn with glass. Yet in this scalding water and on this glass the uninjured sailors walked in their bare feet trying to rescue their more unfortunate comrades.

Messages were sent through the city to call all physicians together. Mayor Sehon arrived to direct relief work and sixty men responded to his request for volunteers to help remove the dead and wounded from the ship.

Open wagons with drivers whipping their horses raced the burned men to hospitals. Fifty-four were taken to the Agnew sanitarium, where they were treated by the town's doctors, and eleven to the old military barracks. All who could talk asked that their companions be cared for ahead of them. Large numbers of women offered their services as nurses. Eleven of the less seriously wounded were soon removed from the sanitarium to St. Joseph's Hospital, but eighteen others died during the afternoon.

The managers of the Isis, Grand, Pickwick and Bijou theaters closed their houses. The City Guard Band postponed its evening concert on the Plaza. President Roosevelt sent a telegram expressing his shock and asking that everything possible be done for the survivors. Acting Secretary of the Navy Charles H. Darling said the accident was the most distressing to befall an American vessel since the blowing up of the MAINE in Havana harbor in 1898.

A fire engine was placed on a lighter and taken alongside the stricken BENNINGTON in the hope its pumps could keep up with the inflow of water through ruptured boiler intake pipes. This failed and as her listing became more pronounced the tug SANTA

FE put a line on board and towed her onto the mud flats. A centrifugal pump used to pump sand for ships' ballast was brought alongside on a Spreckels barge and the water removed. More bodies were found.

An investigation indicated that one boiler gave way and was blown against another, setting off a second blast. A final report listed sixty killed and forty-six injured. After an official Navy investigation into the accident, and the reports of prior trouble with the boilers, the Secretary of the Navy wrote a letter of reprimand to Capt. Young, and while it was not made public, it was not considered too damaging to his career. The BENNINGTON was towed to the Mare Island navy yard for repairs and put back in service.

Funeral services and a mass burial for forty-seven of the dead were conducted on Sunday, July 23, in the post cemetery at Fort Rosecrans high on the hill overlooking the bay and the town. Here also was the last resting place of eighteen members of the First Dragoons who had given their lives at the Battle of San Pasqual in the American conquest of California in 1846. Their bodies had been removed from their temporary graves in the Protestant cemetery in Old Town, to another temporary cemetery behind Ballast Point, and then removed once again about 1888 and reinterred on the hill.

A procession of wagons began loading up the coffins from the various funeral homes at 11 o'clock in the morning. Some carried as many as six or eight coffins. In each of them was a bottle containing a slip of paper on which the name had been written. THE SAN DIEGO UNION reported:

Along the dusty road toward Old Town the procession moved, then skirting the bay the hill on Point Loma side was ascended. All along the way carriages fell into line and by the time the promontory was reached, the procession was over a mile long. Slowly it wound its way along the crest of the point, with the breakers of the ocean pounding against the cliffs on one side and the placid waters of the bay on the other. Some of the wagons were so heavily laden with their human freight that it was necessary to make frequent stops. It was 3 o'clock before the desolate cemetery, surrounded by a rude picket fence, was reached.

A large crowd had gathered, every craft available having been used to bring people across the bay. A trench sixty feet long and fourteen feet wide had been finished minutes before the arrival of the first wagon. Around its sides were seventy-five artillery men from Fort Rosecrans, on the west; the Naval Reserves, bearing flowers, on the north; the BENNINGTON survivors, on the east; and the Universal Brotherhood, on the northeast. Just outside the picket fence the public was gathered. It took about an hour to arrange the coffins in the trench, a task performed by BENNINGTON survivors. The last rites were conducted by the Rev. J. A. M. Richey, rector of St. Paul's, and by Father A. D. Ubach, of St. Joseph's. Three sharp volleys rang out over the bay. Out of the ranks stepped a bugler and taps were sounded. The crowd turned and walked away. Such is the memory of man and the obligation of government that not all of the graves in either the BENNINGTON or the San Pasqual burial were ever individually marked.

Protestant and Catholic services were conducted beside a mass grave on windswept Point Loma for victims of the U.S.S. BENNINGTON *explosion.*

The potential disaster building up in the Imperial Valley did not have an impact on San Diego such as that of the explosion on the BENNINGTON. In their time of need the people of the valley turned to the Southern Pacific Railroad, which was beginning to benefit from the shipment of valley products. In the latter part of the year it was decided to ask for a loan of $200,000, of which $20,000 was to be used in closing the break and the rest in improving the canal system. Harriman agreed but stipulated that the Southern Pacific be given temporary control of the company. This was accepted but Harriman's engineers soon discovered that restoring control of the river would cost more than $200,000; just how much it was impossible to tell.

Though the floods subsided the intake kept widening and further attempts to close it failed. In August, the Southern Pacific

70

took over and constructed a dam of piling, brush-mattresses and sandbags 600 feet long. In November the floods began again. The Gila River which empties into the Colorado above Yuma rose ten feet in ten hours. The dam simply disappeared. The banks of the river crumbled, the crevasse opened up 600 feet and nearly the whole of the river poured down the canal and into the Salton Sink. The sea spread over an area of 150 square miles.

Water also was accumulating in the heart of the lower delta in Volcano Lake, and was slowly moving northward and pushing its surplus into the New River channel that also led to the Salton Sink.

Approval of plans for the installation of the controlling gate finally came from Mexico City, but it was much too late now. Imperial Valley was threatened by rising water from two directions, and another winter and another spring were coming.

That same winter in the early weeks of 1906, John D. Spreckels fell seriously ill in his home in San Francisco. His biographer, H. Austin Adams, wrote in his book, THE MAN JOHN D. SPRECKELS, that a digestive disorder dropped his weight from 175 pounds to 100 pounds and it was feared that he would not live. His death would have had an immediate and most serious effect on San Diego and would have drastically altered its future. It was three months before he began to show some signs of improvement.

On April 18, 1906, at 5:16 o'clock in the morning, San Francisco was rocked by a massive earthquake. Fires rapidly swept

Levees were built and rebuilt in the effort to push the Colorado River back into its main channel and prevent the flooding of Imperial Valley, as this old photograph shows.

71

through the city threatening all that the Spreckels family had built or accumulated.

The original quake was not felt in San Diego but wild rumors swept the coast that both San Diego and Coronado, where John D. Spreckels had invested so much of his fortune, had been engulfed by a tidal wave and had disappeared beneath the sea.

San Diegans learned of the disaster through their newspapers and though a sharp quake was felt at 4:29 that same afternoon, there was no serious damage and Mayor Sehon denounced as "mischievous lies" the stories which had been circulated in Los Angeles about San Diego's total destruction.

As they had to the accident to the U.S.S. BENNINGTON, San Diegans responded to the needs of San Francisco. Sehon sent a telegram to the mayor offering to care for 3000 women and children; William Clayton, the Spreckels companies representative in San Diego, wired that Coronado Tent City canvas would be sent to set up refugee centers; the Ramona Tent City offered 100 tents; public subscriptions exceeded $20,000 in cash, and large amounts of supplies were sent in railroad boxcars provided by the Santa Fe and Southern Pacific.

San Francisco dampened its fires and cleaned up its ruins. The Spreckels' properties in most part survived the shock, but John D. Spreckels, still in a weakened condition, and his wife left for San Diego to make their home in Coronado.

The railroad magnate, Harriman, already feeling the lash of the "Trust Busters" and hard-pressed to repair the damage to Southern Pacific facilities in the San Francisco area, received another request for emergency funds to control the Colorado River. The original $200,000 had vanished and the water in the Salton Sink was still rising and threatening to inundate the Southern Pacific's main line from New Orleans. He agreed to another loan of $250,000 but his own engineers moved in to assume complete charge. Rockwood resigned.

Between Spreckels in the south and Harriman in the north a series of messages began to move. The Southern Pacific had large investments in San Diego County and the Imperial Valley and there were reports from Boston that Eastern financiers were unexpectedly and unexplainably looking with new interest at the proposed San Diego-Eastern Railway to Yuma. The messages resulted in several conferences between Harriman and Clayton, the San Diego representative for the Spreckels interests. Everything was done in secret. "Teddy" Roosevelt was not a President to further antagonize at this time.

The New Liverpool salt works in the former Salton Sink disappeared under sixty feet of flood water with the formation of the Salton Sea. This is a sketch by the French artist Carl Eytel.

By the beginning of summer at the height of the seasonal floods, the whole of the Colorado River was pouring out onto the delta through the cut which had widened to more than a half mile and was collecting into the New River channel and racing down the slope to the Salton Sea. The sea rose seven inches a day over an area of 400 square miles. The New Liverpool Salt Company disappeared under sixty feet of water. The main lines of the Southern Pacific were moved and moved again and again. Irrigation works were destroyed and canals silted. Lands returned to desert. The situation was becoming desperate and the entire nation began to focus attention on Imperial Valley.

The river had not yet displayed all its power and its cunning. The bulk of the water was running down the New River when suddenly it created its own waterfall at the entrance to the Salton Sea and then occurred one of the phenomena of nature — the "cut-back."

The water tumbling over the edge became a cascade and its force cut back the bank. Soon the bank was receding faster and faster, moving upstream into the valley at a pace of 4000 feet a

Flood waters pouring over an embankment created a phenomenon of nature, a "cutback." The action of the water dug out a channel a thousand feet wide in racing backward across the valley.

day and widening the New River channel to a gorge of more than 1000 feet. The roar of the waterfall could be heard for miles as it surged backward, consuming its own bed, toward the towns of Calexico and Mexicali. Farms and homes disappeared in its path.

A second though smaller cut-back formed in the Alamo and another waterfall raced backward across the desert, like a prairie fire, toward a bridge on the Southern Pacific line east of Brawley, which, if destroyed, would paralyze rail shipments and cause more heavy losses to the farmers. The bridge was hurriedly strengthened while farmers worked night and day to harvest and move their crops. The bridge survived.

In the vicinity of El Centro, waters jumped the banks of the main irrigation canal, erased levees and flooded the town of Imperial. At the border, rising water ate away the desert to the edge of Calexico while across the line in Mexicali, homes and buildings already were disappearing.

As the cut-back in the New River sliced its way backward toward the border, with no way of stopping it, it occurred to engineers that if it could be speeded up it might reach the flooded towns soon enough to leave a channel wide and deep enough to draw off the threatening flood waters. They decided to dynamite

Engineers used dynamite to speed the "cutback" on its way across the valley, in the hope it would reach the border in time so the channel could draw off flood waters before towns were undermined or swallowed up.

the ledge, to speed the progress of the cut-back, though it had to be done under martial law and against the angry reactions of frightened farmers.

The speed of the cut-back doubled. As it cut its way past Calexico a corner of the town disappeared. Almost half of Mexicali vanished. But the flood waters drew off into the 100-foot deep gorge which it had left behind and the immediate flood danger passed.

But it was feared if the cut-back were not stopped at the new sea forming in the bed of Volcano Lake in Baja California, it would continue racing backward to the Colorado and then up the bed of the river itself, attacking the town of Yuma and wiping out the government irrigation works at the Laguna site. How far up the river it might eventually go nobody could even guess.

The cut-back was conquered when engineers succeeded in turning it in a circle by placing brush in the shallow Volcano Lake. It broke up into a series of little cut-backs and they soon died away.

The valley was deeply scarred forever. A great chasm still divides the Baja California capital of Mexicali. H. T. Cory, who had succeeded Rockwood in command of the effort to control the river, wrote:

In nine months the runaway waters of the Colorado...eroded from the New and Alamo River channels and carried down into the Salton Sea a yardage almost four times as great as that of the entire Panama Canal...The combined length of the channels cut out was almost forty-three miles, the average width being 1000 feet and the depth fifty feet...Very rarely, if ever before, has it been possible to see a geological agency effect in a few months a change which usually requires centuries.

Homes and farms disappeared during the Colorado River flood. Calexico was partly carried away and nearly half of Mexicali, just below Calexico in Mexico, disappeared.

Engineers then turned to the task of trying to drive the river back into its bed. They built a spur railroad to the site of the crevasse, marshaled special Southern Pacific trains and 300 mammoth side dump cars from the Union Pacific, gathered rock from all quarries within a range of 400 miles, and mobilized Indian desert tribes and laborers from Mexico.

When the flow began to recede a temporary dam was thrown across the channel and much of the water diverted through a by-pass and head-gate, and work begun on a permanent barrier across the intake. But masses of debris carried by the river pounded out the gate in the by-pass and the river burst through and cut a new opening which became the main river.

The engineers began another attempt almost immediately on a round-the-clock schedule. New rail trestles were laid over the water on pilings and 3000 carloads of rock, gravel and clay were dumped into the breach. On November 4, almost two years after it had broken its banks, the river was at last forced back into its original bed and the long struggle seemed to be over.

A little more than a month later a flood came down the Gila, swelling the Colorado once again. The rock-fill dam held, but just below it a levee weakened and gave away, and within three days the entire river was again flowing into the Salton Sea.

The fear arose that the river would forever empty into the valley and in time would drown the entire countryside. It was not a question now of closing a gap but of building a series of dams and levees and it was estimated the cost might run to $1,500,000 or even more.

For Harriman it also was a personal crisis. Only a short time before he had been described by his one-time friend President Roosevelt as an "undesirable citizen" and he was under prosecution by the Interstate Commerce Commission, but to him it seemed that the task of saving the valley had gone beyond the responsibility of the Southern Pacific.

He sent a telegram to President Roosevelt explaining the situation. As far as the government was concerned, the California Development Company had made the cut that let the river loose and the Southern Pacific controlled the company. Harriman received the following reply:

Referring to your telegram of December 13, I assume you are planning to continue work immediately in closing break in Colorado River. I should be fully informed as to how far you intend to proceed in this manner.

Theodore Roosevelt

Though Harriman informed the President that the Southern

Pacific had no vested interest in the California Development Company, and already had spent more than $2,000,000, and was more than willing to cooperate in any government project, Roosevelt replied that as Congress had adjourned for the holidays he had no authority to act and "it is incumbent upon you to close the break again."

Harriman gave in and ordered that the river be brought under control regardless of cost. Roosevelt promised to recommend legislation to prevent a repetition of the disaster and to provide for an equitable sharing of the burden.

The final struggle began. More than 1200 miles of Southern Pacific lines were tied up and commerce in the port of San Pedro came to a virtual standstill for three weeks. The opening to be closed was 1100 feet wide and forty feet deep. Poles ninety feet long were pounded into the river bed to build two railroad trestles and three times they were swept away. Finally it was accomplished and 3000 flat cars and "battleship" dump cars poured rock into the torrent. The scene was described by F. H. Newell, director of the Reclamation Service, as follows:

The stones used were as large as could be handled or pushed from the flat cars by a gang of men, or by as many men as could get around a stone. In some cases the pieces were so large that it was necessary to break them by what are called "pop-shots" of dynamite

Temporary bridges were built across flooding channels and railroad flat and dump cars by the thousands poured rock into the water to build a dike which finally closed a break and forced the river back to its normal bed.

laid upon the stone while it rested on the cars. In this way the stones were broken and then could be readily thrown overboard by hand. The scene at the closure of the break was exciting. Train after train with heavy locomotives came to the place and the stones, large and small, were pushed off by hundreds of workmen as rapidly as the cars could be placed. While waiting to get out upon the trestle the larger stones were broken by "pop-shots," and the noise sounded like artillery in action. Added to the roar of the waters were the whistle signals, the orders to the men, and the bustle of an army working day and night to keep ahead of the rapid cutting of the stream.

The river was checked and its level raised eleven feet and soon it began to flow gradually back into its old channel. The end came on February 10, 1907. As precautionary measures the branch railway was extended and old levees reinforced and new ones built all up and down the river. The upper part of the original Imperial Canal, which had been choked up and temporarily abandoned in favor of the Mexican site, had been dredged and a new steel and concrete gate installed, and water again was being diverted within the United States. An inland sea, forty-five miles long, twelve to seventeen miles wide and eighty-three feet deep remained.

Even before the battle had been won, President Roosevelt went before Congress and castigated the California Development Company. He accused it of criminal negligence in having made the Mexican cut and said that there were between 6000 and 10,000 persons in the valley, that towns had been capriciously laid out, that extravagant claims had been made as to profits to be derived from taking up desert land, and that money from the settlers had been diverted to personal profits rather than to the construction of necessary and permanent irrigation works.

He recommended to Congress that the government acquire the California Development Company and that during the next ten years there should be developed a comprehensive program for the irrigation of the lands of the Colorado River, with adequate storage and control, so that none of the water would go to waste. He as well as his successor, President Taft, recommended reimbursement of the Southern Pacific, but twenty years were to pass before even a token payment was made. In all it had cost the Southern Pacific $3,100,000.

The people of the valley, however, were not to be subdued, either by nature or government. They intended to be their own masters. And they were finished with San Diego as well. Their long trial had received but scant attention in San Diego.

Five

The Auto Challenges the Train and Shapes the City

A. G. Spalding, the sporting goods manufacturer, and his wife were among the early owners of automobiles in San Diego. In a few years roads and politics were inexorably intermingled.

CHAPTER V

Automobiles by 1906 had broken out of the protected confines of city streets and were bumping over dirt roads that had felt the wooden wheels of Spanish carretas and of armed frontier stages. The auto was now a definite challenge to other methods of transportation and it was beginning to be recognized that good roads as well as railroads were essential to progress.

California's first Motor Vehicle Act had been adopted in the previous year and the first chauffeur's license, or Badge No. 1, was issued on May 4 to John D. Spreckels who listed himself as the proprietor of the SAN FRANCISCO CHRONICLE. He was the proud possessor of a White Steamer. The first person in San Diego to obtain a vehicle license was Clyde Adair, who gave his address as 506 E Street and to whom Badge No. 232 was issued for the operation of a Rambler. The City Directory of 1905 gave his occupation as a machinist and the next year as an "automobile operator."

On January 13, 1906, the LOS ANGELES TIMES announced that

there would be an endurance run from Los Angeles to Coronado:

The...."smart set" of motoring is expected to go in for the San Diego run with both feet...the scenery is most picturesque; the mountain driving beautiful in the extreme. It is a trip well worth popularizing.

Both El Camino Real, the original trail linking the Franciscan missions of California, and the usual coastal stage route between Los Angeles and San Diego were by-passed in favor of an inland route because the rivers when they reached the coast were wide and in wet seasons often impassable, and there were many tidal lagoons that might require detouring. It followed generally the historic Butterfield route from Los Angeles to Monrovia, Pomona, Corona, Elsinore and Temecula, and then went up and over the lower western flank of the Agua Tibia Mountains and down to Pala on the San Luis Rey River, a twelve-mile stretch which was considered the worst of the 180-mile journey, though "any good touring car ought to be able to make it, if properly handled."

Two days were allotted and the maximum speed limit was set at twenty miles an hour. A stop of thirty minutes was allowed at Temecula for water and one of five minutes at Pala for water for three consecutive grades that lay ahead. From Pala to Valley Center, a distance of twenty-eight miles, motorists were warned that they must cross the San Luis Rey River, two shallow fords, some sand, and go up a grade into Keys Canyon, over another grade into Castro Canyon, past the schoolhouse and over a third grade to Valley Center.

From Valley Center it was ten miles to Escondido, across the valley and up a short grade to a summit and then "carefully down the five-mile grade to Escondido Valley, then several miles of fine road into the grounds of the Escondido Hotel on the hill."

From Escondido the autos were to follow the familiar wagon road from Escondido over rolling hill country to Bernardo store, then along the stage road to Poway Pass, across the mesa to Murray Canyon and down into Mission Valley, and from there up what was called the hospital grade — which a half century later became part of the Cabrillo Freeway — to University Heights, down Fifth Street to D, or Broadway, and past the Courthouse and to the ferry, and along Orange Avenue to Hotel del Coronado.

It began on January 25 and by 5 o'clock the next evening twenty-two of the thirty cars had arrived in Coronado, and THE SAN DIEGO UNION was jubilant about its high promise:

No one was injured on the run of 180 miles; no serious damage to the machines resulted, and all the contestants were unanimously

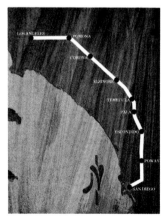

Route of first road race

of the opinion that the run would prove to be one of the most successful ever held, and far-reaching in its effects.

The next day the same cars, along with many others from San Diego, participated in the first annual automobile race meet at the Coronado Country Club, with more than 1000 persons in attendance. First honors went to an Apperson car driven by one W. S. Hook.

Soon afterward, William M. Garland of the Southern California Automobile Club asked the Board of Supervisors of San Diego County to begin construction of a more direct highway connection with Los Angeles, and THE SAN DIEGO UNION commented that the letter indicated "three thousands of automobilists will be glad to pay tribute to San Diego if the coast road between this city and Los Angeles, regarded by many as the most beautiful drive in the world, can be graded and otherwise improved."

In Los Angeles the president of the Chamber of Commerce declared that next to bringing Owens River water to Los Angeles, as was then being undertaken, the road project to San Diego was the most important enterprise for Southern California.

By May auto racing had taken its place alongside horse racing and a fine speedway was under construction around the lake at Lakeside, where Barney Oldfield was to speed a mile in fifty-nine and one-half seconds. The new owner of the Lakeside Inn, J. H. Gay, was projecting a miniature Venice, with canals connecting

This shows a parade of Maxwell autos, with drivers and passengers in typical dress. Where they are going and why is a mystery. But it was supposed to be sporting fun.

the lake and the hotel. The touring season was in full swing and all roads with the exception of the one down the coast were reported in good condition.

The sun was at last rising on the future of San Diego after all those disappointing years, or so it seemed, and building construction in 1906 was double that of the previous year. Among the new buildings started or planned in addition to the U.S. Grant Hotel, were the Spreckels brothers' Union Building between Second and Third Streets on D, or Broadway; the Scripps Building at Sixth and C Streets, built by Frederick T. Scripps, half-brother of the publisher; and the L. J. Wilde Block at Second and D Streets. Though the coaling station had not been completed, the Navy had put into commission in 1906 a wireless station on Point Loma and now was looking over the San Diego area for a second and larger wireless station for fleet communications. Torpedo boats were using the harbor as a port of refuge and capital ships were conducting exercises off the coast. And on September 7 the city turned out to welcome the arrival of the first raft of logs towed down by sea from Oregon for the new Benson Lumber Company sawmill, a practice that was to continue for many years.

Lumber came to port cities in the old days in the form of log rafts which were floated down the coast with the aid of tugs. Here one is entering the main part of San Diego Bay.

The disputes over water began to fade, and faced with a difficult situation of supply with the rapid growth of the community and the failure of the voters to approve development of the El Cajon Valley pumping project, the City Council, over the veto of Mayor Sehon, accepted an offer of the Southern California Mountain Water Company to supply 7,776,000 gallons a day at the low price of four cents per 1000 gallons, to be delivered from the Otay system through the Chollas reservoir. With the signing of the agreement the Spreckels company was to resume construction on Morena dam and the Cottonwood Creek system. San Diego's use of water from the wooden Cuyamaca flume came to an end, and the flume company went into bankruptcy and was taken over and operated at a loss by British bond holders. In the opinion of San Diegans, the water problem had been settled and there was enough for a city of 400,000 persons.

The Chamber of Commerce began to urge the construction of a public highway from San Diego to Yuma as well as to Los Angeles, and the obtaining of a naval training station, and for this, it was emphasized, it would be necessary in the future to elect a congressman directly from San Diego. THE SAN DIEGO UNION stated editorially:

San Diego's population has nearly doubled in five years. The city is rising on the crest of the wave of prosperity, a wave that holds out every promise of landing San Diego in a position to which its numerous advantages give it every right of title, that of one of the largest ports in the world.

In spite of the growth and developing prosperity, the political situation continued to be intense, with Republicans throughout the state as well as in San Diego County defending themselves against charges of corporate domination and political corruption and pleading for party loyalty in a time of restless movements toward new alignments.

Socialists were claiming that they would receive a million votes in the national election of that year, and in a talk in the downtown Plaza, F. M. Elliott and Harry M. McKee, Socialist candidates for state senator and county clerk, respectively, warned that two years before socialism had been pronounced as a foreign importation that would never gain a foothold in the United States, but "it has gained not only a foothold, but a handhold and a tailhold."

A big tent erected at Fifth and B Streets was the site of political debates in which C. A. Barlow, Democratic candidate for Congress, charged that the Southern Pacific had held back development of San Diego, while Sen. George C. Perkins declared that charges of corporate influence being used on James N. Gillett, Republican candidate for governor, and the choice of Harriman, the railroad magnate, were an insult to the intelligence of voters.

An editorial in THE SAN DIEGO UNION pleading for Republican unity, argued:

A great deal is being said about the advantage of nonpartisan action, freedom from party bondage, etc., and the effort is made to create the impression that old-fashioned loyalty to party and ticket is a thing of the past...It is perhaps unnecessary to note that this sort of talk is especially loud in places like San Diego County, where the Democracy, or that part of it which has not gone over to socialism, is so completely in the minority that its only hope of saving something from the coming wreck is through Republican votes cast for Democrats or professed "Independents."

Republican ranks held in California to elect Gillett as governor. He received approximately 125,000 votes; Theodore A. Bell, Democrat candidate, 117,000; William H. Langdon, the Independent candidate, 45,000; and Austin Lewis, the Socialist candidate, 16,000. The reform campaign evidently had a long way to go. Prosperity also had taken the edge off the anti-corporation issue in San Diego County and the normal Republican majority made itself felt, with Gillett receiving 3621 votes; Bell, 2469; Langdon, 564; and Lewis, 974. Leroy A. Wright led the county Republican ticket, for state senator, though he had to beat the Socialist candidate to do it, and S. C. Smith of Bakersfield easily was re-elected to Congress.

For William E. Smythe, politics were over. Having failed to get elected to office or to effect public ownership of irrigation in the Imperial Valley, he retired to selling real estate and then turned his attention to writing another book. He invaded the lair of his old enemy, THE SAN DIEGO UNION AND EVENING TRIBUNE, and with the permission of the general manager, James D. MacMullen, used the offices and newspaper files to write the first detailed History of San Diego that preserved the memoirs and experiences of the early pioneers and settlers.

Before the year had run its course San Diegans at last received the news for which they and their pioneer fathers had been waiting for more than half a century. The Spreckels interests announced on December 14 that they would build the railroad from San Diego to Yuma. There was no mention of Harriman, nor of the Southern Pacific. The incorporators of the San Diego & Arizona Railway Company, with a capital of $6,000,000, were listed as John D., A. B. and J. D. Spreckels Jr., William Clayton, and

Leroy A. Wright

H. L. Titus, an attorney, with the latter three holding only one share each. In a statement, U. S. Grant, Jr., said:

This is only the beginning of good times for San Diego. The thing had to come to pass for which every loyal San Diegan has hoped and prayed since Father Horton's prophetic vision first rested upon the most beautiful bay in the world, and at last men saw the fair and mighty city, which he then dreamed of as a present and imminent possibility.

Mayor Sehon, who had opposed the Spreckels interests, added his congratulations. The Chamber of Commerce passed a resolution, introduced by Fred Jewell, one of the promoters of another railroad building scheme, which extended appreciation to John D. Spreckels and urged everyone to help bring about the railroad's realization. Real estate prices immediately advanced twenty-five percent. Banks began receiving money by telegraph from other parts of the country, and large investors from Los Angeles were reported to be on the way, with their pockets bulging with cash.

Spreckels' home in Coronado

A confident John D. Spreckels began building a $100,000 home in Coronado as well as a public library. Ed Fletcher, as agent for the South Coast Land Company, was laying out a new subdivision at Del Mar, a little to the north of the original settlement, with a large resort hotel first known as the Stratford Inn, and he induced E. W. Scripps to join with his firm in constructing a roadway from San Diego to Del Mar, which would also serve Miramar where the newspaper owner had his estate.

The section from La Jolla to Del Mar was graded up from the beach and along the winding cliffside to the Torrey Pines mesa and through the rare trees and twisted down to the ocean at Los Peñasquitos Creek, which had to be bridged. The stage route that had followed the mission trail from Rose Canyon through Sorrento Valley and back of Del Mar was at last abandoned.

The city was spreading eastward beyond its original pueblo boundaries, and a settlement which was to become a separate town, East San Diego, was rising on the broad mesa which was known as City Heights and had a post office designation as Teralta dating from the boom days of the late 1880's. Just beyond it was the interior valley of La Mesa, with a subdivision started in 1906 by S. C. Grable, where a drier climate was appealing to those afflicted with asthma and sinus troubles.

Stratford Inn at Del Mar

Roads were in everybody's thoughts. The Chamber of Commerce formed a committee for roads and boulevards, with Charles Kelly, livery stable owner, as chairman, and with such prominent members as George W. Marston, E. W. Scripps, A. G. Spalding, the sporting goods manufacturer who now made his home in San Diego where his wife was active with the Theosophists on Point Loma, and William Clayton, representing the Spreckels companies. They recommended and the voters approved a $75,000 bond issue to be spent under the direction of the Chamber committee, for improving roads to La Jolla, Point Loma, Mission Valley, Mission Hills and National City.

Four men from Long Beach made the first auto trip to Imperial Valley, and it required three days to cross the desert from Banning to Imperial Junction. From Brawley, they returned by way of San Diego, negotiating the grade through Devil's Canyon along the main wagon road which still was not in much better condition than it was during the early immigrant days.

Hardly fit for man or beast was the Devil's Canyon road up the San Diego mountains about 1906 or 1907. A few autos made the difficult journey across the desert and up an old wagon road that had served since pioneer times.

The interest of Imperial Valley in San Diego had long since faded, and in the summer of 1907 residents signed petitions to form a separate county and presented them to the Board of Supervisors on July 5. They gave as their reasons that the county was divided by a high range of mountains and it was a great hardship for them to be compelled to come to San Diego on all county, public and legal business, and that San Diego was a maritime city while the valley towns were purely agricultural.

On the following day, the supervisors fixed the boundary lines for the new county and set the date of August 6 for an election. It was estimated that the population of the new county would be 6940 and that of San Diego County about 50,000.

The vote which created Imperial County and also saw the selection of El Centro as the county seat, was a light one, as at the time of registration half the voters had gone to San Diego City to escape the heat. San Diego County lost more than 4000 square miles of territory. San Diego County and Imperial County parted in a friendly manner. Most of the business and finance of the valley already was going to Los Angeles, and it might be long years before the railroad was built between San Diego and Yuma.

But San Diego was to be a great city, no doubt about that, and the manner in which it was to grow occupied the attention of many of its leading citizens. In a talk before a combined meeting of the Art Association and the Chamber of Commerce, Marston suggested that the Plaza be enlarged and converted into a civic center, with public buildings to be grouped around it, and that D Street be made into a handsome avenue to connect the Plaza with an open square and a pleasure pier on the waterfront.

With the landscaping of the city park under way, and the example of San Francisco's rebuilding after its disastrous earthquake before them, the Chamber's Civic Improvement Committee, with Julius Wangenheim as chairman, reached across the country to bring a noted planner and landscape architect, John Nolen, of Cambridge, Massachusetts, to San Diego, to make a study and submit recommendations on what San Diego should do. It was largely financed by Marston. Other members of the committee were George Cooke, Edward Grove, A. Haines, Melville Klauber, E. E. White and Leroy A. Wright.

The past was being left behind. It was in the spring of that year, on March 27, that Father Antonio Ubach died. He was known as the Last of the Padres, a native of Spain who had been ordained in San Francisco and had come to Old Town in 1866 when the Indians still looked to the Church for protection and guidance as they had done since the days of the San Diego Mission.

More than 2000 persons crowded into St. Joseph's Cathedral in the city and filled the street outside on April 3 for the Requiem High Mass in which priests from all sections of California participated. A line of carriages extending a mile and a half followed the funeral procession. Hundreds of Mexicans and Indians walked behind them in the procession to the Catholic cemetery overlooking the bay in what became known as Mission Hills. In his eulogy Right Rev. Thomas J. Conaty, Bishop of the Diocese of Monterey —Los Angeles, said:

The chronicles tell us of long journeys which he made in the mountains, through storm and shine, to carry the consolation of religion to the people of the farthest recesses. What was a journey of 100 miles through a desolate land to him? . . . He was a priest for all that, and no Mexican was so poor, no lonely Indian so far distant, that Father Ubach would not travel into the wilderness to give him the consolation of religion.

The history of the state itself was reaching an important turning point. With Gillett as governor and the Southern Pacific in complete control of the State Legislature, and with graft and corruption widespread, reform movements gathered momentum. Fifteen prominent Republicans met in Los Angeles on May 21, 1907, with Ed Fletcher representing San Diego, and it was decided to call a statewide meeting at Oakland on August 1. Attending the meeting in Oakland from San Diego were Fletcher, Marston and Edgar A. Luce, who had helped Mayor Sehon defeat the Hardy and Spreckels machine in 1905.

The Lincoln-Roosevelt League was formally launched, and a platform was drawn up, pledging:

The emancipation of the Republican Party in California from domination by the political bureau of the Southern Pacific Railroad Company and allied interests, and the reorganization of the state committee to that end...the election of a free, honest and capable legislature, truly representative of the common interest of the people of California.

Immediately afterward a Nonpartisan League was organized in San Diego, with Marston and the hardware merchant, Roscoe Hazard, among the members of the executive committee and it supported a full slate of candidates headed by Grant Conard, a young real estate man who had come to San Diego for his health. John F. Forward, county recorder and owner of a title company, won the Republican nomination. Edgar Luce, one of those who had attended the Lincoln-Roosevelt meeting in Oakland, said:

The success of John L. Sehon in his campaign two years ago, and the splendid record he has made as an independent mayor, caused us to attempt to duplicate it. We expect to draw our strength largely from the mass of...voters...who don't like to wear the collar of a political boss.

Edgar A. Luce

However, with the promise of a railroad to Yuma, and a general era of prosperity, Republicans returned to the Old Guard and elected Forward as mayor. But the State Legislature, perhaps seeing the handwriting on the wall, and acting to avert more drastic reforms, proposed a direct primary, and a constitutional amendment to that effect was adopted by the people in the following year. The reform movement, however, continued to gain strength.

After having his own engineering studies made and acquiring

rights of way, Spreckels disclosed that the railroad to Yuma would go by way of Tijuana and through part of northern Baja California, crossing back into the United States near Tecate, instead of directly east. For a half century San Diegans had tried to convince themselves that there was a railroad route eastward through United States territory, and again it had been proved that it was not practical. Though disappointed, San Diegans celebrated at the ground-breaking ceremonies on September 7, 1907. The principal speech near the foot of Twenty-eighth Street was delivered by Marston, who described the years of alternating hope and disappointment and the frustrating work of the railroad committee of which he had been a member:

It was always felt by the committee that John D. Spreckels was the "Man of Destiny" for the building of this railroad. However much we may have failed in other respects, I am sure that San Diegans, if they knew all the history, would acquit the members of the committee of any failure to make a steady appeal to Mr. Spreckels...Mr. Spreckels kept his own counsel, and independently, by his own knowledge, discernment and business sagacity, had conceived the great enterprise and determined upon its accomplishment.

It would be three years, though, before the rails reached the Mexican border and then the hot springs, or Agua Caliente, beyond the town of Tijuana.

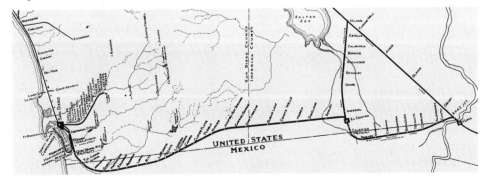

This was the anticipated route of the San Diego & Arizona Railway when it was first projected, and on a map it looked simple enough. But it required years of time and many unexpected millions of dollars.

But those challenging Spreckels were more sure of themselves as a result of political realignments seemingly under way. On behalf of the Huntington interests and over the opposition of Hardy, the local political boss, Fletcher acquired the franchise for an electric line from the foot of F Street and the Jorres wharf and owned by the Bartlett Estate Company with which he was associated, and began building it northward. Just outside of the town proper they would have to cross the electric line being laid to Point Loma, Roseville and Ocean Beach by a Spreckels company of which D. C. Collier was president. Threatened by an injunction, Fletcher made the crossing on Sunday when the courts were closed. He and Frank A. Salmons, his partner and gem mine owner, then picked up rights of way through Rose Canyon to Del Mar and the developments of the South Coast Land Company.

Somewhere on the coast this line was expected to connect with an extension of the Pacific Electric system of Los Angeles. However it was not long before Henry E. Huntington discovered that Harriman and the Southern Pacific had quietly bought out the interests of his partners and were in full control of his system. Even after all of its experiences with railroads and railroad promoters, this news at first was received with welcome in San Diego. It meant, or so it was believed, that Huntington had combined forces with Harriman and assured the carrying out of his ambitious plans.

San Diego would have a second line to the north and a line to the east as well. There was no way of knowing that Harriman had become the silent force in the San Diego & Arizona ostensibly owned by the Spreckels companies, and that there was no intention of sending two lines into the same town. But Harriman's unexpected death in 1909 would precipitate a crisis not only for San Diego but for John D. Spreckels.

Politics and railroad expansion were forgotten for a time when a financial crisis originating in the East rolled across the country, and as had happened so often in the past, struck hard at an expanding and speculative California. Banks in many sections of the state resorted to scrip to meet obligations, but those in San Diego, where progress had been more moderate, weathered the storm. None failed or closed their doors. Money for construction of the San Diego & Arizona railroad temporarily dried up. All work on the U. S. Grant Hotel stopped and the concrete skeleton stood silent and deserted for month after month. G. Aubrey Davidson, a former auditor of the Santa Fe railroad, who had returned to San Diego to open a bank in 1907, took a leading part with

Louis Wilde in a refinancing plan by which the construction work was resumed.

The recession, though, did not dampen the celebration for the arrival off San Diego of the Great White Fleet which President Roosevelt sent around the world. Though San Diego had always welcomed units of the United States Fleet in the grand manner, convinced as it was that some day the Navy would make its home there because of the bay and climate, this observance surpassed even the one in 1871 when the town thought it was to be the terminus of a great transcontinental railroad.

The fleet of sixteen warships rounded Cape Horn, and after a visit at Magdalena Bay 500 miles down the coast in Baja California, it was sighted by watchers on the Silver Strand at 10:57 on the morning of April 13, 1908. Headlines in THE SAN DIEGO UNION proclaimed "Engines of War, Victors of Peace, Arrive; Thousands Awed by Inspiring Spectacle." A news story described how "Sixteen monsters of war dashed out of the South Pacific and cast anchor off Hotel del Coronado."

It was the fleet's first American port since leaving Hampton Roads in December. The Navy responded with equal fervor. The story in THE SAN DIEGO UNION read, in part:

The beauty of the day's spectacle when, with flashing signals and wonderfully executed maneuvers, the ships were brought to

(Next page) The Pacific Coast remembers no celebrations more enthusiastic than those which welcomed the Great White Fleet in 1908. After leaving its first anchorage off San Diego, the fleet sailed north and into San Francisco Bay and a water color by artist Reutendahl, who accompanied the ships, shows what it was like.

anchor in the lazy rolling Pacific waters, was rivaled last night when for three hours every vessel was outlined in fire.

Electric lights were strung along deck lines, up masts and funnels, and down to the water's edge at stems and sterns. The name of each vessel was spelled across its forward bridge in lights and searchlights played shafts of light on the beaches and Hotel del Coronado. On shore, answering red signal fires were maintained by excited citizens.

The commander, Rear Adm. Robley D. "Fighting Bob" Evans, the hero of the Spanish-American War, had left the fleet because of illness, and Rear Adm. Charles M. Thomas received the official greetings extended by Gov. Gillett. At one point Adm. Thomas slipped away to visit the graves of the victims of the BENNINGTON explosion.

San Diego was jammed with visitors and it was estimated that 50,000 saw a two-mile long military parade. At night all large downtown buildings were strung with electric lights. There were formal dinners and grand balls. In four days it was all over, but not forgotten. At midnight before departure for San Francisco, on the 18th, San Diegans fired an admiral's salute of thirteen rockets and lighted thirteen red fires atop Point Loma.

But even before the fleet had arrived and departed a suggested master plan for the development of San Diego was submitted by John Nolen to the Chamber of Commerce. It posed the issue of what a city should be, and what kind of a city San Diego could become.

This night-time photograph, unusual in its day, shows the outlining in lights of the Great White Fleet lying off the Silver Strand. San Diegans in turn decorated their homes and stores and built signal fires on the beach.

It Was Not Yet Too Late to Design a City — or Was It?

*The beauty of Southern California was
its greatest asset, in the opinion of
planners who early urged its towns to
protect their scenery, atmosphere and
way of life. This scene is Sunset Cliffs
where A. G. Spalding left San Diego
a picturesque park.*

CHAPTER VI

It was not too late in the West, as it was with many cities in the United States, to assure a future that would in some measure at least capture the beauty and spaciousness of the great cities of Europe and Latin America.

This was the message of John Nolen. Though the extreme importance of commercial interests must be recognized, to him San Diego was by its nature a play city and the possibilities were indeed challenging. He reported:

The scenery is varied and exquisitely beautiful. The great, broad, quiet mesas, the picturesque canyons, the bold line of distant mountains, the wide hard ocean beaches, the great Bay, its beauty crowned by the islands of Coronado, the caves and coves of La Jolla, the unique Torrey Pines, the lovely Mission Valley—these are but some of the features of the landscape that should be looked upon as precious assets to be preserved and enhanced. And then the "back country"—hospitable to every sort of tree, shrub, root, grain, and flower—is an inexhaustible source of commercial and aesthetic wealth.

But San Diego, in its brief modern existence, from the arrival of Father Horton in 1867 to the rapid building by John D. Spreckels, had listened time and again to the advice of visitors from more unfriendly climes, who said that geography and weather were its greatest assets. With the exception of Hotel del Coronado, little had been done to capitalize on these assets and the years had been spent in a so far fruitless commercial race with Los Angeles. It had left a town without charm, and Nolen wrote:

Notwithstanding its advantages of situation, climate, and scenery, San Diego is to-day neither interesting nor beautiful. Its city plan is not thoughtful, but, on the contrary, ignorant and wasteful. It has no wide and impressive business streets, practically no open spaces in the heart of the city, no worthy sculpture. Aside from the

Cities need not be ugly, planner John Nolen told San Diego, in comparing its tiny central Plaza with the plazas and wide tree-lined prados of Madrid in Spain and other European and Latin American capitals.

big undeveloped City Park, it has no pleasure grounds, parkways nor boulevards, no large, well-arranged playgrounds. It has no public buildings excellent in design and location. It has done little or nothing to secure for its people the benefits of any of its great natural resources, nor to provide those concomitants without which natural resources are so often valueless.

The pioneers laid out the commercial and residential areas of San Diego as promoters have always done, by drawing lines on paper. William Heath Davis, a sea captain and merchant, and Andrew B. Gray, a government engineer, first conceived of moving San Diego from its original site at Old Town to broad flat ground five miles south. This was during the Gold Rush and they marked out streets and lots. With the end of the Gold Rush the project failed and became known as "Davis' Folly." They had provided for only one open space, or park, a block in size. Then fifteen years later came Alonzo Horton who acquired a new site to the east of Davis' Folly, laid out blocks without alleys and streets of only eighty feet in width, and his park was only a third of a block in size. The cost to the future was told by Nolen:

It is too late to make a plan for San Diego based simply upon a thoughtful recognition of the topography, and a skillful consideration of the normal needs of city life and the special needs of San Diego. The street system as a system is fixed almost irrevocably, not only in the built-up sections of the city but for miles beyond. Acres upon acres have been platted through the energy of real estate agents and others, and lots sold to people now scattered all

The uninspired growth of new cities, with narrow treeless streets and formless buildings that were beginning to shut out the sun, distressed the planners of the early 1900's. This was Fifth Street, looking south from C, in San Diego about 1910.

over the country. No topographical map of the city has ever been prepared, and until very recently no contour streets have been laid out.

Cities would remain congested, commonplace and ugly until they understood better the place and function of the street, he warned, and quoted George E. Hooker, secretary to the Special Street Railway Commission of Chicago, as saying that the traffic problem had become a surprise to people in all important centers and "they cannot understand why it should be ever looming bigger than the amplest provision made for it."

San Diego's business streets, Nolen reported, would not meet the demands of the new age of the automobile:

If any citizen of San Diego wishes to see the street problem in an

Downtown Los Angeles was becoming choked with buildings and traffic long before the great in-migrations of the 1920's which would push it on its way to one of the world's largest cities.

A typical street in old Seville

aggravated form, a form in which it will appear in San Diego, let him go to Los Angeles and stand at the corner of Fifth and Spring Streets, or go to other sections of that remarkable city. The problem there is already acute, and yet the provision has been much more ample than in San Diego.

To him, the most serious mistake had been the attempt to implant a rectangular system, almost unrelieved by diagonals, on an irregular topography. He contrasted the streets of San Diego with those of Seville, Spain, the "mother city" of California, where it was said of its seven hundred streets there was scarcely one which did not have a personal character of its own. But in his mind it was still within the power of the people of San Diego to make their city convenient, attractive and beautiful, in recognizing the peculiar opportunity for joy, for health and for prosperity that life in Southern California, and more especially in San Diego, offered to all.

The two central features were the bay and the park, and he suggested that the waterfront could be developed for recreation as well as commerce and aesthetically tied to the improvement of the park. He accepted the existence of the park and designed his plan with it in mind, though he wrote that it was not his purpose to justify the wisdom of withholding permanently so large a tract in the heart of the city, and urged not just one but a series of parks. His recommendations were:

To purchase for a Public Plaza the block from D to C Streets and from Front to First. To form a Civic Centre around this Plaza by some such grouping of public buildings as outlined. To build a sea wall, fill in the Bay Front as suggested, and improve it for the

102

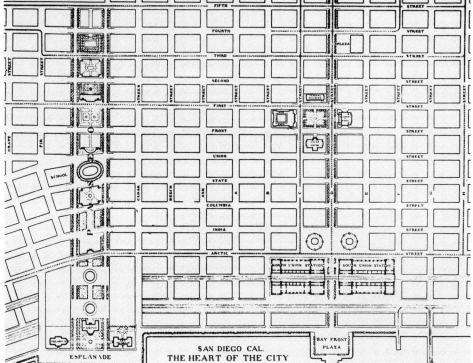

SAN DIEGO CAL.
THE HEART OF THE CITY

This was John Nolen's vision of San Diego. It would have a large central plaza, surrounded by graceful public buildings; a tree-lined avenue leading to another wide plaza on the bayfront, and then a broad prado along Date Street connecting Balboa Park with an esplanade which would be an art and recreational center. Perhaps it was too grand a design for a town that had barely emerged from a frontier settlement.

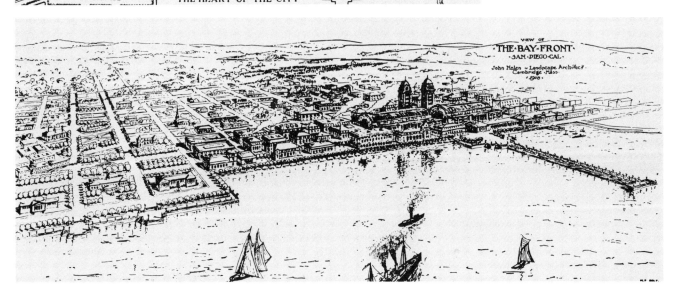

John Nolen

purposes of commerce and recreation. To construct "The Paseo," a pan-handle to the City Park, and so connect the Bay and the park. To establish at the foot of Date and Elm Streets a centre for the more artistic forms of pleasure-making. To improve the railroad and water approaches to the city. To open, ventilate, and beautify the city by increasing the number of small "squares" and open spaces. To provide ample playgrounds for the use of children. To display more differentiation in the location and treatment of streets and boulevards. To establish a system of parks to include the City Park, the Bay Front, Point Loma, a Beach Reservation, La Jolla, Soledad Mountain, Mission Cliff, Fort Stockton, and the Torrey Pines.

Nolen drew on other authorities to establish the artistic value of civic centers and said that San Diego had a rare opportunity to secure a beautiful and permanent grouping of its public buildings. Horton's Plaza, however, was far too small and he contrasted it with the great Plaza of Madrid. He suggested that a new public plaza be created in the block bounded by Broadway and C and Front and First Streets, and that it be surrounded with such buildings as the City Hall, Court House, Federal Building and an Opera House:

It would be easy to name many other cities in California and elsewhere that would eagerly leap to such an opportunity, cities that unfortunately had settled the problems of locations of public buildings in a way that a well-conceived Civic Centre had become an impossibility.

At the end of Broadway, or D Street, on the bay front, he suggested the erection of handsome transportation terminals and another public plaza, with commercial development to be below E Street and recreational developments north to another esplanade centering on the foot of Date Street. Date Street itself would become the main artery, or Paseo, to connect the bay and the park. He urged the acquisition of a dozen blocks between Date and Elm Streets, stretching from the entrance to the City Park west to the bay front:

Here, on this hillside, at comparatively small expense, can be developed what I have called, after the custom in Spanish and Spanish-American cities, "The Paseo," a pleasant promenade, an airing place, a formal and dignified approach to the big central park, free from grade railroad crossings. In itself this Paseo might possess great beauty, each block offering an opportunity for special design, and yet the whole strip brought into harmony and unity. Formal flower beds, pergolas, terraces, would appear from block to

block, and from the City Park to the bay, the cheerful and enliven-
ing influence of water in jets, basins and cascades would give the
final touch of beauty.

At the waterfront, the Paseo would spread out to a width of
1200 feet, where it could command the grandeur of San Diego's
most characteristic scenery, and where the people could establish
the proposed casino, art museum, and aquarium and surround
them with parks and gardens.

For guidance and inspiration there were the ocean, bay and
river fronts of Naples, Genoa, Nice, Mentone, Lucerne, Cologne,
Hamburg, Paris, London, Liverpool and Rio de Janeiro. In the
United States cities fronting on the Atlantic and Pacific, on the
great rivers that traverse the continent, and on the lakes, had not
developed the opportunities their situation afforded:

This contrast has now attracted attention and American cities
of all classes, located in different sections of the country have taken
steps to better utilize their water frontages. Witness the plans for
Boston, Philadelphia, and Chicago, Buffalo, Cleveland, and Detroit,
Harrisburg, Roanoke and Savannah.

In suggesting a system of parks, he said there was a physical
feature the beauty of which it was impossible to estimate, and
that was Point Loma, and while the U. S. Government owned and
occupied the end of the promentory, the city should possess
enough land to command at all times "the marvelous view that
can be enjoyed there." He found it strange that despite its miles
of ocean frontages, including many hard and beautifully curved
beaches, the city owned no beaches whatever. La Jolla was
described as a village within a city and one of the most romantic
and alluring spots on the coast, and that it could be referred to as
"El Nito," the nest, because it seemed to hang like the sea gull's
nest, between the sea and the sky. Fortunately, he said, the city
did control a well-located piece of property for park purposes.

The Chamber of Commerce directors, as is the habit of civic
bodies reflecting the political, economic and personal cross-
currents of a restless city, sat with the report for ten months, and
finally it was released to the public and published in full in THE
SAN DIEGO UNION of January 1, 1909. In an advisory to a printed
version, Nolen also cautioned the people:

The aim and purpose of these drawings should not be misunder-
stood. While their practicality in general has been tested, they are
obviously not offered as a final or constructive plan that can be
executed without further study and revision...Primarily they are
intended to waken and form public opinion.

Waterfronts intrigued city planners and landscape architects. Before 1913 San Diego's waterfront was largely undeveloped, with a few commercial piers, rows of shacks and large areas of mud flats.

In contrast to most of the waterfronts of the United States, the Bay of Naples was held up as an example of providing for recreation and even residential as well as commercial uses.

And so for all practical purposes the first Nolen plan was buried. Perhaps it was too much too soon. It seemed a great deal to expect of a small town at the most southwestern corner of the United States and in time only a few years removed from the frontier of an expanding America. A grouping of public buildings would wait upon another generation, and the broad and beautiful avenues were to remain only sketches in a forgotten booklet. But the idea of beauty combined with utility, and the bay as a central recreational as well as commercial asset would persist and be mirrored in other civic achievements.

Instead, the year closed with San Diego welcoming the growth of industrial development which Father Horton had envisioned with the assurance of a direct railroad connection to the East. The value of manufactured products exceeded that of agriculture. A total of ninety-six firms employing 1082 persons produced products worth $2,819,375, while vegetables and fruits were valued at $1,718,530.

The city had the largest tobacco plant on the Pacific Coast, producing 3,712,000 cigars and 11,480 pounds of smoking tobacco. Other industries were onyx, lapidaries, ostrich feathers, the largest salt works on the coast, broom manufacturing, olive oil and fishing. The cattle industry surviving from the era of the Silver Dons of the Spanish and Mexican land grants produced 500,000 pounds of hides and 1200 barrels of tallow. Orchards and farms produced 451,152 boxes of lemons and limes, 2,000,000 pounds of grapefruit, 3,601,000 pounds of grapes, 4,180,000 pounds of raisins and 3,682,000 pounds of olives. Orange production was only 99,840 boxes. The fish catch was valued at $131,510.

A new business building, the Timken Block, was under construction at Sixth and E Streets and a ten-story office building was projected for Fifth and D Streets by Los Angeles and San Diego capital. La Jolla had witnessed the building of thirty-five new structures. Congress at last had appropriated $250,000 for a wharf at the coaling station on Point Loma, and San Diego was sure it was the result of the visit of the Great White Fleet, and military officers assigned to duty at Fort Rosecrans were finding service in San Diego so pleasant they were retiring in the town, or planning to do so.

All of this building and renewing of faith and energy must have brought deep satisfaction in the last days of the man who had foreseen it all, Father Horton. He fell ill in late December and died on January 7, 1909, at the age of ninety-five. The town's oldest citizen, he was a familiar sight on the downtown streets up

until the time of his last illness, and though the city had left him little in a material way, he never looked backward and never publicly regretted the speculative experiences that saw him swiftly rise to wealth and fall to near poverty just as fast.

As he was not a devout church-goer, though of a religous family, funeral services were conducted from the Elks Lodge where the eulogy was delivered in the eloquence of the times by the past exalted ruler, John B. Osborn. He described Father Horton as a "plain, typical American...and his faults therefore we will write upon the sands, his virtues on the tablets of our love and memory." The funeral procession, led by mounted policemen, passed through silent streets, with most offices, stores and business houses closed, and after it disbanded, his body was taken to Mount Hope cemetery for burial in the Horton family plot.

Except for the Church, there were few to mourn the Indians who had been driven from their land with the coming of the pioneers and builders, and Bishop Conaty began returning pastors to some of the crumbling missions around which a few Indians were still clustering. Government reservations represented banishment and not hope. In 1910, Fr. William Hughes wrote in the INDIAN SENTINEL:

Of the thirty thousand Indians at one time attached to the missions, and the uncounted thousands in the hills never converted, the official census shows less than three thousand of their descendants in Southern California today.

Among the old missions, a few only have any Indians in attendance at all. San Diego, the first of the missions to be established, which, at the zenith of its glory, in 1800, numbered over fifteen hundred, now has less than fifteen souls. San Luis Rey, which in 1810 had a thousand neophytes, musters now only as many as can be counted on the fingers of two hands. At San Juan Capistrano, in 1812, there were nearly fourteen hundred souls; today there are not more than five families...Of the ASISTENCIAS, or chapels, originally offshoots of the main missions, San Antonio de Pala has about 250 Indians; though very few are children of the original inhabitants. Mesa Grande and Santa Isabel (the latter being now comprised in the Volcan Reservation) contain, the one, seventy-five and the other, one hundred families. For the rest, the remnants of the Mission Indians are found in small numbers in the mountains above Warner's Ranch, around San Jacinto, or on the desert below Banning. A poor torn band of forty are huddled together on San Manuel Reservation near San Bernardino, which comprises six hundred and forty acres, which is described in a calm, judicial

(Opposite page) The fading beauty and dignity of the old Franciscan missions of California were reminders of the passing of time and of the neglect of governments. At the top is a sketch of the ruins of Mission San Luis Rey and below, of the ruins of Mission San Juan Capistrano. They were drawn in 1910.

Government report as "worthless, dry hills," and which constitutes all that remains of the once happy out-missions of San Gabriel.

Bishop Conaty placed resident pastors at Pala, San Diego and San Juan Capistrano, encouraged Father O'Keefe at San Luis Rey, provided for more spiritual attendance at the distant chapels of Campo and Mesa Grande and Warner's Ranch, and continued work among the Yumas along the Colorado. Fr. Hughes wrote:

Driven from the fertile valley of San Felipe, above which their deserted homes and chapel now hide themselves in sorrow among the ancient oaks; evicted from the great plain of Warner's Ranch and the almost sacred Agua Caliente, in order to be transported to bleak Pala; forced, by the encroachments of white men even upon the desert, to find refuge in cold Cahuilla, and pressed back by degrees from the mesa of San Jacinto till they have taken up their last stand on the sand-dunes of Soboba; is it any wonder that they are a sad and demoralized race?

The land left to the Indians failed to provide them with a means of earning their own living, but there were those who still believed that an industrious and humble family could wrest a livelihood from even an acre of land.

A "back to the soil" movement was gaining strength in the country and with his history of San Diego finished, William E. Smythe returned to his causes and was instrumental in the organization of a cooperative farming community which became known as the "Little Landers." Smythe and George P. Hall, a former agricultural commissioner of San Diego County, selected a site in the Tia Juana River Valley where the old border town of Tia Juana was located before the flood of 1891. Smythe wrote:

A man can make a living from a little land...It is marvelous but true, that upon as little as one acre, in any part of the United States, the average industrious man...can make better provision for his family than half the citizens of the country are doing now.

With a campaign of a "little land and a living," Smythe raised enough money to purchase 550 acres of valley and hillside land valued at $15,000 and launch a nationwide publicity program. His community was renamed San Ysidro in honor of the Plowman Saint, a name that also had been originally applied to a Spanish or Mexican land grant in the area that had never been patented. A headquarters was established in an old adobe house that had served as a stage station and was located on the line of the San Diego & Arizona Railway.

The grand opening for sale of lots was on January 11, 1909. Acres were priced from $350 to $550 and lots at $250. By sundown

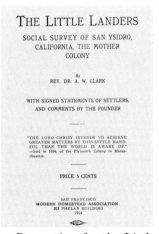

THE LITTLE LANDERS

SOCIAL SURVEY OF SAN YSIDRO,
CALIFORNIA, THE MOTHER
COLONY

By
REV. DR. A. W. CLARK

WITH SIGNED STATEMENTS OF SETTLERS,
AND COMMENTS BY THE FOUNDER

"THE LORD CHRIST INTENDS TO ACHIEVE
GREATER MATTERS BY THIS LITTLE HAND-
FUL THAN THE WORLD IS AWARE OF."
—Said in 1654, of the Plymouth Colony in Massa-
chusetts.

PRICE 5 CENTS

SAN FRANCISCO
MODERN HOMESTEAD ASSOCIATION
303 PHELAN BUILDING
1914

Promotion for the Little Landers

110

lots had been sold to twelve families. In one of the many speeches in front of the old adobe house, Smythe said:

When he heard that the Declaration of Independence had been adopted, Samuel Adams cried, "This is a glorious morning!"—and this is a glorious morning for San Diego for it marks the beginning of a new and solid industrial era in which men shall deliberately sow the seeds of industry before seeking to reap the harvest of profit. It is the second serious industrial era in our history. The first was inaugurated by the Mission Fathers who conquered two generations of prosperity from the fertile soil of our valleys.

The early days of the colony were difficult ones, because of inadequate irrigation, and most of the settlers were barely able to pay for their land and build temporary shelters. There were few farmers among the idealistic colonists who came from all walks of life. Teachers, lawyers, doctors and other professional people, however, provided the community with a distinct social life for such a small and isolated venture. Produce was to be sold at a Little Landers market in San Diego, there was to be a cooperative store in the village, and the colonists were to share in the dividends from both. But for several years most of the colonists had to seek outside work in order to sustain their experiment.

In the new year, 1909, the Board of Supervisors created a new County Road Commission with an unusual body of men, all millionaires—E. W. Scripps, John D. Spreckels and A. G. Spalding— and all vigorously in opposition politically and philosophically. The people of the county approved a $1,250,000 bond issue for roads, and one of the roads to be graded and graveled was to circle the bay from Coronado to Point Loma. The State of California created a state highway system and provided for an $18,000,000 bond issue for 3000 miles of construction.

Auto roads were being laid out or graded from San Diego to El Cajon Valley, north to Santee, Lakeside, Ramona and Julian; and from Julian to Cuyamaca, through Green Valley to Descanso and Pine Valley. Northward, roads were laid out to Fallbrook and up the San Luis Rey Valley through Pala and Rincon and on up to Warner's Hot Springs, and from there to Santa Ysabel. Escondido was connected to Oceanside on the coast, by a route through Vista, and to Ramona by way of Clevenger Canyon. Between Los Angeles and San Diego, autos now were able to go by way of Del Mar, Encinitas, and Oceanside, with six bridges along the route, and then north across Rancho Santa Margarita y las Flores, at last abandoning use of remnants of the historic El Camino Real.

The first step in establishing a favorable auto road to Imperial Valley was taken with the improvement of the road eastward through the mountains to Jacumba and Boulder Creek but stopping short of the descent down what is known as Mountain Springs into the desert.

Los Angeles, watching San Diego's road-building activity toward Imperial Valley which threatened to put direct routes into southern Arizona and open the door to transcontinental auto travel and trade, hastened work on a route to the valley by way of San Bernardino and Mecca. With the arising of competition from Los Angeles, San Diegans again sought contributions from concerned citizens and raised $60,000 to extend the new road from the San Diego County line to the desert floor in Imperial County.

John F. Forward Sr.

Interest in political and governmental reform revived and City Charter amendments were adopted reducing the number of councilmen from nine to five, to be elected at large through direct primaries with all party labels banned, and installing a modified commission form of government, the first such in California, in which councilmen divided and assumed direct responsibility for city operations as "commissioners." However, the subsequent city election saw Republican Progressives help bring about the narrow defeat of John F. Forward as mayor and the election of Grant Conard. In the primary the Socialists turned out a large vote for William J. Kirkwood which went to Conard in the general election. Kirkwood was named city building inspector.

The defeat of Forward also reflected the continuing dissatisfaction with the town's seeming inability to advance as rapidly as its rivals on the coast. G. Aubrey Davidson, the banker, later related that he became convinced that San Diego would "never get to first base unless the city did something unusual to direct attention to what could be found here."

The Nolen Plan had been for an uncertain future, for a time that might find them all gone from the scene, and at a meeting of the Chamber of Commerce on July 9, 1909, Davidson suggested that in view of the completion in a few years of the Panama Canal, when San Diego surely would become a principal port of call in a great new Atlantic-Pacific sea trade, it might be a good idea to stage an exposition in the city park. This would not only provide for a major attraction but for park development as well.

Grant Conard

San Francisco and Los Angeles also were keying future plans to the Panama Canal. Los Angeles had annexed the port towns of Wilmington and San Pedro and was engaged in building breakwaters to make sure that it, and not San Diego, for example, would get the anticipated sea trade through the Panama Canal. San Francisco was considering how best to capitalize on the opening of the canal and would come up with plans for a world's fair of its own.

Though the era through which the country was passing was a turbulent one, it also was a creative one and civic and regional energy was finding expression in fairs and expositions which captured the imagination of people all over the country. San Diego was proud of the gold medals its products had won at the St. Louis, Portland and Jamestown Expositions.

San Diego was not aware at first of any plans of San Francisco though it learned soon enough, and the exposition idea took hold quickly. The Panama-California Exposition Company was incorporated in September and D. C. Collier became director-general.

G. Aubrey Davidson

The disappointing census figures of 1910 convinced San Diegans that they were losing a population race. The city's population was given as only 39,578, far below the estimates of the previous year which had ranged as high as 50,000. Population of the county was given as 61,655. Though the town's population had doubled in ten years, it was still not as large as it was in the Boom of the Eighties. San Diego had passed San José in size but had failed to overtake Sacramento. San Francisco had grown to 416,000. As for Los Angeles, its population had tripled in the same time, to 319,000.

In his memoirs, Wangenheim wrote:

One night, in about 1910, our doorbell rang, and there were a number of "prominent citizens" of San Diego, wanting a rush signature for directors of an exposition to be held here in 1915. The rush was probably to get ahead of San Francisco, which was also planning to hold one at that time. Anyway, I signed (I was president of the bank and hence a "prominent citizen"). Charley Collier was the moving spirit of the whole venture, and worked on it dynamically all the while. It started ambitiously, with the goal of a whole million dollars, the largest amount that our minds could grasp at that time, and one that was almost synonymous with infinity. Plans were laid out for buildings all over the park. That was easy. But when the sponsors got around to figuring the costs, they found that a million not only wouldn't cover the project; it couldn't even make a fair start. The plan was grandiose in scale and had to be somewhat curtailed, but future expansion was still a factor, and little by little more millions were needed and demanded.

A sum of $1,000,000 was raised by private subscription and a city bond issue of $1,000,000 was voted for improvements to the

113

Architecture in the classic manner was highly esteemed in Western towns struggling for their place in the sun. This was the ladies' foyer in the U. S. Grant Hotel, a symphony of marble and statuary.

park. Its name was changed to Balboa Park on November 1, 1910. Who suggested the name is not known.

New life flowed through the community and under Louis Wilde, who now owned a half interest, the U. S. Grant Hotel was completed and opened for business on October 15, 1910. U. S. Grant Jr., who had conceived and promoted it, was in New York but sent

114

The Spanish heritage of Southern California was something to be forgotten, and the town Plaza's fountain was more likely to be of formal design, as this one was in San Diego.

his congratulations. The structure had cost $1,100,000 and the furnishings $250,000. The cost of operation was estimated at $1000 a day. It had two swimming pools and the top floor was a ballroom proclaimed as the equal of any on the coast. The opening night ceremonies attracted 400 visitors from Los Angeles and 100 from Pasadena. It was a civic achievement for San Diego as well. Citizens had subscribed $600,000 to assist in the financing and another $100,000 to help buy furnishings.

Across the street in the Plaza on the same evening, Wilde presented to the city a fountain designed in classic style by the architect Irving J. Gill, and it was accepted on behalf of the city by Judge M. A. Luce, president of the Board of Park Commissioners. Colored lights on the cascading water suggested a future that seemed at last within the grasp of the present generation and which had escaped their fathers and the city's pioneers.

There was one task yet to be completed in the opinion of many and that was to rid the town of "boss rule" and the corporation domination under which it was supposed to have been suffering.

Though Theodore Roosevelt had been succeeded as President by Republican William H. Taft, the zeal of reform was still running high. In California the Lincoln-Roosevelt League and Republican Progressives chose Hiram W. Johnson, a lawyer who had won renown in San Francisco graft trials, as their candidate for governor, and Gillett, fearing defeat, decided not to run for re-election. John D. Spreckels threw his support to the secretary of state, Charles Forrest Curry. Johnson, campaigning on a platform to "kick the Southern Pacific out of politics," and supporting the initiative, referendum and recall, swamped his Republican opposition in the primary and began the final drive toward the State Capitol.

In San Diego, he promised that if he were elected the government of the state no longer would be tied to a locomotive wheel. A thousand persons in Germania Hall heard him say:

We have heard that certain interests are making ready to deliver certain votes in this city and county to the corporations. Can it be true? Can any man or body of men deliver the votes of the citizenship of this great city and county—in the most beautiful spot on this footstool of God—to a boss in San Francisco? I say, No! Never!

The people loved it. With Harriman dead, and the Southern Pacific political machine in actuality already in swift decline, John D. Spreckels and his newspapers bowed to the inevitable and urged a straight Republican vote, though the endorsement of Johnson was not with any visible enthusiasm. The vote, on November 6, 1910, in San Diego in favor of Johnson was almost two to one over his Democrat opponent and made the county one of the strongest Republican centers in California.

Ed Fletcher in his memoirs said his support of Hiram Johnson and the Progressives earned him the enmity of both Spreckels and Hardy and it lasted for years, until Hardy's death. Spreckels, be-

Hiram W. Johnson

set on all sides, now also found himself involved in a personal matter that disclosed for all to see a bitter family rift that had ranged brother against brother for fifteen years. The death of his mother in San Francisco had brought to public light a will in which she disinherited two of her five children, John D. and A. B. Spreckels, and while it said they had been provided for by their father before his death, it was made clear she was cutting them out of her $6,000,000 estate and making sure they could never share in it. San Francisco newspapers reported the two other brothers, Rudolph and Claus, had tried to prevent John D. from seeing their mother before she died.

At about this time San Diego Electric Railway, a Spreckels company, made the mistake of asking for a fifty-year franchise to use the city's streets. Before this fight had run its course, the town was almost torn asunder. The SAN DIEGO SUN, owned by Scripps, charged that Spreckels would try to ruin the town if he did not get his "half-century's monopoly of its streets:"

We look John D. Spreckels squarely in the eyes and say: We defy you! Upon that issue there can be no middle ground. Either you are the master and hold in your hand the welfare of every man, woman and child in this town, or the people are their own masters, and will know how to deal with your insolent challenge.

THE SAN DIEGO UNION agreed that the people had to make a choice between Spreckels and Scripps, but answered that before the choice could be made, Scripps should make a firm commitment as to how many millions he expected to invest in San Diego.

The discord greatly troubled Louis Wilde, who had invested heavily in the completion of the U. S. Grant Hotel, as well as Marston, who in a letter to William Clayton, manager of the transit system, wrote that while he trusted Spreckels personally he was apprehensive over what might happen if the great power of the Spreckels interests fell into less conscientious hands:

If rightly handled and safeguarded all this power is for good. Our interests are mutual; the city needs the capital investment and your companies need the good will and cooperation of all citizens ...To secure the freedom for efficiency and profit on the one hand, while maintaining for the city its rightful securities for the future on the other hand, is one of the difficult tasks of our city life.

A mass meeting was called for Germania Hall by the Chamber of Commerce which had offered an alternative to the franchise proposal. A number of San Diego's labor unions, most of them still in a formative stage and beset by Socialists and anarchists of various sorts, were supporting the alternative. But after several

William Clayton

117

of their leaders had spoken, and been accused of being employes of Spreckels, a body of Socialists invaded the hall, tried to disrupt the meeting, and then retreated outside to regroup for another charge.

Upon their return they were accompanied by Capt. Sehon, who since retiring as mayor had become a member of the City Council and, under the new modified commission plan, commissioner of police, health and morals. Arriving with him were four police detectives and a member of an Eastern soap manufacturing family and political radical, Joseph Fels. Fels had been ranging the United States and England promoting the Single Tax theory of Henry George and establishing labor colonies.

When the uproar was at its height, Fels clambered onto the stage, and there were those who said it was with the help of Sehon, and offered to buy out all the Spreckels interests and turn them over to the city in twenty-five years. Under questioning, he acknowledged that he had arrived in the city at 1 o'clock that afternoon and knew little of the franchise issue for which the meeting had been called.

At an election the voters on February 15, 1911, overwhelmingly approved the Chamber's franchise alternative, which provided for revocation by voters and a maximum period of fifty years, but with exact time to be set by the City Council. In the aftermath it was alleged that before he invaded San Diego, Fels had been a guest of Scripps at Miramar ranch, and Sehon threatened to sue THE SAN DIEGO UNION for libel for accusing him of participating in the effort to break up the Chamber of Commerce meeting.

The issue of domination, whether by Spreckels or by Scripps, or whether in truth such an issue was a valid one, had not been settled. Scripps would soon tire of civic controversy. To Spreckels, however, San Diego was his life and he refused to accept defeats. The death of Harriman of the Southern Pacific meant little to the residents of a town that had taken at face value the promise of the scion of the California sugar family that he would bring to San Diego the railroad that had always seemed so important. But a financial crisis was swiftly moving upon Spreckels and perhaps in the exposition's promise of commercial and recreational developments he could see the means to overcome it. San Diegans were not aware of this; neither were they aware that the San Diego & Arizona was not Spreckels' railroad and that the new management of the Southern Pacific did not look with any enthusiasm upon the future of the port of San Diego. They would learn soon enough.

Seven

Beauty Wins a Round in Parks and the Exposition

*The airplane was wedded to the ship
when a Glenn Curtiss biplane, fitted with
floats, was hoisted from the water and
taken aboard the U.S.S. PENNSYLVANIA
in San Diego Bay.*

CHAPTER VII

High over the harbor of the sun a few little airplanes of wood and
fabric circled and dipped in the steady though gentle wind. They
were flown from North Island, where Glenn H. Curtiss, a pioneer
flyer and manufacturer, had established a private flying school
on land obtained without charge from John D. Spreckels through
the cooperation of the Aero Club of San Diego, composed of a number of leading citizens who had become excited about the possibilities of flight. Curtiss had been attracted by the same wind and
climatic conditions that had intrigued Octave Chanute.

Curtiss arrived at North Island in the winter of 1910-1911 and
invited the Army and Navy to send officers for free instruction as
"aeroplane pilots." In San Francisco Bay on January 18, 1911,
Eugene Ely, employed by Curtiss, landed and took off in a Curtiss
pusher-type plane on a specially-constructed wooden deck on the
cruiser PENNSYLVANIA. But Secretary of the Navy George Von L.
Meyer remained sceptical and had a different concept of the possibility of naval employment of airplanes in scouting at sea, and

Glenn Curtiss' hydroplane skims over the waters of San Diego Bay, with Point Loma in the background, as the curious watch excitedly from their boats.

informed Curtiss:

When you show me that it is feasible for an aeroplane to alight on the water alongside a battleship and be hoisted aboard without any false deck to receive it, I shall believe the airship of practical benefit to the Navy.

On January 26, after fitting a float to his plane at the suggestion of a naval officer, and thus converting it into a "hydro-aeroplane," Curtiss took off and landed on the waters of San Diego Bay. On February 17, he maneuvered the float-equipped plane alongside the cruiser PENNSYLVANIA, was hoisted aboard, and then lowered to the bay, from where he lifted off for a return flight to North Island. In March the Naval Appropriations Act provided $25,000 for developing naval aviation.

Curtiss' pilots staged aerial circuses at Coronado which jammed the bay ferries with spectators from all over Southern California. On a damp day on January 28 with 1500 persons in the stands of the Coronado polo grounds, according to THE SAN DIEGO UNION:

All eyes were turned toward the hangars on North Island. Suddenly on the mist-laden breeze there came a whirring, pounding noise not unlike the flushing of a covey of giant birds, and almost instantly a great salvo of cheers rent the air as a big Curtiss racing biplane lifted itself above the sagebrush across Spanish Bight and ascended higher and higher as its daring driver guided it over a circuitous aerial route, westward toward Point Loma headland.

At the controls was Eugene Ely. After executing a spiral turn, in which "it seemed the machine must lose its intangible grip on the upper ether," he landed and was reprimanded for his daring by Curtiss. The climactic event of the day was an aerial race in which a "terrific" speed of sixty miles an hour was attained.

The following day, with an improvement in the weather, 10,000 persons witnessed spiral dips, ocean wave dips, altitude climbs, grass-cutting swoops and races. One of the participants was Lieut.

Three ages of transportation are evident in this photograph taken on San Diego Bay. Glenn Curtiss flies his hydroplane over a Navy vessel which has both steam power and sails.

One of the first aerial races was that between Glenn Curtiss and Eugene Ely in an air show at Coronado early in 1911.

T. G. Ellyson, who had been sent to North Island for training with Curtiss, as the Navy's first aviator.

In a land where the winter sun was warm Joseph Jessop strolled across the empty blocks of Coronado and scattered the seeds of the wild poppy of California. Golden flowers sprang from the sandy soil and covered the island with a blanket of glory, to give Coronado its name of the "Poppy City."

Jessop had brought his family to San Diego from a drab manufacturing town in England, where tuberculosis had always come with the rain and the fog, and his children, browned and healthy, were marrying into prominent families of the community in which he had begun a new life at his old trade as a jeweler.

Along the cliffs between La Jolla and Del Mar north of the city grew the Torrey Pines, one of the rarest trees in the world. They are found in only one other place, on Santa Rosa Island, one of the Channel islands southwest of Santa Barbara. Dwarfed, gnarled, twisted and beaten almost to the ground, these trees are

The United States Navy's first aviator, Lieut. T. G. Ellyson, prepares to lift off in a biplane at Curtiss' training school on North Island.

relics of another age, of a different climate and a different soil, and have made their last stand in the rugged canyons and painted cliffs of an area of little rain.

In 1889 the Common Council of San Diego had set aside 369 acres to preserve part of the Torrey Pine forest, but when commercial development threatened the trees growing on adjacent lands, E. W. Scripps and George W. Marston persuaded Ellen Browning Scripps to acquire the privately-owned areas to protect the trees forever, and she did.

On a promontory overlooking both San Diego and Mission bays were the ruins of the first White settlement on the Pacific Coast, where Don Gaspar de Portolá founded a Spanish Presidio and Fr. Junípero Serra raised the first Christian church in a pagan land. The old adobe walls were slowly melting back into the earth and it was apparent that the historic site soon would be enveloped by a surging tide of residential growth. Publication of William E. Smythe's HISTORY OF SAN DIEGO was to awaken interest in events that had happened before San Diegans or their parents had been born. To them the mud heaps on Presidio Hill had been merely sad and rarely noticed remnants of a nation which long since had forfeited its claim to the land and its riches. In 1907 Charles Kelly, Spalding, Spreckels, Scripps and Marston acted to protect the site and purchased it with the expectation that eventually the city would share their interest and enthusiasm and publicly acquire it as the Plymouth Rock of the Pacific Coast.

The development of Balboa Park had been steady though often plagued with indifference or disagreement. It was difficult to sustain interest amid the clamor of civic progress or disappointment and there were charges that more money was being spent on planning than on planting.

But after he had laid out the basic design of Balboa Park, Samuel Parsons Jr. returned to San Diego from New York several times and always was enthused over what had taken place. In a letter to the NEW YORK POST he said that one of the notable developments of the enterprise and intelligence of the Pacific Coast was to be found in the interest taken in parks, from Portland, Oregon, to San Diego. He said that the Golden Gate Park in San Francisco already had become one of the few really great parks in America, and, he went on:

My special object in writing this letter is, however, to give the readers...some idea of another great park, which is now being developed in San Diego. So rapid is the growth of plants in that favored region that this new park bids fair, in the next decade, to be a successful rival, in some particulars, of the parks of the world ...It is pleasant to think of a city of the moderate size of San Diego ...setting out in earnest to build a park of the first class...How many populous cities in the country, with far greater resources, have never dreamt of starting out on such an enterprise. But this is also true, that in no other place in the United States does such a magnificent park territory serve to tempt the enterprise of its citizens.

Over the years the dry hard ground was broken open, with blasting often required, and the southwest corner became green and inviting, and tall eucalyptus trees were embedded in the deep canyons. Water was taken up to the mesas to water shrubs and acacias and peppers. Roads were laid out and dust eliminated by oiling.

The unfortunate death in 1908 of George Cooke, the partner of Parsons who had settled in San Diego to live with the park, as the result of an accident with a runaway horse, and the approach of the exposition, had significant effects on the future of the park. The great open vistas with a panoramic view from Point Loma to Mexico, which Parsons had envisioned, and which to him belonged to the imagination "like the stately pleasure domes of Xanadu decreed by Kubla Khan as seen by Coleridge in his opium dreams," would largely be shut off. There would be a different park, though still a magnificent one.

The tall and graceful eucalyptus trees, like the geranium flower, were becoming symbolic of San Diego and both had been brought from far off places. The eucalyptus is a native of Australia and Tasmania and its seeds had been brought to Southern California by Boston ships of the fur and hide trades during Spanish and Mexican times. Geraniums of many hues found their way to Southern California from South Africa by way of Europe and most certainly were cultivated in the old gardens of the San Diego Mission.

The geranium thrived in a climate very similar to that of its native country. The eucalyptus, however, did not always fare well and suffered during droughts. During a time when easily available lumber was becoming scarce and it was feared that our forests might be disappearing, the Santa Fe Railroad purchased nearly all of the lands which once formed the 8000-acre San Dieguito Rancho of the Osuna family, and had planted 4000 acres with 3,000,000 eucalyptus seeds and seedlings from which they expected to grow hardwood for railroad ties. Growth in a country with an average rainfall of ten inches a year was slow, and without irrigation few of the trees reached any size. The experiment

Irving J. Gill

126

proved to be a costly one. When Oregon fir became more plentiful and proved, with proper treatment, to be superior to eucalyptus wood for railroad ties, the rancho was turned over to Fletcher to manage in 1909. He leased the land for grazing cattle, developed sources of water for farming, and laid out roads through the rolling hills with a view of someday subdividing it.

As the scenery and character of the town changed, so did its homes and its buildings. The stately and ornate "gingerbread" houses of the Victorian Age were no longer being built. Almost gone too were the prim homes built by the early settlers who had brought with them the architecture of New England. In their places appeared for a time a classic Grecian style and then a mission style that borrowed from a past that went back to an era before the first American settlers. Throughout California railroad depots and municipal buildings appeared with the arches and red tile roofs of the crumbling California missions.

At about this time Irving Gill, who had designed the classic fountain in the Plaza and was struggling to make a living as an architect in San Diego, began to develop a style which was called a radical simplification of the Spanish Colonial, and which was to gain for him a national reputation, though it came long after his death. Among the larger buildings which he designed were the Bishop's School for Girls, the Community House and the Woman's Club, all in La Jolla; the residence of Ellen Scripps, also in La Jolla; and the homes occupied by George Marston and Melville Klauber.

The reaching for new forms of expression and the striving for beauty in cities, no matter the difficulties of a public consensus or the uncertainty of course, affected the plans for the Panama-California Exposition.

San Diegans were aware that they could not compete with San Francisco in staging a world's fair and narrowed their ambitions to an exposition that would be regional in character. They again turned to Boston and Massachusetts as they had so many times in the past. John Nolen, the city planner, had come from Cambridge, a suburb of Boston, and San Diego now invited the Olmsted brothers, of Brookline, Massachusetts, to be the landscape designers for both the park and the exposition.

It was the idea of Collier, the director-general, to create an exposition in keeping with the history and culture of Southern California, and to him that meant a miniature city with its buildings in the style of the missions and its gardens suggesting the atmosphere of Old Spain, and buildings and exhibits featuring

The Arthur Cosgrove home of the Gingerbread Era

E. W. Scripps built his Miramar home in the style of Trieste Castle

George Marston's home was in Irving Gill's early style

Irving Gill's architecture reached its height in Ellen B. Scripps' home

D. C. Collier

Frank P. Allen Jr.

John P. Morley

the products and arts of the Southwest and Latin America. Charm and beauty were to be preferred over size and variety.

In a way Collier's plans were expressive of the revival of interest in the Spanish and Mexican heritage of California. State and county fairs had featured everything from pyramids to classic temples and the Pasadena Tournament of Roses the chariot races of ancient Rome. But the history of Spanish and Mexican occupation now became something to be exploited and not concealed. Even the Indian was to have a place in the exposition.

The exposition company's building and grounds committee selected a site in the southwestern section of the park centered on what was known as the "Howard" tract. It was the area west from the site on which later was built the United States Naval Hospital and north of the San Diego High School. The Olmsted brothers, John C. and Frederick Law Olmsted Jr., were in agreement with the committee's plans as to the site for the exposition as they believed, as had Samuel Parsons, that any buildings should be erected only along the edges of parks.

While in Los Angeles, the Boston architect Bertram Grosvenor Goodhue learned of the plans for the exposition and visited San Diego and influenced the committee to adopt a Spanish Colonial instead of the primitive mission style. During his life, Goodhue designed or contributed to the design of some of the country's most famous buildings, among them the United States Military Academy at West Point, the Nebraska State Capitol, the Museum of Art at Honolulu, the California Institute of Technology, St. Bartholomew's Church in New York, and a number of other cathedrals in the United States and Latin America. An artist as well as an architect and designer, he had become enchanted with the cathedrals and baroque governmental buildings of Mexico and in sketches had created imaginary cities of Moorish and Oriental splendor. He was promptly hired as designing and consulting architect and Irving J. Gill as his assistant. Because of his experience with the Seattle World's Fair, Frank P. Allen Jr. was hired as chief engineer and director of works. John P. Morley left Los Angeles parks to become San Diego's superintendent of parks.

The modified form of commission government had left the mayor a figurehead with only the power of the veto. By 1911 there was a general dissatisfaction with Conard's administration, so much so that support began to crystallize behind a conservative Democrat attorney, James E. Wadham, a resident of San Diego for forty years, who said he was against a "one man town" but had never "associated or affiliated with the Lincoln-Roosevelt League or the

128

so-called 'push crowd.'"

Councilman Sehon, the former mayor, rallied liberals and Socialists behind George A. Garrett for a City Council seat and when he was defeated THE SAN DIEGO UNION proclaimed the end of Sehon as San Diego's political boss. Wadham was elected but soon found himself embroiled in trouble.

The exposition company originally had been organized with U. S. Grant Jr. as president, John D. Spreckels as first vice president, A. G. Spalding as second vice president, and including among the directors Lyman J. Gage, a former Secretary of the Treasury who also had come to San Diego to make his home. In 1911 Collier was delegated to tour the country to promote interest in the exposition and to carry on negotiations with Congress, the U.S. Government and the State Legislature for recognition and support. For that purpose he was elected president and J. W. Sefton Jr. took over as acting director-general.

J. W. Sefton Jr.

Assurances were given to San Francisco that the San Diego exposition would supplement and not rival its fair and an understanding presumably was reached. All mention of the word "international" was eliminated and the exposition became merely the Panama-California. A resolution was introduced in Congress calling upon the United States to invite Mexico and the Republics of Central and South America to participate at San Diego.

In an appearance before the House of Representatives Committee on Industrial Arts and Expositions, Collier testified that San Diego was willing to wait until the President had first issued the invitations to all countries of the world to participate in the San Francisco fair. Collier said:

We are working in absolute harmony with San Francisco at this stage of the proceedings. It has not always been so, but it is to-day. We feel there is a community of interest between us, and...I further believe this resolution is as strongly endorsed by the men of San Francisco as it is by the men of San Diego, and I bring you the positive assurance that the men of Los Angeles do approve it.

Collier endeavored to reassure the committee that while it was true San Diego had a metropolitan population of only 50,000, its citizens had shown what they could do by approving many bond issues for civic and park improvements and by individually subscribing a million dollars for the exposition and $700,000 to help complete and furnish the U. S. Grant Hotel.

While the exposition would be twice the size of the one in Seattle, its total cost would be only between $5,000,000 and $6,000,000; it would not be commercial in the strict sense, but largely have to do with agriculture and reclamation and the resources of the Southwest and Latin America, and while the State Legislature had authorized all counties to levy a special tax in order to participate, the federal government was not being asked for any financial assistance:

I want to say without fear of successful contradiction...that we have brought together an organization for the purpose of constructing our exposition that has never had a superior, and...we went out into the highways of the world and gathered the best talent that money could possibly hire, to perfect all the features of the exposition.

Collier was congratulated on his presentation and felt secure in his belief that all was well with the exposition and that in due time the resolution would be forthcoming. At home, however, conflict had developed over a question of authority.

The Park Commission had formal jurisdiction over Balboa Park and though a division of responsibility and work had been agreed upon, new park commissioners appointed by Mayor Wadham soon challenged the authority of the exposition directors. The directors resigned in protest and the fate of the exposition hung in the balance. Within ten days, however, the park commissioners were forced to resign themselves and Wadham appointed a new commission composed of Julius Wangenheim, John Forward Jr. and F. J. Belcher Jr.

The groundbreaking ceremony was scheduled for July 19, 1911. The date was only three days after the 142nd anniversary of the formal founding of the first San Diego Mission, a crude structure of sticks and reeds, on Presidio Hill. The official program stated:

The fourth epoch of California begins with the rebuilding of San Diego coincident with the first permanent development of San Diego, the marvelous progressive movement in Southern California and the awakening of imperial enterprise throughout the Southwest; closing with the completion of the Panama Canal and the San Diego & Arizona Railway, thus concentrating the traffic of a continent and the commerce of a great ocean in the harbor of San Diego, the nearest point on Pacific tidewater to the Middle West and the Southern states and the first port of call in American territory north of the canal.

F. J. Belcher Jr.

San Diego was crowded with visitors for the groundbreaking ceremony. Notables were greeted by flower-decked autos and fire engines and escorted through an "arch of welcome" erected across the foot of D Street, or Broadway. At 7 o'clock in the evening in Washington, D.C., which was 4 o'clock in the afternoon in San

Diego, President Taft pressed an electric button in the East Room of the White House which unfurled an American flag at the site of the ceremony. John Barrett, director-general of the Pan-American Union and envoy of President Taft, wielded a silver pick and shovel. Bishop Conaty came from Los Angeles to celebrate a pontifical military mass, the first in San Diego since 1769, in honor of Fr. Serra.

A formal dinner followed in the U. S. Grant Hotel and there were three days of masked balls and street and water carnivals. One feature of the celebration literally never got off the ground. An aviation experimenter by the name of C. H. Toliver had floated a bond issue and built a dirigible, 250 feet long and 40 feet in diameter and with four gasoline engines and six propellers, which he proposed to inflate with hydrogen gas and take off with forty passengers on a flight that would astound the world. He never succeeded in inducing it to rise and the city, fearing the gas might explode, declared it a public nuisance. Later, Toliver and his wife were shot to death by Toliver's secretary.

A preliminary sketch showing how the exposition might appear had been submitted by the Olmsted brothers, but it was not long before Goodhue and Allen became dissatisfied with the size of the site and its terrain, and proposed a new location in the central portion of the park. Collier and the majority of the directors agreed to the change. The Olmsteds, who believed that buildings were unnatural intrusions upon parks, were flatly opposed. In September in a letter to Wangenheim, chairman of the Park Commissioners, they announced their withdrawal:

This is contrary to our advice and will interfere with other por-

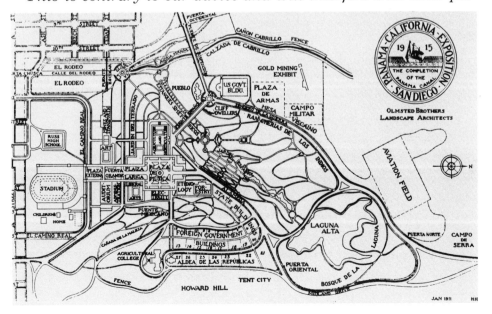

This sketch shows the original exposition grounds and layout as designed by the Olmsted Brothers for a location in the southwest section of Balboa Park.

tions of the design proposed for Balboa Park by us. We regret that our professional responsibility as park designers will not permit us to assist in ruining Balboa Park. We tender herewith therefore our resignation.

A new plan for the new site was drawn by Allen and Goodhue and recommended by the exposition's building and grounds committee on October 25. Gill resigned as assistant architect and was replaced with C. M. Winslow, of New York. Goodhue designed the group of permanent buildings, Winslow the temporary structures, and Allen conceived and designed the high bridge to span the canyon and connect the exposition area with Sixth Street. In Goodhue's sketches of the exposition there was a feeling of the mysticism and splendor of the imaginary towns he so liked to draw.

This is a dreamy sketch by architect Bertram Grosvenor Goodhue of the approach to the exposition which he created and to the permanent buildings which he designed.

The progress on the railroad that was expected to mean so much for San Diego upon completion of the Panama Canal and opening of the exposition continued to be agonizingly slow, though construction work also had been started westward from the New River in the Imperial Valley, from a temporary connection with the valley's inter-city line to El Centro. The suspicion grew that the San Diego & Arizona might only get as far as El Centro and a permanent connection with the Southern Pacific line.

Autos were becoming a necessity and 325 new cars had been delivered to San Diegans in 1910. The route of new roads and which of the existing ones were to be improved pitted areas as well as individuals against each other, as roads would determine what sections of the county were to be opened for sale and settlement.

One day the millionaire members of the County Highway Commission found themselves out of office with the expiration of the first year of their second term. No provision had been made for them to serve until appointment of their successors, and the Board of Supervisors, unhappy over the selection of a route near Ramona and the work of the commission's engineer, quietly let their terms run out.

In a statement issued in their names, Spreckels, Spalding and Scripps charged that their terms had been deliberately shortened:

We conclude, therefore, that we have been legislated out of office by the Board of Supervisors. We are perfectly confident, from expressions of certain supervisors, that our services are neither appreciated nor desired.

The supervisors, however, in the face of public protest, beat a hasty retreat and, blaming it all on an error, hastily reappointed all three of the commissioners. But Spreckels had had enough, not only of the Board of Supervisors but of his co-worker, Scripps:

I will not again sit on the highway commission or any commission with Mr. Scripps who is inimical to my interests and to the best interests of the city.

When Spalding also presented a formal resignation, an angry supervisor, Joseph Foster, countered:

I'm not going to be riff-raffed by these millionaires because I'm a poor rancher. I am tired of the abuse of these people...Gentlemen, I move we accept Mr. Spalding's resignation.

Scripps, however, reversed himself and repudiated the letter of protest to the supervisors and agreed to serve again on condition that no members be appointed with whom he did not care to serve. He promptly fired the controversial engineer, Austin B. Fletcher, and became, in the words of THE SAN DIEGO UNION, "monarch of the roads of San Diego." Scripps' reign lasted about six months, when he was caught in another quarrel with fellow commissioners over personnel and quit, with the following comment:

I've patched up a good many things in my time. I suppose I'm a great patcher, but this is one of those things that won't patch.

Transportation by sea and land was the key to the future, and when the Pacific Navigation Company's steamship YALE arrived with 400 excursionists at the west Santa Fe wharf on March 4, cheers and whistles resounded along the waterfront, and the ship's officers and passengers were taken on a trip around the city in automobiles. The autos were decked with Yale and Harvard pennants representing the two new coastal steamships. When the ship departed, the pilot of an airplane from the Curtiss flying

E. W. Scripps

133

school bombarded it with oranges.

The need to improve docking facilities for the expected trade by sea resulted in Gov. Johnson's signing on May 2, 1911, legislation giving San Diego control over its tidelands from National City

Steamer day was one of high excitement, in the era before super highways and airplanes. The YALE *and* HARVARD *carried passengers between San Diego, Los Angeles and San Francisco ports. Here the* YALE *arrives with hundreds of persons on hand.*

to the military reservation on Point Loma on condition that $1,000,000 be spent on harbor improvements. Control of the tidelands had rested with the state since its jurisdiction had been firmly established following the efforts of land speculators to gain possession of them in the early days of the railroad booms.

A campaign to gain approval of a million dollar bond issue was organized under the leadership of the City Council and the Chamber of Commerce, and a proposal was made by City Engineer Edwin Capps, the former mayor, to dredge and fill along the waterfront and build a pier at the foot of D Street.

The designation of the foot of D Street for a commercial pier and the bayfront just to the north of it for related facilities was in direct conflict with the Nolen Plan that had called for all commercial structures to be south of E Street and all recreational development north of it. The Civic Improvement Association telegraphed Nolen and asked him to appear in San Diego. But Frederick J. Lea, manager of an onyx company and chairman of the executive committee of the bond campaign, warned:

I don't believe there is a reputable taxpayer or citizen or business man in San Diego who has the nerve to help openly to defeat these bonds. If they secretly oppose the bonds, we will find it out and their names will be published.

A week later, the Civic Improvement Association began a retreat and announced that it had decided to support the bond proposition, even if it had to "swallow the Capps plan" but did not mean it would cease its opposition to the site chosen by the city engineer.

Nolen arrived from Sacramento and a mass meeting was held in Germania Hall, with Lyman Gage, the former Secretary of the Treasury, presiding. George A. Garrett, a printing firm executive who had been defeated for a seat on the City Council, said that the press had misrepresented the views of the association:

We are a tourist city. We'll always be a tourist city, and while it is good to see new smokestacks going up and more ships entering the harbor, what we want is not more smokestacks and ships as much as we want to make things attractive and pleasant for the tourists.

It had been four years since Nolen had visited San Diego and he told his audience that it was gratifying to see the progress San Diego had made in commercial and residential building:

In public improvements, some progress has been made...but...the really big opportunities have not yet been grasped...Above all, it needs to begin a practical, well-considered business-like improvement of its great bay along modern lines and requirements, especially for commercial purposes...the older cities in the United

*States have made mistakes in the development of their waterfronts
...it is a pity to have smaller and newer cities repeating their mistakes.*

A petition was presented to the council requesting that the question of the pier location be settled by the council after the election. It was signed by Gage, Garrett, Fletcher, Marston, Alfred D. Robinson, Julius Wangenheim, Charles N. Andrews, Gordon Gray, Ernest E. White, and John M. Ward. It was ignored and the bond issue carried almost unanimously in the election on November 14, in which women voted for the first time. Smokestacks had won again.

While the city quarreled over plans for its development, and its leading citizens fought for power over roads, Los Angeles, with its railroad lines and developing harbor, was moving to realize ambitions of becoming as well the terminal of continental highway systems slowly being put together. San Diego was advocating a route from Arizona to the coast and Los Angeles by way of San Diego which Los Angeles did not favor. San Diego was at a distinct disadvantage in this crucial struggle. The steepness of the mountains had defeated the early railroad schemes though now the engineers of the San Diego & Arizona were planning to penetrate a canyon of almost overwhelming ruggedness, Carrizo Gorge.

The highest elevation on the lowest pass of the mountain mass on the direct Yuma-San Diego route was about 4000 feet. Just east of Jacumba the elevation was about 3200. For several years road crews had been hacking out a new highway down the mountains from Jacumba. The old wagon road, which had been used by autos for a decade, left Jacumba Valley and went northeast and then almost directly south to reach Mountain Springs, dropping about a thousand feet in three miles; then it followed the bed of Devil's Canyon, a virtual tunnel between towering red rock hills and dropping another thousand feet to the upper desert floor. Any auto caught in this narrow gap in a desert cloudburst could be picked up by rushing water and battered to pieces against the walls.

*Lonely ruins at
Mountain Springs*

The new road was following what eventually became Highway 80, clinging precariously to the sides of precipitous mountains, dipping in and out of their scalloped sides and reaching Mountain Springs from the south, a drop of a thousand feet. Avoiding Devil's Canyon, it was turning down Myer Canyon, or In-Ko-Pah Gorge, for another thousand feet, again clinging to a narrow ledge cut out of the mountain sides, and was to reach the desert floor near Ocotillo. In time both the Devil's Canyon and Myer Canyon routes would become divided sections of Interstate Highway 8.

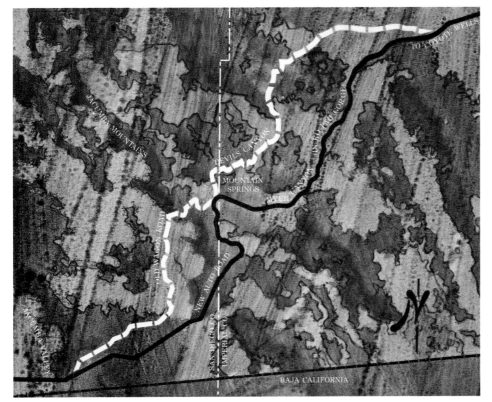

This map shows the old wagon road and the newer auto route over San Diego's mountain barrier, from Jacumba and down Mountain Springs to the desert country.

All of the Myer Canyon section was in Imperial Valley, as were sections of the upper road. Residents of San Diego's county towns began a movement to have the proposed Imperial highway, as it was known, approach Mountain Springs by way of El Cajon, Lakeside, Alpine and Descanso to Clover Flat instead of along the old stage route nearer the border which led to Campo and then to Jacumba.

In contrast to San Diego's new road, Los Angeles was offering a route which followed in part the tracks of the Southern Pacific Railroad, from Yuma to San Bernardino by way of the Salton Sea, and had the advantage of a gradual rise through the low San Gorgonio Pass. Road races were popular ways of emphasizing the importance of national highways and one from Los Angeles to Phoenix, by way of San Diego, brought the cheering news that "San Diego will awaken this morning with the full realization that it is on the automobile map." The race attracted sixteen motorists who pledged to maintain a speed limit of six miles an hour through cities and towns but on the highway "only the drivers, their mechanicians and the startled rabbits and other field and tree creatures knew at what terrific rates they traveled."

A month later, an Ocean to Ocean Highway Association convened in Phoenix, with eighty-four delegates from California, Arizona and New Mexico. A delegate from Los Angeles was president.

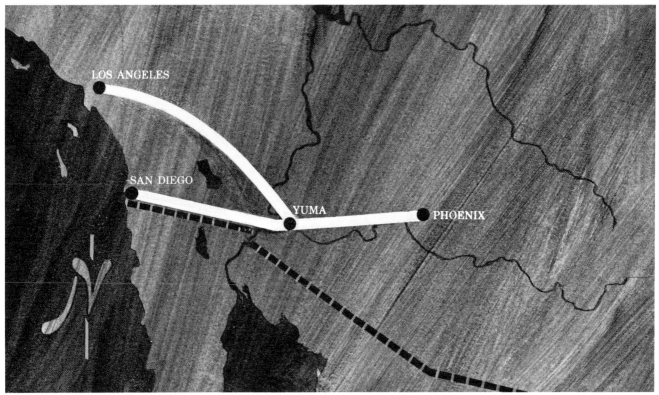

Los Angeles and San Diego competed to be the terminus of a southern transcontinental highway. The way by San Diego was shorter but more difficult.

San Diego was represented by Spalding, as first vice president for California, and Rufus Choate of the Chamber of Commerce. The object of the meeting was to work for the construction of a highway through the three states which would link with a highway system through the Middle West and East.

The Arizona and New Mexico delegates had no trouble agreeing on a route through their states but the Californians were divided on whether it should go directly from Yuma to Los Angeles, by way of the Salton Sea and San Bernardino, or by way of San Diego. San Diego lost, and the decision also removed the principal towns of Imperial Valley, El Centro, Holtville and Calexico, from the proposed national road system. An article in the AMERICAN MOTORIST of February, 1912, protested that 130 miles of the route would be through absolute desert conditions:

From El Centro, which is located fourteen miles south of Brawley, a perfectly feasible route now leads via Coyote Wells through Devil's canyon to Campo... This route may be improved at not an excessive expense owing to the proximity of road material. The distance is seventy-three miles from El Centro to Campo. From Campo to San Diego through a beautiful mountainous country, there already exists a splendid boulevard, a distance of fifty-two miles. San Diego is a charming city, offering many advantages both as a business and residential city... Already a road 133 miles long connects San

Diego with Los Angeles, and is improved for a major part of the distance.

The route by way of San Diego had ninety miles less of desert though it was about thirty miles farther than by way of the Salton Sea and the mountain barrier made it slow and much more difficult.

Disappointments were not new to the little border city and its people would fight as hard for a highway connection with the East as they did for a railroad. The year had been a good one, with bank clearings up by $20,000,000 and the value of building permits by $2,000,000. Exports through the port exceeded $1,000,000 for the first time. The growing of fruit and the manufacture of fruit products were the county's largest source of income despite the growth of industry. In fishing the year's catch was nearly 6,000,000 pounds and the Portuguese with their gasoline-powered boats largely had taken over from the Chinese. In 1911 one of the boats brought in a load of an unusual tuna, but as there was very little market for that type of fish it was cooked to keep it from spoiling. The taste after cooking was similar to that of chicken. It was albacore tuna.

Artists and musicians as well as retired or semi-retired industrialists and philanthropists were building homes and enjoying

It was like a different world. Here are children at the Theosophical School on Point Loma when the experiment was at its height about 1910.

139

Madame
Schumann-Heink

the sun, among them, Madame Ernestine Schumann-Heink, the opera star, and Carrie Jacobs Bond, a composer. At the Theosophical headquarters on Point Loma, Greek pageants were being held yearly and the lure of a serene closed little community also was attracting people from around the world. Among those who arrived after 1910 were William Edmond Gates, a Mayan scholar; the poet Kenneth Morris, of Wales; the English novelist Talbot Mundy; and Maurice Braun, a Hungarian immigrant artist, and his wife, Hazel Boyer Braun.

In the Imperial Valley, with nearly 200,000 acres under cultivation, the farmers tired of the continual troubles of the California Development Company, organized the Imperial Irrigation District and under the leadership of the county's vigorous young district attorney, Phil D. Swing, moved to acquire the canal system on which they were so dependent. Swing's greater work still lay ahead, in the taming of the Colorado River.

The menace of the river was ever present. In the winter of 1908-1909, it changed its channel about twenty miles below the border and began emptying into Volcano Lake situated on the plateau of the delta. With its water came the silt which slowly began filling in the bed of the lake at the rate of about a foot a year. All concerned knew that if the river's course was not changed, and its water and silt diverted to the Gulf of California, the rising deposit of silt would lift the water pouring into Volcano Lake and let it flow once again into the Imperial Valley, to re-create the ancient Lake Cahuilla.

San Diego's population now was estimated at 55,000 and the rush of downtown traffic gave the city what was described as a metropolitan air. A time limit was proposed on auto parking in the downtown area. Merchants didn't like the idea, but W. B. Hage told a hearing in the City Council that "I can remember the day, and it was not so very long ago, that moving pictures in Los Angeles would show a donkey and a scissors grinder in some one of our streets with the inscription 'San Diego's Busy Day.'" One citizen complained, however, that under the proposed thirty-minute limitation a surgeon performing an operation in his office in the Granger building would have to leave his patient and rush outside and move his vehicle. It was a drastic proposal and needed more debate.

During the same year of 1911 gunfire had sounded along the border and radicals who had aligned themselves in one way or another with a revolution in Mexico were to blow the reform movement in California into disorder and angry recriminations.

Eight

The Wobblies and a Story No One Likes to Remember

A revolutionary movement, the I.W.W.'s, sang THE REBEL GIRL *and* NO FLAG BUT THE RED FLAG *and brought rioting, gunfire and vigilantes to peaceful border towns.*

CHAPTER VIII

With the beginning of the Mexican revolution led by Francisco I. Madero in 1910 and 1911 a number of conspirators in Los Angeles started slipping arms across the border into Baja California to carry out a separate insurrection of their own, by which they hoped not only to overthrow the dictator Porfirio Díaz but society as well.

They were members of the Liberal Party which had alienated itself from the main Mexican revolutionary spirit. Their leader was Ricardo Flores Magón who had just been released from prison in the United States for violation of neutrality laws and was one of the followers of Karl Marx who went beyond the Socialists to advocate direct action.

Their cry was "Bread, Land and Liberty" and their aim was the redistribution of land, seizure of the means of production and the abolishing of paid hand work. Similar uprisings by the Liberal Party took place simultaneously in thirteen Mexican states and help was confidently expected from Socialists in Europe. It was

143

six years before the Communist revolution in Russia.

In Los Angeles they had received sympathy and financial help from the I.W.W., or Wobblies, as members of the Industrial Workers of the World were known, who also believed in direct action and had infiltrated California in large numbers to agitate among the unemployed and agricultural workers and engaged in such violence as the seizure of freight trains.

Baja California in 1911 was an isolated territory with most of the Northern area still in the hands of foreigners who had received gigantic land concessions from indifferent Mexican governments. The largest holder was an English firm which had acquired 18,000,000 acres from the original grantees and subsequently had sold or leased some of it to American interests. Harrison Gray Otis and his son-in-law Harry Chandler, of the Los Angeles newspaper family, held a tract of 832,000 acres lying below Mexicali and extending all the way to the Gulf of California.

Northern Baja California

Development had been slow, in no way matching the growth of Upper California or even of the Southern territory. The population of the Northern territory was perhaps 7000 or 8000, with the capital, Ensenada, seventy-five miles south of San Diego, having about 1000. Mexicali, just across the line from Calexico in the Imperial Valley, and Tijuana, also on the border and fifteen miles below San Diego, each had somewhere between 500 and 1000. Tecate was a settlement a short distance from Campo on the American side where the Gaskill brothers had shot down a group of Mexican bandits in 1875.

Mining had declined, roads were poor or nonexistent and the climate, except along the coast, was unfavorable, but, as in Imperial Valley, the possibilities in the irrigation of arid lands were beginning to be realized. The San Diego & Arizona Railway tracks were creeping into the territory on the way to El Centro and Yuma and connections with the Southern Pacific to the east and to Los Angeles, and promised to open more lands to agriculture and trade.

That was the situation when Flores Magón dispatched a tiny revolutionary army of eight men, led by José María Leyva and Simon Berthold, toward Baja California. At Holtville in Imperial Valley they conferred at I.W.W. headquarters and then slipped across the border and at the Laguna Salada, the bed of a dry desert lake, they were joined by a dozen Mexicans and Indians and entered and captured Mexicali on January 29.

The capture of Mexicali, though not impressive, as they had failed to find any gold in the customs house, greatly excited California radicals and at a meeting in Los Angeles on February 5,

Jack London, the writer, circulated a manifesto proclaiming:

We socialists, anarchists, hoboes, chicken thieves, outlaws and undesirable citizens of the U.S. are with you heart and soul. You will notice that we are not respectable. Neither are you. No revolutionary can possibly be respectable in these days of the reign of property ...I for one wish there were more outlaws of the sort that formed the gallant band that took Mexicali.

José María Leyva had nominated himself a general and permitted a reporter for the ASSOCIATED PRESS to witness an inspection of his troops:

The rebel soldiers presented a grotesque appearance. Only eight of the men were mounted. Some were astride horses, without either saddles or bridles, and using only halters to guide their steeds. Four White men were in the company, having the appearance of typical Western ranch hands. All of the men were armed with rifles and small arms and appeared to have an abundance of ammunition.

Though it had not penetrated the peninsula of Baja California, the Madero revolution on the mainland was violent and widespread and President Taft ordered 20,000 American troops to patrol the border, thus cutting off a heavy arms traffic. Army units from Fort Rosecrans patrolled the border from San Diego to Calexico.

A war message, perhaps the first to be delivered by airplane, was dropped from a French Antoinette monoplane flown by a millionaire aviator Harry S. Harkness. Harkness, a captain in the New York division of the United States Aeronautical Reserve, flew his monoplane from Curtiss' flying school at North Island to the border near Tijuana, dropped a packet containing orders from Maj. G. H. McManus at Fort Rosecrans to Lieut. George Ruhlen Jr., and then flew back, averaging, THE SAN DIEGO UNION reported, "fully sixty miles an hour" for the round trip.

A short time later the Aeronautical Reserve proposed to the War Department that aviator Eugene V. Ely, who had flown the first airplane off an improvised landing on a naval ship, and a number of other pilots be engaged to reconnoiter along the boundary line, and it was expected that the success of this mission might have a great influence on the War Department's decision on scouting by aviation.

After picking up reinforcements and supplies the rebels were expected to march on Ensenada and Tijuana. Various reports had them being joined by hundreds of Cocopah Indians and an "American Legion" made up mostly of I.W.W. members with red ribbons on their sleeves. Tijuana was in a state of excitement. Many resi-

Tijuana, just below the border in Baja California, was becoming a busy trading town at the time of a small-time revolution.

dents crossed into American territory, taking their valuables with them. The town was patrolled by an armed guard of citizens under Lieut. Gov. Juan Larroque and the Mexican government had a force of about fifty, many of whom also were Americans, patrolling the border to prevent the smuggling of arms to the revolutionaries.

At about this time a curious aspect of the border "war" began to unfold. Richard Wells Ferris, one-time actor and promoter, had been employed to publicize the ground-breaking ceremonies for the Panama-California Exposition and had promised San Diegans that he would "dream up" some lively publicity stunts. Advertisements began to appear in newspapers in New York recruiting volunteers to participate under "General Dick Ferris" in a campaign to "annex" Baja California and he sent telegrams to Mexican generals insisting that the peninsula rightfully belonged to the United States and that if not surrendered "the Panama Pacific Expedition will sail from San Francisco at an early date."

The Mexican government as well as the rebels merely reacted with irritation and for a time Ferris disappeared from the newspapers, but a woman named Flora Russell, of Los Angeles, rode into the territory and planted a flag of her own design proclaiming

146

a republic observing women's rights.

The rebels pressed on, capturing Tecate on March 12, but Federal troops were becoming active. Tecate fell to them a few days later and José María Leyva was forced back to Mexicali. In a raid on the mining town of El Alamo, Berthold, a veteran Magonista who had been active in Los Angeles labor struggles, was fatally wounded. On April 8, an American I.W.W. named Stanley Williams led an attack against the Federals south of Mexicali and also was fatally wounded. Jack Mosby, a deserter from the United States Marines and an active member of the I.W.W., assumed temporary command of the rebels and plundered much of the country in the triangle between Mexicali, Tijuana and Ensenada. An election among the rebels conveyed command to a Welsh soldier of fortune who had served the British Army in India and South Africa. His name was Caryl Ap Rhys Pryce and he was the first leader not connected with the I.W.W.

Support for the rebel cause was urged in San Diego by Emma Goldman, the woman anarchist whose speeches and writings had incited the assassin of President McKinley. In a talk in Germania Hall before about 200 persons, Miss Goldman also accused Wall Street of being responsible for the presence of American troops on the border and the shutting off of guns and supplies for the Madero revolution. She said:

I call upon you as Americans to use every effort to call on the President to withdraw the American troops. You Americans who preach liberty and boast of independent freedom should not allow American interference. Let the Mexicans fight it out among themselves.

"Splendid Emma," as she was known among anarchists, was assisted in her San Diego appearance by two members of a newly formed Anti-Interference League, the Socialist Kasper Bauer and the liberal lawyer E. E. Kirk. The SAN DIEGO SUN was carried away by what it thought was the idealism of the Americans participating in the revolution against "Barbarous Mexico" and suspecting it was largely a filibustering expedition similar to those of the 1850's, exclaimed in an editorial:

Texas was conquered by Americans. It is American yet... If Lower California should wake up some morning to find the Stars and Stripes floating over it, San Diego would suddenly become more than ever a City of Destiny.

Recruits were sought openly on the streets of San Diego and I.W.W. halls and they were promised $1 a day and 160 acres of land. The battle for Tijuana drew near and the United States took unusual precautions along the border. Rear Adm. Chauncey

Revolutionist Caryl Ap Rhys Pryce

147

Thomas, commander of the Pacific Fleet, arrived at Coronado early in March and was quoted as follows:

The cruisers are now at anchor, the gunboat YORKTOWN *arrived tonight, and the transport* BUFFALO *with 500 Marines aboard is expected before morning. We don't know where we are going; we don't know what we are going to do, but we are ready for our orders.*

A force of 4500 naval and marine personnel was being assembled at San Diego and all shore leaves were canceled and every ship kept steam up. A provisional Army brigade, composed of the 8th and 30th Infantry and auxiliary troops, arrived by train from San Francisco and tents were put up in neat rows west of the main

Smoke rises from burning buildings in Tijuana after a battle in which the town was captured by revolutionists. Americans watch and U.S. soldiers stand guard on the border.

road between Roseville and Fort Rosecrans. Brig. Gen. Tasker H. Bliss, commander of the Department of California, visited border towns and made his headquarters at the fort. By mid-April San Diego was an armed camp and the entire Pacific Fleet was in the bay. The ships formed a line almost two miles long.

The long-expected attack on Tijuana began on May 8 and curious San Diegans lined the hills above the town to watch the drama. The defenders of the town numbered somewhere between seventy and 150 and they had little ammunition. The rebel army had filled out its ranks to about 220 assorted radicals, drifters, adventurers and criminals, with Mexican citizens in the minority.

After some preliminary maneuvering and exchanges of fire, Pryce ordered a general attack at dawn on May 10. Soon after 8 o'clock it was all over and the rebels held Tijuana. Estimates of the number of dead varied, but twenty or more of the Federal defenders were killed and perhaps a dozen or more of the rebels. One of the dead was the lieutenant governor, Juan Larroque, whose body subsequently was buried in San Diego's Catholic cemetery in Mission Hills.

A Red flag was raised over one building, though other store owners hoped for protection by raising the American flag as well as the Red flag. Pryce sent a message assuring San Diego that no men had been burned at the stake. Though he ordered all liquor in the town destroyed, there was considerable looting both by rebels and spectators from the American side. Two criminals es-

caped from the San Diego county jail and rode bicycles to Tijuana to join the insurrection.

A Red Flag with the slogan "Land and Liberty" was hoisted in Tijuana after the border town had been captured by revolutionists led by the I.W.W.

Trains of the San Diego & Arizona, which were running to construction camps near Agua Caliente and hauling some freight as well, were harrassed by rebels and the reports of Conductor W. G. McCormick tell of encounters with mixed bands of Americans, Negroes and Mexicans. At one point a train was stopped and McCormick and a company agent, C. E. Crowley, were summoned before Gen. Pryce who wanted to know if Spreckels was building the line. When informed that he was, Pryce said:

Well, Mr. Crowley, war is war, and we must have supplies for man and beast, and I will not draw on you for more than is necessary and will receipt for everything taken, but as Spreckels has millions and large interests in this section, it is my intention to make

Jack Mosby

him and other large holders contribute heavily to the support of my army.

On May 17, Pryce, accompanied by his adjutant C. W. Hopkins, slipped across the border and registered at the U. S. Grant Hotel as "Mr. Graham," but his identity quickly became known and he was introduced to many San Diegans. Warned of imminent arrest on orders of Gen. Bliss, Pryce and Hopkins attempted to flee but were intercepted and taken to Fort Rosecrans.

Dick Ferris, the publicity promoter for the exposition, and Kirk, the liberal lawyer, went to Pryce's aid and in court challenged the Army's right to hold him and his adjutant in the absence of martial law and Superior Judge W. A. Sloane granted a writ of habeas corpus. They as well as all other rebels were released, including the American Jack Mosby who had been found on this side of the line.

As a result of the publicity, ranks of the rebels grew with the arrival of more California I.W.W.'s, Italian anarchists from the Northwest, and Indian and Mexican bands from Sonora. The cause of the Liberal Party, however, was not advancing elsewhere in Mexico and the revolutionists led by Madero were taking the country. Díaz made peace with Madero and resigned as President. Former Federalist forces in the peninsula, however, were gathering to attack the rebels and in June Pryce secretly crossed the border again to meet with Magón and other conspirators in Los Angeles to decide on what to do.

In his absence Dick Ferris stepped back into the picture and one of the rebels by the name of Louis James is supposed to have suggested that he proclaim himself in command of the army, which he did, at least in publicity releases, and he advised the rebels to haul down the Red flag and abandon Socialism and anarchism and "every other ism that you have got into."

Ferris then returned to his office in the Exposition headquarters and James continued to speak for him and announced his election, in absentia, as President of Tijuana. Ferris designed a flag with two horizontal bars and a white star and proclaimed the new Republic of Lower California. The Liberal Party's Junta from Los Angeles arrived in Tijuana, without Pryce, who realized that the cause had been lost. Jack Mosby was elected commander of the army. Ferris was declared persona non grata and his flag publicly burned. An appeal for volunteers was published by the Liberal Party Junta in the I.W.W.'s INDUSTRIAL WORKER which said that five months had passed since the Red flag had been raised over Mexicali, and that while victory had followed victory, more men and money were needed and there could be no "peace in Mexico until the Red flag flies over the workingman's country and Capitalism shall have been overthrown." Pryce, however, wrote to the rebels advising them to disband.

The Junta refused to come to terms with representatives of Madero and Mosby undertook his own negotiations, demanding for each of his men $100 as well as the dollar a day and the 160 acres of land that had been promised them when they joined the Magón revolution. But the end was to come from another direction. A force of 560 Mexican soldiers and volunteers advanced on Tijuana from Ensenada. Mosby gathered his 155 men and commandeered a five-car San Diego & Arizona work train for his infantry, and with the cavalry riding alongside, moved to meet the advancing Federalists. The battle on June 22 on the approach to Tijuana just north of the hot springs, lasted three hours and a defeated Mosby, with thirty of his men dead and "weeping like a child," fled across the border into the United States. With him went his American and alien followers. THE SAN DIEGO UNION reported:

Lined up in single file, they marched through the gateway of the custom house, and proceeded to the camp of the American soldiers about an eighth of a mile beyond...Late in the afternoon, they were placed aboard a train and brought to San Diego...The government boat LIEUT. GEORGE M. HARRIS...*conveyed them to Fort Rosecrans ...There are ninety-three of them in the barracks...and four in the hospital.*

When the rebels were interned temporarily at Fort Rosecrans, twelve of them were identified as deserters from the Army, Navy or Marines, including Mosby. Ricardo Flores Magón and his brother Enrique and other Junta leaders were convicted of violation of neutrality laws and sent to prison. Pryce and Ferris also were

Units of a minor revolutionary army move out to face a Mexican Federal force advancing on Tijuana. The rebels were defeated.

Defeated rebels claiming citizenship in the United States of America are led across the border by U.S. soldiers for internment at Fort Rosecrans.

indicted, but in time the charges against them were dropped. Pryce played cowboy roles in Hollywood and in World War I served in the British and Canadian armies. Ferris, after resigning from the exposition company, capitalized on his notoriety, appeared on the stage as THE MAN FROM MEXICO and then turned to various promotional schemes. Mosby was shot and killed while trying to escape when being transported to prison as a deserter.

Many of the I.W.W.'s remained in the area and with rising unemployment in the country they were joined by other agitators in street corner meetings and were in general calling for the overthrow of capitalism and in particular endeavoring to destroy craft unions which were in a state of organization. A pamphlet written by a recognized representative of the I.W.W. and a resident of San Diego, Laura Payne Emerson, was circulated under the heading, "The Crack of Doom or the Fall of Capitalism," and it read, in part:

Industrial unionism, the capitalist well knows, spells the abolition of the wage system...When the workers who make these great industries possible get ready for action they will no longer beg for some master to give them enough to live on, but take what belongs to them.

San Diego was known as a tolerant city but agitators became such a nuisance that sixty-five merchants on December 8 petitioned the Common Council to prohibit assemblies in a forty-nine block zone centering on Fifth and E Streets. Another petition was submitted by 250 Wobblies and Socialists and their liberal sympathizers insisting on a right of free speech anywhere at any time. While the Council hesitated, the situation grew tense.

152

On a Saturday night, January 6, 1912, a real estate man by the name of R. J. Walsh attempted to drive his auto through a mob of about a thousand Wobblies, Socialists and spectators on E between Fifth and Sixth Streets, and the response to the honking of his horn was the slashing of a tire. Police Chief Keno Wilson and a riot squad rushed to the scene in the department's black touring car and when the crowd refused to disperse began making arrests on charges of inciting to riot. It was an hour before the streets were cleared. Councilman Sehon, commissioner of police, watched but took no part. It was a difficult time for him, torn perhaps between his liberal views, military background and his responsibility as a city official.

The Socialists and I.W.W.'s returned to the scene the following night but the crowd was orderly and listened to speeches by Laura Emerson, Kaspar Bauer and E. E. Kirk, who had figured in the border revolutionary events, and later they adjourned to Germania Hall where the Rev. A. Lyle De Jarnette urged the socialization of the church. Kirk said:

The police caught us napping Saturday night, but tonight we were ready for them, and we had cash money on hand to use in case arrests were made. The fight for free speech in San Diego has but begun and it will be a fight to the finish.

On Monday the Council passed a modified version of the ordinance sought by the merchants which banned street corner speaking in an area bounded by C and F Streets and Fourth and Sixth Streets, but enforcement was delayed when the city attorney questioned the legality of an emergency clause suspending the usual thirty-day waiting period. The ordinance was almost a duplicate of one in effect in Los Angeles and its constitutionality had been upheld as being within the ordinary police powers of a city. So what began as a challenge to the restriction of a right of free speech soon turned into a license to create disorder.

No arrests were made when Socialists and Wobblies invited arrest in street corner speeches, so they and their supporters prepared for a showdown by organizing a chapter of the California Free Speech League and elected Wood Hubbard, of the I.W.W., as secretary. "Free speech" meetings advocated open violation of the law but the city attorney advised them that they would be free to talk on any street corner in any other section of the city.

The day after the ordinance went into effect, on February 9, the police arrested forty-one men in the forbidden zone. Chief Wilson said:

All these men have violated some law, whether they are street

Police Chief Keno Wilson

speakers or not, of that I am sure. So I'm going to charge some of them with disturbing the peace and others with offenses which I shall figure out by tomorrow.

A call for help went to all I.W.W. chapters in California and soon radicals and hoboes began pouring into the city. On February 13, Commissioner Sehon moved into action and ordered a roundup of all vagrants. Seven more persons were arrested when they attempted to speak before a street audience of more than a thousand. All of those arrested demanded jury trials to clog the jail and the small number of available courts and from their cells they yelled or sang "no flag but the red flag."

The attention of the nation was focused on the situation when Mayor Wadham received a telegram from Vincent St. John, general secretary of the Industrial Workers of the World, from Chicago, which warned:

This fight will be continued until free speech is established in San Diego if it takes 20,000 members and twenty years to do so.

At that very moment, according to the later testimony of Chief of Detectives Joseph Myers, there were at least 150 men on the road between Los Angeles and San Diego and hundreds of others were reported leaving all parts of the country for San Diego. They came by auto, by railroad passenger cars or jammed in box cars. The Board of Supervisors ordered the hiring of an armed guard to patrol the San Diego County line and conveyed authority to disperse gatherings of three or more persons. Sheriff Fred M. Jennings refused a request of District Attorney H. S. Utley to swear in a number of deputies and so Harry Place, a constable, organized an armed body of men, according to later testimony of Fred H. Moore and Marcus W. Robbins, attorneys for the Free Speech League, and maintained a border guard and stopped and searched autos, wagons and trains. The city rapidly was reaching a state of hysteria. Gov. Hiram Johnson rejected a plea to call out the State Militia. The EVENING TRIBUNE commented:

Why are the taxpayers of San Diego compelled to endure this imposition. Simply because the law which these lawbreakers flout prevents the citizens of San Diego from taking these impudent outlaws away from the police and hanging them or shooting them. This would end the trouble in an hour.

A climax came on March 10 when protestors gathered in the morning before the city jail on Second Street, with speakers, among them Mrs. Laura Emerson, haranguing the police from soap boxes and hundreds of spectators flocking to the scene until there was a crowd of almost 5000 persons. The situation was be-

James E. Wadham

154

yond the control of a force of less than a half hundred police officers and Fire Department engines arrived and firemen hooked up their hoses and sprayed the crowd with water. Some of them held their ground for an hour. News reports in other cities painted a picture of injustice. The OAKLAND WORLD reported:

For a full hour hundreds packed themselves in a solid mass around Mrs. Emerson as she stood upon the speakers stand. Bending themselves to the terrific torrent that poured upon them they held their ground until swept from their feet by the irresistible flood.

An old gray haired woman was knocked down by the direct force of the stream from the hose...A mother was deluged with a babe in her arms.

An awestruck American patriot wrapped himself in the flag to test its efficacy against police outrage, but he was knocked down and jailed and fined $30.00 for insulting the national emblem.

An investigation conducted later at the instigation of Gov. Hiram Johnson found that the water treatment had been effective and there had been no serious consequences in the way of illness or injuries.

An announcement signed "The Vigilantes" appeared in THE SAN DIEGO UNION of April 12, 1912. It read, in part:

The constitution of the State of California guarantees the right of free speech and public assembly...but it denies that right to all those who have no respect for law or order, or of the officials who

Rioting members of the I.W.W. were routed in San Diego when police and firemen drenched them with streams of water from fire hoses.

are charged with the execution of the laws...We propose to keep up the deportation of these undesirable citizens...as fast as we can catch them, and hereafter they will not only be carried to the county line and dumped there, but we intend to leave our mark on them in the shape of tar rubbed into their hair, so that a shave will be necessary to remove it, and this is what these agitators (all of them) may expect from now on, that the outside world may know that they have been to San Diego.

The police, with the city and county jails overflowing and more hoboes and Wobblies on the way, sent prisoners to jails in Santa Ana and Riverside and turned loose late at night others against whom charges could not be immediately substantiated. The Vigilantes took care of them, and a number of them subsequently described their experiences in testimony taken by Harris Weinstock, named by Gov. Johnson as a special commissioner to investigate the disturbances in San Diego. They were taken in groups in autos to Sorrento Valley where they faced scores of men, unmasked and carrying lanterns, who forced them to kneel and kiss the American flag or sing the National Anthem, and then they were taken to San Onofre, where they were herded for the night into cattle pens. In the morning they were made to run through double rows of men armed with clubs, whips and guns, and repeatedly beaten, and then, after the flag-kissing episode had been repeated, sent on their way along the railroad tracks with a warning never to return.

Others trying to enter the county were hauled off box cars, beaten, and driven back along the tracks. Some persons innocent of participation were seized in police or Vigilante raids on I.W.W. headquarters. It was claimed that one man was kicked to death in the jail but an autopsy indicated he had died of natural causes.

One of the most publicized incidents concerned A. R. Sauer, editor of a weekly newspaper which had borrowed its name from the original SAN DIEGO HERALD published in the 1850's, and who had spoken out against the Vigilantes. This was on April 5, and the report of Commissioner Weinstock stated:

Emboldened by the support and approval of some of the leading San Diego daily newspapers and its leading commercial bodies, members of the so-called vigilance committee became so reckless in their contempt of the law and for the provisions of the Constitution that, antagonized by his bold and, to them, distasteful, utterances, A. R. Sauer, editor of the SAN DIEGO HERALD, was kidnapped by the so-called vigilantes. Sauer who was on the way home from his office in the evening, before darkness really had fallen, was

Editor A. R. Sauer

accosted by a number of men, placed in an auto and hurried out of town. Arrived at the outskirts, the editor was compelled to descend, followed by his captors, who placed a rope about his neck. The other end of the rope was flung over the limb of a tree, and Sauer was hauled clear of the ground. In view of which treatment he was constrained to promise that he would leave San Diego and never return. The threat was made, according to Sauer's story, that if he divulged the names of his captors he would suffer the penalty of death.

Sauer made his way to Los Angeles and soon afterward returned to San Diego and resumed publishing of the newspaper. He promised to identify the Vigilantes whom he had recognized but never did so.

In a public address, Superior Judge Sloane, who later was to become a member of the State Supreme Court, warned that while "in this day and land of initiative, referendum and recall there is no excuse for organized disobedience and defiance of the enforcement of law...I would urge with equal earnestness it is the duty of those who enforce the law, to act within the law..."

Judge William A. Sloane

It was then that an aroused Gov. Johnson finally sent Weinstock, a business man, to San Diego to investigate and he conducted hearings in the Grand Jury chambers from April 18 to 20, in which a great deal of voluntary testimony was taken, and all public officials with the exception of District Attorney Utley cooperated except as to self-incrimination or identification of Vigilantes. The American Federation of Labor at San Francisco also sent a committee and reported a number of conversations with San Diego business men in which Spalding was quoted as saying, "We are going to run this element out of town," and J. M. Porter, a real estate man and identified as a leader of the Vigilantes, as asserting that, "We are fighting for our homes...We don't care about Weinstock or Gov. Johnson...Only troops can stop us."

Weinstock found that while the I.W.W.'s had been careful not to commit overt acts, they had deliberately invaded San Diego to disrupt normal government and the processes of law, and that they were committed to revolution; the police were above average in intelligence, and in character and personality, and there was no evidence of mistreatment of prisoners in the crowded jail, but acts of brutality had been committed away from the jail. He warned that radical tactics and philosophy imported from Europe, which had led to violence in Spokane and Fresno as well as San Diego, could menace the peace and welfare of the entire country.

After Weinstock had departed, conditions quieted down for a

while, though Wobblies still sought entrance to the town and arrests continued. In one incident in which there was conflicting testimony, a European-born radical by the name of Joseph Mikolasek was shot during an encounter with two police officers who had been watching the I.W.W. headquarters. This was on May 8. The officers, H. C. Stevens and R. M. Heddon, said that two men jumped out of the darkness and started shooting at them. Stevens was wounded but managed to shoot back and the assailants fled. Heddon was felled by a blow from an ax wielded by a third man who had come running out of the I.W.W. headquarters and who was identified as Mikolasek. Bleeding and on the ground, Heddon raised himself and fired three bullets into Mikolasek who staggered away and collapsed on a porch a few blocks away. Before dying he said that when he heard the shots he thought the officers were after him and were going to resume beating him, and he had acted in self defense.

The shots resulted in a city-wide riot call. Maybe the revolution had come. Repeated blasts of the powerhouse steam whistle summoned hundreds of citizens to the police station where they were armed with billy clubs and divided into patrols. Though the assailants who had shot at the police were never identified, the violence that the I.W.W. leaders had sought to avoid in order to frustrate the law in a campaign of civil disobedience, had at last occurred, and many of their more timid followers and transients began to desert. The liberals who had believed they were championing the right of free speech began to have second thoughts on the subject. A mass funeral planned for Mikolasek as a martyr to free speech was transferred to Los Angeles when police refused to permit the paraders to carry Red flags through the streets.

The last chapter came on May 14. In view of the shooting of Mikolasek and the effort to transform him into a martyr Emma Goldman moved up the time of her next lecture engagement in San Diego, and ignoring telegraphic advice from Chief Wilson that she remain away, she boarded the train to San Diego with her manager and traveling companion, Ben Reitman. There was a large crowd at the depot, but Mr. and Mrs. E. E. Kirk, who were to have met them, were nowhere to be seen. Slipping unnoticed out of their car, Emma Goldman and Reitman boarded the U. S. Grant Hotel's doubledeck autobus and proceeded to the top section where they found the Kirks. In her autobiography, LIVING MY LIFE, she tells what happened:

We had barely taken our seats when someone shouted: "Here she is, here's the Goldman woman!" At once the cry was taken up by the crowd. Fashionably dressed women stood up in their cars screaming: "We want that anarchist murderess!" In an instant there was a rush for the autobus, hands reaching up to pull me down. With unusual presence of mind, the chauffeur started the car at full speed, scattering the crowd in all directions.

With police assistance Miss Goldman and Reitman entered the hotel and were assigned a large suite of rooms. Toward evening there was a bedlam of auto horns and whistles and a thousand persons filled the street below waving flags and singing patriotic songs, and she was informed that city officials wished to confer with her in another room:

I entered a room filled with men. The window-blinds were partly drawn, but the large electric street light in front disclosed an agitated mass below. The Mayor approached me. "You hear that mob," he said, indicating the street; "they mean business. They want to get you and Reitman out of the hotel, even if they have to take you

San Diego Socialist supporters welcomed anarchist Emma Goldman to San Diego despite a mob scene. Atop hotel bus, left to right, are E. E. Kirk, of San Diego; Emma Goldman, Mrs. Kirk and Miss Goldman's companion, Ben Reitman.

by force. We cannot guarantee anything. If you consent to leave, we will give you protection and get you safely out of town."

Other reports indicate that the conference with city officials did not concern a threat to her safety but an anxiety to avoid further demonstrations, and Mayor Wadham was not present but was represented by Chief Wilson and Commissioner Sehon. Another person present was the chief of the California division of the United States Secret Service. In her version of the incident, however, she insists that she demanded that the officials enforce the law and disperse the crowd. She returned to her quarters to find Reitman missing. The hotel manager, J. H. Holmes, who she said had been sympathetic, now pleaded with her to leave San Diego. She went to the station to take the Owl Train leaving at 2:45 in the morning and again heard the sound of a mob:

"Hurry, hurry!" someone cried: "get in quick!"

Before I had time to make another step, I was picked up, carried to the train, and literally thrown into the compartment. The blinds were pulled down and I was locked in. The Vigilantes had arrived and were rushing up and down the platform, shouting and trying to board the train. The crew was on guard, refusing to let them on. There was mad yelling and cursing—hideous and terrifying moments till at last the train pulled out.

In their publications the Wobblies, who had only contempt for the anarchists whom they considered undependable, charged her with having been more frightened than defiant and retreating before an imaginary danger from a crowd more interested in hissing and jeering than in harming her. In Los Angeles she was reunited with Reitman, and in her autobiography she quotes him as reporting he had been taken on a twenty-mile auto ride and then:

When we reached the county line, the auto stopped at a deserted spot. The men formed a ring and told me to undress. They tore my clothes off. They knocked me down, and when I lay naked on the ground, they kicked and beat me until I was almost insensible. With a lighted cigar they burned the letters I.W.W. on my buttocks; then they poured a can of tar over my head and, in the absence of feathers, rubbed sage brush on my body...They forced me to kiss the flag and sing THE STAR SPANGLED BANNER. *When they tired of the fun, they gave me my underwear for fear we should meet any women. They also gave me back my vest, in order that I might carry my money, railroad ticket, and watch. The rest of my clothes they kept. I was ordered to make a speech, and then they commanded me to run the gauntlet. The Vigilantes lined up, and as I ran past them, each one gave me a blow or a kick. Then they let me go.*

The city had been saved, the Wobblies and itinerants vanquished, and in a short time it seemed as if it all had been a bad dream. Prisoners held in jails in Orange and Riverside counties as well as in San Diego slowly were released. The last of them pleaded guilty during a smallpox epidemic in the jail and received suspended sentences. Federal investigations were launched in a desultory manner and nothing came of them. There are no accurate reports of how many persons answered the call of the radicals and actually invaded or tried to invade the town but estimates ran as high as several thousands. It had been a high point of a revolutionary movement.

In a few years the people of this small town in a distant corner of a vast country, who had reacted with such fury, and outside the law, to a shapeless threat to the order of their ways, brought about a civic and cultural achievement that would leave a heritage known around the world.

Nine

San Francisco Shows How Politics Should Be Played

This painting by Jonas Lie in the Metropolitan Museum of Art in New York shows the great Culebra Cut for the Panama Canal. Pacific Coast cities were staking their future on trade through the canal.

CHAPTER IX

Though construction work on the Panama Canal was being delayed by cave-ins and dirt slides, and by the long effort of draining swamps and eradicating disease, two rival cities rushed ahead with their plans to celebrate its completion and to capture the anticipated trade.

San Diego was rallying support for its exposition from other Southern California counties and in Washington the House of Representatives passed the resolution asking President Taft to invite the participation of Latin American countries. It was a moment of triumph for D. C. Collier, the exposition's temporary president, who had remained in Washington to lobby for its passage.

As had been agreed upon, President Taft issued the invitation to all countries of the world to participate in the San Francisco fair, while the resolution for participation in San Diego's exposition moved to the Senate on its own way to the White House. A local attorney, Sam F. Smith, returned from Washington and reported on Collier's successes.

In a newspaper interview he told San Diegans:

Collier is a power in Washington and those who knock him and sneer at him in San Diego should be ashamed of themselves. Official Washington is especially interested in the reclamation of arid lands and irrigation, and accordingly takes much interest in this feature of the San Diego fair.

The very next day came word that a United States Senate committee had ruled unfavorably on the resolution. As San Francisco was to hold a fair in the same year to which the nations of the world already had been invited to participate, the committee felt that an invitation to another exposition would be inadvisable. Collier was stunned. The blame was placed with San Francisco and politics. It was charged that President Taft had been induced to discourage Senate approval by the promise of San Francisco to deliver to him the support of California in the struggle between the Old Guard and the Bull Moose Party movement with which Theodore Roosevelt was seeking to break the Republican Party and return himself to the White House. In a telegram to THE SAN DIEGO UNION Collier stated:

The war is on. San Diego accepts the challenge of San Francisco ...for many months I have seen that the limitations of the agreement with San Francisco, which we considered binding on us, seriously jeopardized the success of our exposition. The shackles are now stricken off and our hands are free; and we will build an exposition of which the whole United States will be proud.

In San Diego, Joseph W. Sefton, the acting director-general, spoke for the exposition's officers and directors:

San Francisco has shown by her latest action what she has proven by practically all of her past acts—the right to the proud title of Judas Iscariot...It was San Diego which first started the exposition idea; it was San Diego who first advertised California as the exposition state; it was San Diego, who realizing that she was not large enough to build the greatest world's fair this country has ever seen, for the honor of the State of California, gave precedence to San Francisco. And for this we get a knife in the back.

There was no intention of surrendering so easily and California Sen. John D. Works, who once had been a resident of San Diego, promised to carry on the fight for official recognition. The word "international" was returned to exposition advertising and the capitalization was increased from $2,000,000 to $3,000,000 as the result of an over-subscription of stock.

Stimulation of the economy was apparent on every hand. In the harbor, in preparation for the line of commercial ships expected to soon rise above the horizon, dredges were pumping silt from the bay bottom and depositing it behind a long bulkhead, from D Street, or Broadway, to Date Street, and two blocks wide, to create sixty acres of new land west of the railroad depot. The new pier over which there had been such controversy was being readied to handle the cargoes of the world. It was obvious, however, that it could not be finished before the opening of the exposition. The Marston Company opened a new store in April at Fifth and C Streets. Street car lines were being extended and the Consolidated

How San Diego's waterfront came into being is shown in this photograph of the dredging and filling in from just a little west of the Santa Fe Railroad tracks.

Gas & Electric Company was spending a million dollars to meet demands for its services. Though Spreckels privately was in desperate need of money, he went ahead with two new six-story structures on Broadway, the Hotel San Diego and the Spreckels Building with a theater with ornate boxes and two balconies.

The Southern Pacific Railroad brought suit against John D. and A. B. Spreckels to compel them to purchase all of its interest in the San Diego & Arizona Railway and to recover $2,800,000 it had expended on construction. The suit confirmed what financiers knew and most of the public had suspected. The San Diego & Arizona was a creature of the Southern Pacific and there had been no intention on its part, regardless of the hopes of Spreckels, of extending its line beyond El Centro to the Colorado River and thus competing with its own main line into Los Angeles. The Southern Pacific previously had withdrawn all support for the proposed electric railway from Los Angeles to San Diego and to the coastal subdivisions which Fletcher had laid out for the Huntington interests.

Spreckels proposed to sell to the city for $2,500,000 more of the water system that he had been building for years, the Barrett intake dam and reservoir site, the Dulzura conduit, the Otay lakes and the Chollas reservoir system, and to lease the Morena reservoir with an option for purchase any time within ten years. Clayton, Spreckels' representative, wrote in an article in THE SAN DIEGO UNION:

...there are several people in San Diego, some who own considerable property, who came here with the knowledge and understanding that Mr. Spreckels was building the Arizona road, and now that the road has been dragging along for several years, they find in reality that the Southern Pacific was building it, and have very little confidence in its completion, and are consequently inclined to be peeved...No matter what may happen, long after he has paid the debt of Nature, there will be people in San Diego who will have a very kindly feeling toward the memory of the man who did so much towards its upbuilding.

In August of 1912 the voters approved bonds for the purchase of the water facilities which it was said would provide the city with a municipally-owned system from "mountain to meter."

The opening of the Spreckels Theater on August 23, under the management of J. M. Dodge and H. C. Hayward, was a social and cultural event unmatched since the boom days of the 1880's. That evening street curbs were lined for blocks with autos and carriages, as gaily gowned parties arrived to enter a foyer which news reports described as "luxuriously fitted with rare Persian rugs and hangings, palms, ferns and the stately Egyptian lotus," and took their seats in a theater of "a gleaming harmony in old ivory and gold." After the Star Spangled Banner had been rendered, the audience began a spontaneous ovation for John D. Spreckels and he reluctantly left his box to make his way to the stage. The audience arose in greeting and he was presented with a large basket of red roses. He expressed his appreciation in only a few words. It was not a night to recall all that had been said against him. In building the theater he said he had endeavored to give San Diego something which would be a testimonial of the high esteem in which he held the city and its people. The citizens of San Diego had so often expressed confidence in him and appreciation of his enterprises that he wished to reciprocate and had been able to think of no better way to do so than to build the playhouse.

Though Los Angeles had been joined by San Francisco in seeking to thwart the ambitions of San Diego, the town had no intention of being isolated from the main current of the times. It decided to put itself back on the national highway map by proving that the Yuma-San Diego route was the most practical way to reach the Pacific Coast from Phoenix. Transcontinental highways as well as railroad terminals were vital for a port with ambitions to become a center of Pacific Ocean trade. A committee composed of Ed Fletcher, F. B. Naylor and Fred W. Jackson raised $3000 as prize money and challenged Los Angeles to a race. The autos from Los Angeles would go by the way of San Bernardino, Indio and the Salton Sea; the cars from San Diego by way of Mountain Springs and El Centro. Phoenix citizens also contributed $1000.

For reasons not at first very clear, sanction for the race was slow in coming from the American Automobile Association, so in the meantime, the LOS ANGELES EXAMINER issued a challenge for a preliminary pathfinder race and it was accepted by the SAN DIEGO EVENING TRIBUNE. Also interested was C. H. Akers, publisher of the PHOENIX GAZETTE, who was carrying on a campaign to have San Diego and Imperial counties annexed to Arizona. The San Diego entry became the TRIBUNE-GAZETTE auto and was driven by Ed Fletcher. The LOS ANGELES EXAMINER driver was given the privilege of selecting any route that he wished, and decided to race for Phoenix by way of the Blythe crossing on the Colorado River, which was eighty miles above the Yuma crossing. It was a longer route. From San Diego to Phoenix by way of El Centro was about 360 miles; from Los Angeles to Phoenix by way of Blythe,

A trail-blazing auto was sent out to prove that the Yuma-San Diego route was the best way to reach the Coast from Phoenix instead of by way of the Salton Sea and Los Angeles. Promoter Ed Fletcher is in the left front seat.

about 425 miles.

After negotiating sections of the new road to the desert and crossing the bridges over the wide barrancas cut by the Colorado River flood, Fletcher drove his four-cylinder, air-cooled Franklin through El Centro and toward the distant sand hills which more cautious motorists always avoided. He let some air out of the tires and plunged ahead. He had taken no chances and had stationed six horses in the sand hills, and when his auto bogged down, a horse team pulled it through four and a half miles of sand. At Yuma he crossed the Southern Pacific Railroad bridge at night, kept driving through a cloudburst, forded streams swollen by rain, and finally arrived in Phoenix nineteen and a half hours out of San Diego. The Los Angeles entry was nowhere to be seen. It had broken down in the desert and never reached Phoenix.

When AAA sanction for the race to Phoenix finally had been received, arrangements for the competition were completed. However, when the autos were about ready to start it was learned that a subsequent AAA ruling required that the cars be held up at Yuma for a checkout for the last lap to Phoenix. This meant that the San Diego autos would have to wait at Yuma for the ones from Los Angeles to arrive before continuing the race, and thus it might be difficult to present dramatic proof of the superiority of the more southerly route.

Twenty-two cars started from Fifth Street between D and C Streets, and went by way of Fifth and University, thence east through La Mesa, Descanso, Mountain Springs, Coyote Wells, El Centro and Holtville. Only twelve of the twenty-two finished the race. A San Diego auto, a Stevens-Duryea, driven by D. W. Campbell, an auto dealer, was the first to reach Phoenix, two hours ahead of the first Los Angeles auto. However, though the route from Los Angeles was sixty-five miles longer, in actual running time from the starting city to destination, the Los Angeles auto beat Campbell's time by fourteen minutes.

As usual, San Diegans suspected that the influence of the LOS ANGELES TIMES somehow had been exerted against the community. There was no doubt that San Diego was lacking in political influence and it was time to do something about it. The Republican Party was badly split, in San Diego as elsewhere in California, between the Progressives and the Standpatters, and when Sylvester C. Smith, of Bakersfield, who had represented the Eleventh District in Congress, decided to retire, a Democrat, William Kettner, was asked to make the race. He was a director of the Chamber of Commerce and in the insurance business, and in his younger days had mined gold and driven a horse car.

When a candidate from Riverside defeated Lewis R. Kirby of San Diego for the Republican nomination, GOP leaders swung the support of San Diego behind Kettner and he was elected in November of 1912. He would represent six other counties as well: Imperial, Riverside, Orange, San Bernardino, Inyo and Mono.

There was some measure of satisfaction to the promoters of the exposition when President Taft failed of re-election. Theodore Roosevelt split the Republican Party with his Progressive movement in which Gov. Hiram Johnson of California was his vice presidential candidate. In California, the Progressives who dominated the machinery of the Republican Party entered the same electors on both the Progressive and Republican tickets in the presidential primary and virtually eliminated Taft supporters. San Francisco had not been able to deliver the state to Taft as supposedly promised in return for support for its world's fair, and his name did not even appear on California ballots. The nationwide political divisions resulted in the election of a Democrat, Woodrow Wilson, as president. California gave a majority of several hundred votes to Roosevelt, while San Diego County's majority for Wilson was about 1600.

One of Kettner's first acts was to obtain full Congressional recognition of San Diego and United States participation in the Panama-California Exposition. It was too late, however, to expect any general participation from Latin America. Only Brazil had shown any real interest. The Panama Canal promised no blessings for the west coast of South America. Its opening would cut the ties of Chile and Peru with California that had existed since the days of the greatness of Spain. Their ports had been important points on the long route from Spain and around Cape Horn to San Diego and Monterey, and they had benefitted for a century from the growth of American shipping.

Even the weather seemed to conspire against the town and on January 6 and 7, 1913, a severe freeze damaged citrus crops. The temperature fell to 25 degrees and was lower than 32 degrees for twelve hours. The water in Wilde's fountain in the Plaza froze

THE DAY THE FOUNTAIN FROZE *is the title of this civic event. The natives had never seen anything like it. Southern California's cold spell in 1913 found water in the San Diego Plaza fountain coated with ice thick enough to stand on.*

over and San Diegans came from long distances to see it.

In the following Spring of 1913 hopes rose with the weather and the new Mountain Springs road was dedicated in a ceremony that attracted 800 excursionists. In commending San Diegans for private contributions for work within Imperial County, J. J. Carr, chairman of its Board of Supervisors, said:

Imperial County is growing by leaps and bounds. This stretch of road is just what it needs. I fail to find words to express the gratification of Imperial Valley residents. Products of the valley

170

will be hauled to San Diego for market. Your coffers will in a few years team with the valley wealth.

Frederick J. Lea, representing the San Diego Chamber of Commerce, said that "today is just like commencement day at college. We have just begun the good roads movement." Fletcher said San Diego certainly would realize its dream of being the western terminus of the ocean to ocean highway.

The ambitions for economic importance and for size and population, which had brought about the exposition, the campaign for

highway connections, the reclaiming of tidelands and building of a commercial pier at the city's front door, dominated the debate in the city election of 1913. The issue of what kind of a city San Diego was to become, and whether it could have both beauty and industry, came to a head after years of discussion and argument.

A group of citizens, including E. S. Babcock, who originally had built Hotel del Coronado as a resort, Wangenheim, M. A. and Edgar Luce, Sefton, Fletcher, Lyman Gage and Spalding, most of whom, if not all, had been backers of the Nolen Plan, induced

The flivvers of another day chugged over the mountains for the dedication of the Mountain Springs grade which all hoped would draw tourists and traffic to San Diego instead of Los Angeles.

171

Marston to be a candidate for mayor, or signed his petition. Those who favored more commerce and industry at the expense of tourists and resorts entered Charles F. O'Neall, a real estate agent.

The campaign supporters for O'Neall stated that he was for payrolls first and civic beauty next and represented the backbone of the city instead of merely the "aristocracy," that he belonged to the element which in recent years had come to the city and with new energy and new inspiration had largely helped to develop it and made possible the fancy prices the old timers were now getting for their property.

Marston was forced to defend past actions. One of them was in regard to the original Santa Fe line into San Diego, which for a time was expected to become the western end of its main transcontinental route. Floods had washed out the section through Temecula Canyon in the 1880's and Los Angeles became the terminal, with a branch down the coast to San Diego. Marston and other merchants agreed, though reluctantly, to the change. Marston also had been traveling in Europe when the exposition was formulated and acknowledged that at first he had some reservations about it.

In speeches in his own behalf, Marston promised that he would accelerate the building of the railroad to Arizona and said he supported the harbor improvements and the exposition. To him the city could be both beautiful and prosperous, but beauty could be its greatest asset:

I have been criticized for advocating the "city beautiful" idea, and I hereby plead guilty to the indictment, if indictment it be. I am for the city beautiful. I'm for it because it pays in dollars and cents. I believe in a city beautiful because we want more than selling real estate; we want comfort for our citizens.

Women entered the campaign in large numbers and a former suffragist leader, Mrs. Earl Garrettson, told a gathering of 300:

The women of San Diego realize the importance of preparing for the great influx of immigration which the opening of the Panama Canal will bring...there are more than 350,000 people in southern Italy and Russia booked for passage to San Diego. These people will have to be housed properly...they will have to be given employment. George W. Marston is the man to solve these and many other problems and to make San Diego, which heretofore has been a good little city, become a good big city.

Louis Wilde, the banker, who had come to San Diego from Los Angeles, came out against Marston:

O'Neall is progressive, not narrow, conservative...Mr. Marston

Louis J. Wilde

...means well, but he has not got it in him to do broad things for anybody...somehow or other every time a big vital movement has been started for the advancement of the city, Marston has been quietly against it...Marston, for instance, has been talking the "city beautiful" ever since I have been here, and he has not even managed to keep the streets clean...We don't want San Diego to be the "amen corner" of the United States.

Seven other bankers, however, immediately came out in support of Marston. Spreckels remained aloof and gave equal news space to both sides. Scripps and his SAN DIEGO SUN supported Marston who continued to answer his critics. In a letter to Fletcher he wrote:

Charles F. O'Neall

Despite the fact that I have been accused of favoring the aesthetic rather than the practical, and that I am a dreamer of dreams in which neatly kept lawns and attractive posy beds play a prominent part, I beg to assure you that the speedy completion of our wonderful harbor resources has been often in my thoughts. I have for a long time favored the construction of a great dry-dock in San Diego, for I believe it will do much to bring to San Diego that recognition as a seaport of prominence which it deserves.

The establishment of a dry-dock would also be one of the most effective arguments possible for the establishment of a naval coaling station in San Diego bay. Eventually San Diego is destined to become a great naval station, with a training school on North Island, and the harbor as a haven wherein our fighting craft can repair and replenish.

The primary produced several surprises. O'Neall led with a vote of 6840. Marston had 4738. The Socialists were back in political strength and produced 3015 votes for their candidate, Jacob Beckel. In the general election, O'Neall was elected mayor by a majority of 668 votes. The Socialists, with no candidate for mayor in the final election, concentrated successfully on defeating their old friend, Councilman Sehon, to punish him, as the news stories reported it, "for suppressing the lawless Industrial Workers of the World a year ago, and quenching the flaming tongues of Kasper Bauer, Harry McKee and other advocates of government without courts."

The approach of the exposition and a revelation of the difficulties of the Spreckels companies soon took the people's minds off the central issue, but it would be fought out again. Marston's interest in San Diego was not diminished by political defeat. His partners in the ownership of the site of the old Presidio had withdrawn and he acquired sole possession. In 1913 the Order of

173

William Kettner

A. B. Spreckels

Panama, with his permission, erected a cross to Fr. Junípero Serra. It was built with tiles taken from the ruins. President Wilson designated the old lighthouse on Point Loma as the Cabrillo National Monument in honor of Juan Rodríguez Cabrillo, the discoverer of California.

In Congress, Kettner engineered his appointment to the House Rivers and Harbors Committee and was successful in obtaining from Adm. George Dewey, the commander of the Navy and president of its General Board, a letter which, though it reaffirmed the board's view that it would not be wise to establish a second naval station on the coast below San Francisco, said it was certain that naval use of the port of San Diego would increase with the years and it would be desirable to deepen the inner harbor where there was room for at least sixteen capital ships. The Senate Commerce Committee thereby consented to adding an appropriation of $259,000 for San Diego. Within a short time he also had obtained appropriations to complete the Naval Coaling Station on Point Loma, for the proposed new Naval Radio Station at San Diego, to strengthen coastal defenses at Fort Rosecrans and to map the offshore kelp beds. When he returned to California to visit his district, his train was met at Oceanside by a civic band.

Construction work on the San Diego & Arizona was continuing despite the legal maneuvering as to who really owned it, and Spreckels again found himself in financial difficulties and made a second appeal to the citizens of San Diego.

The holdings left to John D. and Adolph Spreckels by their father, Claus, in California sugar interests, shipping, and various Hawaiian and Philippine plantations, had been valued at $25,000,000. But they were not producing money fast enough to satisfy John D. Spreckels' ambitions to exceed the enterprise of his father. Adolph had never been in good health and it was the elder brother who dominated the firm of J. D. & A. B. Spreckels. He had little interest in the sugar industry, as such, and before his father's death he had begun building the great fleet of the Oceanic Steamship Lines, and then spent ten years as publisher of the SAN FRANCISCO CALL. It was San Diego, however, and the opportunity to build a city, which drew most of his attention and which demanded more and more money from the other family enterprises.

On May 3, 1914, Clayton put all of the cards on the table and wrote a long newspaper account of the railroad's problems and how they had come about, and it made interesting reading for a town that had taken John D. Spreckels at his word:

*The San Diego & Arizona Railway was projected by the South-
ern Pacific Company under policies adopted by the late E. H. Harriman. For reasons which I am unable to explain...Mr. Spreckels
came out and announced he would build the San Diego & Arizona
Railway...He was to direct all its affairs, but the money was to be
found by the Southern Pacific, while the title remained ostensibly
in the hands of J. D. Spreckels.*

There was a time after the death of Harriman when the Southern Pacific asked Spreckels to slow down but he said he could not
do so. The Southern Pacific then withdrew its support. Spreckels
entered into an agreement with the Southern Pacific whereby he
acquired an option to purchase the San Diego & Arizona within
twelve months. He turned to the Rock Island Railroad, which
had built toward Arizona and which at one time had begged for
the opportunity of participating in the San Diego & Arizona in
the hope of reaching tidewater on the Pacific. But the Southern
Pacific had entered into secret agreement with the Rock Island
to forestall this possibility. Clayton continued:

*At the end of twelve months, Mr. Spreckels told the Southern
Pacific he would not exercise his option. The Southern Pacific said,
"You bought this railroad." But Mr. Spreckels replied, "No, I did
not. I signed nothing but an option." So the Southern Pacific sued
him and said he had bought it.*

So, Clayton said, Spreckels found himself up against it. He
used the $2,500,000 obtained from the sale of his water system
to the City of San Diego as collateral to borrow money to keep the
work going. So far the railroad had cost him $5,000,000.

Requirements by the State of California for the issuance of stock
and bonds would require heavy further investments by Spreckels.
It was suggested that the citizens of San Diego be asked to sub-
scribe money but it was pointed out they already were heavily
committed by the exposition. An appeal was made for the city to
take up the option to buy Morena reservoir for $1,500,000, and
Spreckels pledged that the money would be used for construction
of the railroad and that he would continue his efforts to find additional means of financing. The bonds for the purchase of Morena
passed by a vote of six to one on May 5, 1914. Spreckels was
deeply moved by the margin of approval and said:

*The result of this election demonstrates that in one portion of
this great country is a community which is not hostile to capital
and will assist in a legitimate public enterprise. Capital will be
inspired by such a result and will be attracted to a community so
eminently fair and liberal minded.*

The San Diego & Arizona still faced the most difficult and costly section of its road, the descent to the desert through the Carrizo Gorge, and it was feared the cost of the line between San Diego and El Centro would rise to $15,000,000. An extension to Yuma would cost another $10,000,000. These costs were far above the original estimates for the entire line of less than $5,000,000. Spreckels hoped to sell bonds to meet these heavy costs and he promised San Diego that somehow he would find a way to complete the line to El Centro by the time of the exposition opening. Sixty-five miles of track had been laid from both ends and seventy miles more remained to be built. The work went on while Spreckels and the Southern Pacific engaged in further legal maneuvers.

A reputation as a center of aviation was being won. In 1912 the Navy had established a base on North Island, with three airplanes, three tents, and three fliers, Lieuts. John H. Towers, Victor Herbster and T. G. Ellyson; Howard Morin, a Navy electrician, installed the first radio set in an airplane; on Thanksgiving Day the Army Signal Corps established an aviation school on North Island and named it Rockwell Field; Lieut. H. A. Erickson took the first aerial photograph. In 1913, Lincoln Beachey, a civilian flier trained by Curtiss, made the first loop-the-loop; Army Lieut. T. C. Macaulay made the first night flight; and the first aerial bomb was dropped by Riley Scott, a former Army officer with the North Island unit, and Army Lieut. L. E. Goodier. A Curtiss airplane established an altitude record of 16,798 feet over San Diego.

After several years of struggle, the Little Landers Colony in the Tia Juana River Valley and adjoining hillsides had grown to more than 400 persons and Smythe, its founder, was carrying the message of communal life to other towns and cities of California. To him, San Ysidro was the "mother colony." Clayton, after visiting the colony in the company of Spreckels, said he was amazed at its progress and that it would be a good thing if San Diego County had 500,000 Little Landers. It had been found, though, that some persons worked harder than others, that some persons more radical than their fellow colonists agitated continually for a more communal life than merely the cooperative marketing of products raised on small privately-owned plots, and that success of such a venture depended on the nearness to cities, the larger the better. They could not exist in a world of their own.

Through all these years Ed Fletcher had quietly proceeded with establishing rights to the water of the San Diego River which came through state filings. The river passed directly through San Diego and had wasted its flood waters into the sea. The city had

(Opposite page) Steady as she goes! Lincoln Beachey prepares for history's first aerial loop-the-loop which he made over San Diego in 1913.

177

pumps in Mission Valley and also once had relied on the privately-owned wooden flume which brought water from Cuyamaca Lake on a tributary of the San Diego River. When the flume company went bankrupt Fletcher and J. A. Murray, a millionaire owner of water systems in Montana and Idaho, acquired it for $150,000 and later offered it to the city. But Spreckels had his own water system to sell and city officials looked the other way. Fletcher and Murray began serving the La Mesa, Lemon Grove and Spring Valley Irrigation District and went ahead with plans to build dams and reservoirs on the San Diego River and to supply the newly organized town of East San Diego. This set the stage for a future struggle over the paramount rights to the water which the city would finally claim by rights coming down from the King of Spain and the Royal Presidio of San Diego. Warner's Ranch was purchased by William G. Henshaw and Fletcher induced him to acquire sites for dams and reservoirs on the San Dieguito River system by which frost-free coastal areas, which Fletcher had begun developing for the former Huntington interests, could be served with water.

H. Austin Adams

Of much more momentary interest was liquor and not water, and whether the "wet" zone, or the area in which liquor could be sold, should be widened. The liberals were out in force again, and Austin Adams emerged as their leader for an "open" town. He declared:

We must decide at once whether San Diego is to be a Middle West village controlled by the narrow minded and bigoted provincialism of a small minority, or by those broad and sane views of modern civilized life which obtain in the really great cities of the world ...what may be all very well for a backwoods Kansas tank town will not do for a cosmopolitan city at the very moment that we are inviting the whole civilized world to come here and spend a year (and all the spare cash possible) in our midst.

The City Council passed an ordinance widening the zone of sale but a referendum petition was filed under leadership of the Anti-Saloon League which caused it to be held in abeyance until a future election.

The assassination of President Madero had released once again the forces of revolution in Mexico and that unhappy land was torn by intensive warfare and humiliated by United States intervention. Mexican bandits raided the border town of Tecate in March and killed the town's postmaster, Frank Johnson, and set fire to buildings. By late 1914, Col. Esteban Cantu, in the name of one of the revolutionary armies, seized control of Tijuana without firing a shot. United States Cavalry units again patrolled the border as they had done during the Magón insurrection.

In Europe Archduke Franz Ferdinand and his wife were assassinated in Sarajevo, on June 28, 1914. On July 28, Austria declared war on Serbia. On August 1, Germany declared war on Russia. On August 3, Germany declared war on France, and on August 4, England declared war on Germany.

The outbreak of war at first had a severe impact on business and much of the building activity in San Diego, with the exception of that in the exposition, came to a halt. There was no general feeling at the time that the United States would become involved and on the Pacific Coast there was great rejoicing when the steamship ANCONA passed through the Culebra Cut and became the first ocean-going vessel to navigate the Panama Canal. On September 6 the pleasure yacht LASATA arrived at San Diego, after having passed through the canal, and its owner, Morgan Adams, of Los Angeles, said that other vessels would soon be following the LASATA to San Diego.

G. Aubrey Davidson was elected president of the exposition, with Collier returning to his post as director-general, and the first high-ranking government official to visit the grounds was the Assistant Secretary of the Navy, Franklin D. Roosevelt. His car was the first to pass over the new bridge spanning Cabrillo Canyon. A fever of excitement brought a boom in land speculation and development. An encouraged Spreckels undertook the development of Mission Beach, then a strip of sand dunes covered with

Even the mud flats of Mission Bay held possibilities for recreation and a Venetian City with islands and waterways was designed to lure tourists to Southern California.

scrub brush, by connecting it to Ocean Beach with a wooden bridge, and creating, at least on paper, a Venetian city that would have done credit to the imagination and enthusiasm of a John Nolen or a Bertram Goodhue. An open air pavilion in Balboa Park also was being completed to house the great outdoor organ which Spreckels was presenting to the city. The Santa Fe Railroad and the San Diego & Arizona Railway combined resources to construct a new depot in a style compatible with the architecture of the exposition. A stadium for nearly 30,000 persons was being built in a canyon, a natural amphitheater where the hillsides served as walls, with money from a $150,000 bond issue.

The opening of the exposition was set for midnight of January 1, 1915. That would be several weeks ahead of San Francisco. At last everything was ready and a pearl gray city with towers and domes of brightly colored tile rose out of history.

The old Santa Fe station comes down as a new one in the Spanish style is opened to welcome visitors to the Panama-California Exposition.

Ten

A "Magic City" Surprises Even Those Who Built It

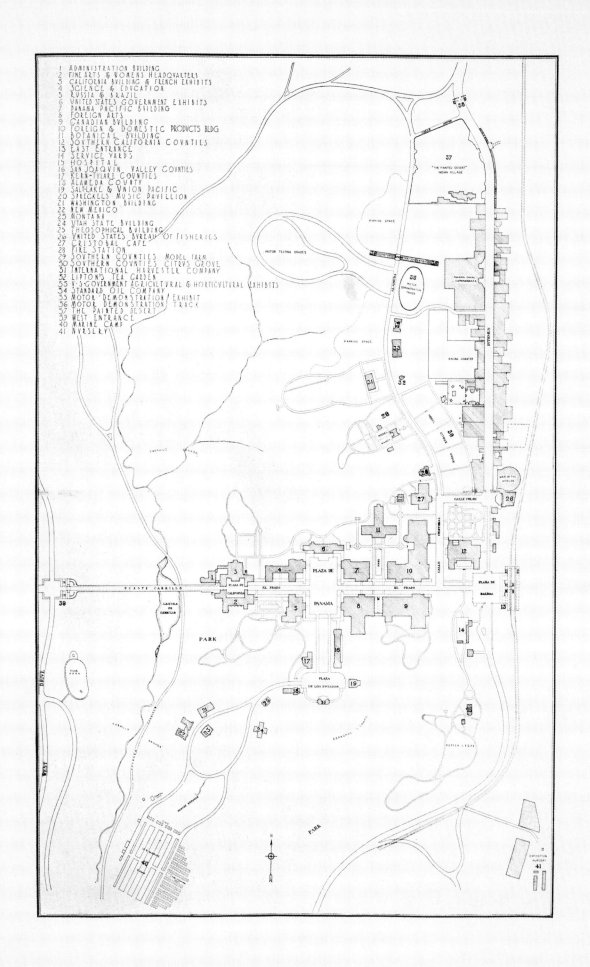

1 ADMINISTRATION BVILDING
2 FINE ARTS & WOMENS HEADQVARTERS
3 CALIFORNIA BVILDING & FRENCH EXHIBITS
4 SCIENCE & EDUCATION
5 RVSSIA & BRAZIL
6 VNITED STATES GOVERNMENT EXHIBITS
7 PANAMA PACIFIC BVILDING
8 FOREIGN ARTS
9 CANADIAN BVILDING
10 FOREIGN & DOMESTIC PRODVCTS BLDG.
11 BOTANICAL BVILDING
12 SOVTHERN CALIFORNIA COVNTIES
13 EAST ENTRANCE
14 SERVICE YARDS
15 HOSPITAL
16 SAN JOAQVIN VALLEY COVNTIES
17 KERN-TVLARE COVNTIES
18 ALAMEDA COUNTY
19 SALT-LAKE & VNION PACIFIC
20 SPRECKELS MVSIC PAVILLION
21 WASHINGTON BVILDING
22 NEW MEXICO
23 MONTANA
24 VTAH STATE BVILDING
25 THEOSOPHICAL BVILDING
26 VNITED STATES BVREAV OF FISHERIES
27 CRISTOBAL CAFE
28 FIRE STATION
29 SOVTHERN COVNTIES MODEL FARM
30 SOVTHERN COVNTIES CITRVS GROVE
31 INTERNATIONAL HARVESTER COMPANY
32 LIPTON'S TEA GARDEN
33 V-S-GOVERNMENT AGRICVLTVRAL & HORTICVLTVRAL EXHIBITS
34 STANDARD OIL COMPANY
35 MOTOR DEMONSTRATION EXHIBIT
36 MOTOR DEMONSTRATION TRACK
37 THE PAINTED DESERT
38 WEST ENTRANCE
39 MARINE CAMP
41 NVRSERY

CHAPTER X

President Woodrow Wilson, 2600 miles away, touched an electric button that turned on a light suspended by a balloon and bathed an area of three square miles in a glow in which the "Magic City" was visible for miles at sea. The guns of Fort Rosecrans and those of Navy cruisers in the harbor sounded in unison with the explosions of 1000 mines planted around the grounds to herald the opening of the Panama-California Exposition.

A fire works display atop the Spreckels Organ Pavilion was timed to coincide with the opening of the gates to an exhibit of a replica of the Panama Canal, from which emerged the prow of an imaginary ship labeled "1915" and then, outlined in flame, was the phrase "The Land Divided—the World United—San Diego the First Port of Call." At a brief ceremony before the opening, conducted on the steps of the Sacramento Building which faced the main Plaza de Panama, D. C. Collier told his audience:

We are here tonight to celebrate the culmination of five years of hard work, of meeting and defeating obstacles which have been flung in our way, and discouragements which seemed always a little greater than we could overcome.

(Next page) A light suspended from a balloon was turned on and bathed buildings and towers in gold to officially open the Panama-California Exposition. The beauty of its architecture and the warmth of its colors would linger with all those who walked the grounds.

*Secretary of the Treasury
William Gibbs McAdoo
at the exposition
opening*

To Mayor O'Neall, the future of San Diego as the metropolis of the West seemed assured, on a foundation of geographical location, harbor, climate, soil, and the benefits sure to flow from the exposition itself. To George W. Marston, the beauty of the architecture of Bertram Grosvenor Goodhue was a treasure for a city to enjoy. Gov. Hiram Johnson was on hand to present to the citizens of San Diego the California Building and California Tower and they were accepted by G. Aubrey Davidson, president of the exposition. Formal ceremonies were conducted the next day, with Secretary of the Treasury William Gibbs McAdoo representing President Wilson and Count del Valle de Salazar representing King Alfonso XIII of Spain.

It was the first unified exposition held in the United States. It did not, as other fairs had done, seek to bring together as many varied products and dissimilar achievements of the world as possible, but in the words of Goodhue himself:

At San Diego, the case was different. Though rapidly increasing in population, San Diego cannot yet be considered a great city…yet it did project and did carry out a smaller exhibition, not a World's Fair in the strictest sense of the term, but rather one that was cultural and regional. It endeavored to reflect the past of that great section of the country of which it forms the natural seaport, and to obtain insofar as this was possible, something of the effect of the old Spanish and Mission days and thus to link the spirit of the old seekers of the fabled Eldorado with that of the Twentieth Century.

As had John Nolen and Samuel Parsons before him, Goodhue believed that Southern California's assets were climate and location, and that these attractions were limited to a very few areas of the world, the Riviera, the bays of Naples and Salerno, some of the Greek islands, certain mountain valleys of India, the Vega of Granada and the parallel one of Shiraz. He wrote:

Yet…except for the charm that comes from works of man softened by centuries of use, the glamour given by ages of history, the tender respect always commanded by things that are venerable — in Southern California may be found every attraction possessed by those areas.

The population of the city at the opening of the exposition was estimated at about 74,000. This had not been enough to command large national or international participation. No foreign countries were represented by buildings, though there were many trade craft and archeological exhibits. Only six other states, Washington, Montana, Utah, Kansas, New Mexico and Nevada, participated. Arizona had not gotten around to it in time. But the representation did comprise most of the West. Larger buildings had combined exhibits from Sacramento Valley Counties, San Joaquin Valley Counties, Kern and Tulare Counties and Southern California Counties.

The success of the exposition was not in its exhibits but in its buildings and in the gardens and park grounds. In many instances its buildings suggested the architecture or distinguishing feature of historic structures in Spain, Italy and Mexico. However, many of the buildings had been reduced in scale from original plans because of cost and lack of anticipated financial participation. In some instances patios were eliminated or left unfinished. In the early years of planning and building, 50,000 trees and shrubs had been set out and when the opening approached, a million and a half more specimens as well as flowering plants were placed in harmony with the buildings and their feeling of serenity and beauty.

Bertram Grosvenor Goodhue

The central and dominating group of buildings were the permanent structures which enclosed the Plaza de California and which included the California Tower. But the plan as a whole was designed to suggest a typical Spanish city with its tree-shaded Prado and lines of stately buildings and frequent open plazas. The Prado purposely was made narrow to help create the atmosphere of 17th Century life before the advent of the steam engine and the automobile. The principal approach was from the west over the bridge spanning Cabrillo Canyon. It was 900 feet long, 120 feet high and forty feet wide. The graceful arches were not true arches but a series of connected "T" structures. In a later book of tributes to Goodhue, George Ellery Hale, after whom the famed Hale telescope on Mount Palomar was named, and who had urged the employment of Goodhue as architect for the California Institute of Technology, wrote:

I discovered Bertram Goodhue when I first walked across the great causeway that leads to the San Diego Exposition. This superb creation, so Spanish in feeling — yet so rarely equaled in Spain, with its stately approach, its walls springing from the hillside, its welcoming gateway, its soaring tower, and its resplendent dome, foretelling all the southernly privacy and charm of the courts that live beyond...reveal...his constructive imagination, overflowing with the vision of the Orient and South, impatient of rule and convention, free at last to utilize without restraint the exotic setting of a one-time Spanish colony.

What Goodhue and his assistant Winslow had accomplished was to be recorded by Clarence S. Stein in a small book published

(Next page) Arising from the still rather dry and barren mesa the exposition appeared to many as a mythical city out of some childhood fable. The only developed section of Balboa Park was in the southwest corner.

in 1916 on THE ARCHITECTURE AND THE GARDENS OF THE SAN DIEGO EXPOSITION. He wrote:

The architectural styles of Spain in all its various periods have been strongly marked by characteristics that differentiate them from those of Italy and France. While we find in Spain both Classic and Gothic work, whose general forms are obviously derived from these other nations, the manner of their use is characteristically national. The Oriental heritage, due to the long sojourn of the Moors in Spain, had a profound influence on the taste of the people. From these Oriental invaders the Spaniards derived the great surfaces of blank wall with occasional spots of luxuriant ornament that characterize nearly all their work. From them also comes the love of bright color shown in the use of polychrome tiles and rich fabrics, and in the painting and gilding of sculpture and ornamental motifs.

But the delicate Plateresque style of fine ornamentation, in the manner of the ancient silversmiths, which was to be found on so many historic and magnificent Spanish buildings, practically had been abandoned at the time of the erection of the great cathedrals and public buildings in Mexico. It was replaced with a baroque which in Mexico became even more ornate and more exuberant. Stein continues:

A truly great architecture grew up in Mexico after the time of the Conquest of Cortez. It was probably not on account of any lack of desire on the part of the early Fathers that this architecture was not transplanted to California in the days of the Missions. It is apparent in their simple crude touches of ornament, that the Padres were trying to simulate the richness of the churches of Mexico and Puebla …they were pitifully limited, however, not only in wealth but also in the skill of the workmen they had at hand.

This was a view of the exposition buildings looking east from the California Tower. Colorful Moorish turrets and Spanish towers surmount pearl-gray buildings, not all of which withstood the ravages of time and change.

191

During three centuries Aztec and Mexico artisans developed a style of artistic workmanship that combined not only the crowded — almost Oriental — splendor of Aztec carving, but much of the best of the artistic inheritance of the Spanish masters.

The advanced baroque style was the basis of Mexican-Spanish Colonial architecture and was identified as Churrigueresque, after the Churriguera architectural family of the old city of Salamanca, Spain. There were many who called it depraved in the richness and elaborateness of design and execution, but in a sun-drenched country it provided an interplay of light and shadow contrasted with the plain surfaces of walls and towers.

As with all fairs, there was an amusement area which was located on an arm of the mesa stretching to the north, and it featured an Indian Village similar to that of the Pueblo of Taos, New Mexico. Constructed by the Santa Fe Railway, it was known as the Painted Desert and was a striking recreation of an ancient pueblo.

To the south from the central Plaza de Panama was the Spreckels Organ Pavilion, also a permanent structure. The peristyle of the pavilion was a colonnade in the Corinthian style which provided a dramatic and sweeping view of the city, bay, ocean and Mexico that all of the early planners of Balboa Park had so urged be protected.

One of the outstanding and permanent exhibits was "The Story of Man Through the Ages." In 1912 Dr. Edgar L. Hewett, director of the School of American Archeology in Santa Fe, New Mexico, and Collier had conceived the idea of a major cultural display and enlisted the aid of Dr. Alés Hrdlicka of the Smithsonian Institution. The exposition appropriated $100,000. Data was assembled from all over the world and an expedition was sent to Peru to collect osteological material illustrating prehistoric pathology and surgery of the American aborigines. A large group of sculpture by M. Mascré of Belgium was the result. Dr. Hewett himself was interested in the Mayan civilization of Central America and sent another expedition to Guatemala where casts were made of four steles and two other massive pieces. These were set up in the rotunda of the California Building. Ten other inscriptions and reliefs of ancient Guatemalan and Yucatan civilization were made and displayed.

In scope San Diego's Panama-California Exposition did not compare with San Francisco's Panama-Pacific Exposition which opened on February 20 and which attracted exhibits from twenty-three foreign nations, including six from Latin America, and from

Carleton M. Winslow

192

The rival World's Fair in San Francisco which also celebrated the opening of the Panama Canal was more traditional and formal — but how many persons after the passing of half a century recalled it with nostalgia?

twenty states of the union. Its fair, with an ultimate cost of nearly $25,000,000, was done in the grand manner of traditional world fairs as befitting a city of more than a half million population and which, despite the rapid growth of Los Angeles, still dominated the financial, economic and cultural life of the Pacific Coast.

It was some time before the word of the San Diego exposition spread across the country. The early attendance figures were disappointing. The average daily attendance in the first month was 4783. In early February it dropped to 4360. It was recalled that Mayor O'Neall had promised that if elected, and regardless of the exposition, he would bring about industrial development to assure the future of the city. San Diego did have many visitors, though not as many as had been expected, and they brought no new businesses nor smokestacks. The improvements to the harbor, on which the trade through the Panama Canal was to depend also had lagged behind schedule and Edwin Capps had been fired as chief engineer.

Capps vowed vengeance and entered the race for mayor, but the influence of Collier, the director-general of the exposition, was thrown behind John S. Ackerman. In a statement, Collier pointed out:

We feel that Mr. O'Neall, with the best of intentions in the world,

193

has been lamentably lacking in execution. It is not through any fault of intention, perhaps, but it is a fact nevertheless, that little has been accomplished, and that the opportunity for change in the mayor's office is to be welcomed. The time is ripe for a new business mayor...If we want factories for San Diego, if we want great improvements of other sorts, if we want a metropolis, in brief, Ackerman is the man we should elect.

O'Neall withdrew. However, Ackerman failed of election. Capps, long an advocate of promoting the tourist business though it was he who had planned the waterfront development which violated the original Nolen Plan of beautification, became mayor of San Diego for the second time. By March, however, exposition attendance was improving and Interior Secretary Franklin K. Lane, while a guest at a luncheon at the exposition, said:

You have done something here that the whole world will know about and before very long you are to have a larger number of people in summer than in winter. They are to learn by personal experience how equable this climate is and that the Pacific Coast has a summer climate that has not its equal on the Atlantic.

Soon afterward came Vice President Thomas Riley Marshall, who had been President Wilson's representative at the opening of the San Francisco Fair, and Franklin D. Roosevelt, assistant Secretary of the Navy, for his second visit to the grounds. Roosevelt took the occasion to announce that a Naval dirigible base probably would be established at San Diego and that the United States' main battleship fleet soon would pass through the Panama Canal and San Diego would be the first port of call.

The great and near-great were there. Standing together, and wearing top hats, are, left to right, Thomas Riley Marshall, Vice President of the United States; G. Aubrey Davidson, president of the exposition; and Franklin D. Roosevelt, Assistant Secretary of the Navy.

While attendance perhaps was not all that had been hoped for, the exposition was beginning to return dividends of another kind. Present at the time were the Second Battalion of the Fourth Regiment of United States Marines, under the command of Col. Joseph H. Pendleton, and a squadron of the First Cavalry of the United States Army. At a luncheon in the exposition's Cristobal Cafe, Col. Pendleton told San Diego's representative in Congress, William Kettner, that he had been advocating a site in San Diego for location of a second Marine Advance Base. In his memoirs Kettner says that it was he who first suggested a site in the tidelands area known as "Dutch Flats," along the north shore of the bay. When the commandant of the Marine Corps, Maj. Gen. George Barnett, visited the exposition, Pendleton took the matter up with him and won his support. They soon had the help of Roosevelt who already had become enthusiastic about San Diego and believed that the Naval Training Center should be moved there from Goat Island in San Francisco Bay.

Col. Joseph H. Pendleton, U.S.M.C.

By April, Davidson, as president, was able to announce that the exposition had made a profit of $40,000 in the first three months, and effectively quieted rumors that it might be closed.

The SATURDAY EVENING POST delivered the national recognition that San Diego so needed. In an editorial, it stated:

Speaking of expositions, we hope that none of those who are attracted to the coast by the fair at San Francisco will miss the one at San Diego. The buildings there are beautiful, the setting is lovely...you can fall in love with it...the note of San Diego's fair is simply charm.

But to Dick Ferris, the discharged publicist who had sought to capitalize on the revolution in Baja California, it was a "grand show for the highbrows."

San Diegans were moving quickly to capitalize on the exposition and to make sure that the city became the terminus of the proposed Southern auto route to the Pacific Coast. Congress was expected to appropriate huge sums for participation with the various states in creating a national highway system and Los Angeles was advocating a route through Phoenix and crossing the Colorado River at Blythe instead of going through Tucson and crossing the river at Yuma.

The State of California had agreed to share in the costs of bridging the Colorado at Yuma with Arizona and the federal government but at the last moment Gov. Johnson abruptly withdrew his state's support, on the contention that the bridge would cost more than anticipated. Angered San Diegans raised $25,000 through donations to meet the state's promised share of the cost and the bridge was completed. Later, they were reimbursed by the State Legislature.

On this side of the bridge, however, were the sand hills. They required a detour of forty-six miles on the route from Yuma to San Diego and often were the reason for the diversion of auto traffic to Los Angeles by way of the Salton Sea and San Bernardino. A number of years before roads within Imperial Valley had been laid with brush and it was suggested that the same technique could be used on the sand hills, by laying a road of planks. Again this required voluntary action and contributions. Supervisor Ed Boyd of Imperial County diverted funds available in his road district and obtained volunteer labor, and Fletcher and other interested San Diegans raised $17,000 and residents of Yuma $3,000 to pay for the lumber. The first spike was driven on February 13. Within three weeks a flimsy, two-track road of planks had been laid for six miles across the rolling, yellow sand. It was made of two-by-twelve planks nailed to cross ties which provided two tracks each twenty-five inches wide. It required a steady hand at the wheel to keep an auto on the tracks in the face of adverse weather and terrain.

The original plank road across the sand hills lying between the Imperial Valley and Arizona was made of two tracks and rare the driver who could negotiate the six miles without at least one plunge into trouble.

It demonstrated, however, that a modern road could successfully be built across shifting sand hills. When the new bridge at Yuma was dedicated on May 24, San Diego and Imperial Counties had a usable route running directly from Yuma to the mountains, to press their bid for inclusion in the proposed Southern highway route.

May brought the largest exposition attendance since the opening, 179,440, and an average daily attendance of 5800. By July the total attendance was approaching the million mark. A visit by William Jennings Bryan was followed by one by Theodore Roosevelt, the former president, who interspersed criticisms of the foreign policies of President Wilson with praise for San Diego and its exposition. In an address to a nighttime crowd at the Organ Pavilion on July 27, he said:

We would not be here today had peace been bought at any price ...the building of the canal to make a short route between the Atlantic and Pacific had been talked about for centuries, or ever since Balboa discovered the Pacific. If we had continued the conversations, you in San Diego would not this evening be holding an exposition.

He said that San Diegans had created a beautiful exposition in a place made beautiful by nature:

It is literally an astounding feat for a city which we hope in the lifetime of you present will reach a half million population, but which doesn't quite come up to that mark now. It is so beautiful that I wish to make an earnest plea...I hope that not only will you keep these buildings running for another year but you will keep these buildings of rare, phenomenal taste and beauty permanently ...I hope that you of San Diego whose city is just entering on its great period of development will recognize what so many old communities have failed to recognize; that beauty is not only well worth while for its own sake, but that it is valuable commercially.

Then, as a president who fought the trusts and advocated conservation and the public development of the arid West, he warned San Diego that its waterfront was an asset to be treasured:

Keep your waterfront and develop it that it may add to the beauty of your city...and do not let a number of private individuals usurp it and make it hideous with building and then force your children to pay them an exorbitant sum to get rid of the ugliness they have created.

The next day was an important one in the naval history of the community. The first battleship squadron ever to enter the harbor, comprised of the U.S.S. MISSOURI, OHIO and WISCONSIN, dropped

Theodore Roosevelt and G. Aubrey Davidson

anchor in man-o'-war fashion, bringing the first, second and third classes of midshipmen from the United States Naval Academy, on the first such visit to the Pacific Coast, and they were reviewed by Roosevelt in Plaza de Panama.

Roosevelt's suggestion that the park buildings be retained had not entered public discussion, though with the arrival of summer tourists, who swelled exposition attendance to 229,604 in August, there was considerable discussion about extending the fair for another year. The fair at San Francisco was due to close after a year of operation and it was thought that some of the national and foreign exhibits could be brought to San Diego.

"Uncle Joe" Cannon,
Speaker of the House,
and John D. Spreckels

The principal buildings, other than those of the California quadrangle, were considered of temporary construction and even their creators had no illusions about their permanency. As Goodhue himself wrote:

It must be remembered that exposition architecture differs from that of our everyday world in being essentially of that fabric of a dream—not to endure but to produce a merely temporary effect. It should provide, after the fashion that stage scenery provides, illusion rather than reality.

The designs of the bridge, the California State Building, the California Tower and the Fine Arts Building were intended to express permanence, and the gardens, avenues, pathways, pools and watercourses had been laid out so that when the other sites were cleared of the temporary structures, the whole could easily be brought into a general park design.

Emily Post in COLLIER'S MAGAZINE wrote vividly of her impressions:

The composite impression of it is a garden of dense shiny green in great mass and profusion against low…buildings of gray white, no color except gray and green until you come into the central plaza filled with pigeons as in St. Mark's in Venice, and see a blaze of orange-and-blue striped awnings, stripes nearly a foot wide…In curtains hanging behind the balustrade of another building just around the corner the same vivid sweep of blue repeats again…the San Diego Exposition was pure delight. Its simplicity and faultless harmony of color brought out all its values startingly.

Former President
William Howard Taft
with G. Aubrey Davidson

On September 16, former President Taft addressed a large audience at the Spreckels Organ Pavilion and recalled his long familiarity with San Diego, where his father, mother and sister had lived for some time. Though he did not directly allude to the circumstances in which Congress had failed to approve an invitation to Latin American countries to participate in the exposition, Taft did say:

You may feel great satisfaction that you have had courage in the face of all the obstacles that have presented themselves in the creation of this beautiful city, that you had nerved yourself to go on, and have vindicated yourselves before the world against what we may call ill-judged criticism.

By this time the interest of Los Angeles in San Diego's exposition had become considerable, as it was drawing southward the Eastern and Midwestern visitors who had come to see the San Francisco fair. Forgotten for the time were old rivalries that had found San Diego bested at every turn by the commercial ambitions of its larger neighbor. In October a hundred prominent Los Angeles citizens, among them Harrison Gray Otis of the LOS ANGELES TIMES, met with San Diego exposition officials and pledged to raise $150,000 as a contribution to assure its continuation for another year. Guy Barham, publisher of the LOS ANGELES HERALD, said:

We all agree that this is a big thing for Southern California and ought to be done. Then let's get in there with that old-time California spirit and do it. I've heard enough to say to these San Diego men: "Go back and tell the people of San Diego that the exposition goes on for another year."

It was William Randolph Hearst, the publisher, who was instrumental in seeing that the Liberty Bell was sent to the San Diego exposition in November, as he had helped to defray the expense of bringing it to the Pacific Coast and the San Francisco fair. He assured Davidson that he was so impressed with the exposition his newspapers would do everything possible to publicize it.

To stimulate interest in driving to the exposition over the Southern route, following the building of the bridge across the Colorado River and the plank road over the sand hills, but primarily to emphasize San Diego's campaign to be the terminus of a Southern national highway planned under anticipated congressional appropriations, a cross-country auto tour was organized by the Cabrillo Commercial Club. Ed Fletcher warned that as far as federal funds were concerned, San Francisco's Lincoln Highway Association might get there "first with the most" if San Diego did not act quickly. An auto bearing Fletcher, Wilbur Hall, a magazine writer, and William G. Gross, a former actor after whom Grossmont was named, and with Harry Taylor as driver, left San Diego on November 2. While Fletcher did not make the entire journey, the car arrived in Washington, D.C., after twenty-three and a half days, for an average of 133 miles a day. They

It was "On your mark!" in San Diego as the community readied its send-off for a transcontinental auto trip to demonstrate the importance of a southern highway from Washington to San Diego

carried a message of the importance of a national highway from New York to San Diego by way of Washington, El Paso, Phoenix and Yuma. That they had crossed the country at the approach of winter, and had experienced no difficulties, told its own story to the nation's capital.

The future, though, was uncertain. The war in Europe was rising in intensity. The Panama Canal was not yet experiencing a heavy commercial traffic, because of continuing physical problems. In San Diego, many of those who had signed pledges for exposition stock had defaulted and legal action was begun to collect more than $200,000. The average monthly attendance had never come up to expectation, though the total attendance for 1915 was to reach almost 2,000,000. But by December the books had been balanced, all operating debts paid, and with the assurance of many new exhibits from San Francisco and the financial help of Los Angeles, a decision was made to continue the fair through 1916. The increasing possibility of United States involvement in the war was having an effect on travel and then, even before the 1916 fair had hardly gotten under way, nature took a hand and lashed San Diego and Southern California with prolonged storms of tremendous proportions.

And out of the storms came one of the most enduring stories of the many bizzare happenings of a Southern California whose eternal sunshine encouraged the experimenter in nature as well as attracting the faddist, the cultist and the health seeker.

Eleven

The Rainmaker – and Who Caused the Big Flood?

*There were some mighty angry farmers
as Charles Hatfield refused to stop
his rain-making activities which
some blamed for floods that destroyed
crops, washed out bridges and drowned
a number of persons.*

CHAPTER XI

For four years the runoff into the local rivers had been below normal and it appeared that another prolonged drought was under way. There still was water in the storage reservoirs but the early settlers had never forgotten the periodic dry spells that had brought disaster to cattle and crops in past years.

From time to time from 1912 to 1914 the town Council had received recommendations, particularly from a real estate agent named F. A. Binney and from the Wide Awake Improvement Club, that Charles M. Hatfield be employed to produce rain, as they insisted he had been doing successfully since 1904 from Los Angeles north through the Central Valleys of California and in the wheat fields of Oregon, Montana and Alberta, Canada.

As 1915 drew to a close the city's reservoirs, Morena, Upper and Lower Otay, and Chollas held more than ten billion gallons. A dry November sharply reduced the supply. Rain in the first few days of December held out hope that the drought might be over, but only Morena added any appreciable amount of storage.

On December 8 the Common Council received a letter from Hatfield offering to produce at least forty inches of rain in the vicinity of the Morena Reservoir without expense to the city. On instructions of the Council, City Clerk Allen H. Wright sent a telegram to Hatfield, who was then in Eagle Rock, near Los Angeles, asking if he could be present at a meeting of the Council the next day. In reply, Hatfield forwarded the following offer:

I will fill the Morena Reservoir to overflowing between now and next December 20th, 1916, for the sum of ten thousand dollars, in default of which I ask no compensation; or I will deliver at the Morena Reservoir thirty inches of rain free of charge, you to pay me $500 per inch from the thirtieth to the fiftieth inch—all above fifty inches to be free, on or before the 1st of June, 1916. Or I will forty inches (sic) during the next twelve months, free of charge, provided you pay me $1000 per inch for all between forty and fifty inches, all above fifty inches free.

Accompanying the offer was a photograph of a lake in Stanislaus County which Hatfield said had been filled by his efforts for the first time in its recorded history. He was not without credentials. The Hatfield family was of Quaker stock and had come to California from the Midwest, settling first in Los Angeles County and moving to a ranch in Gopher Canyon, in San Diego County between Bonsall and Vista in 1894. Dry years in Los Angeles County had aroused the interest of Steven Hatfield's two sons, Charles and Paul, in meteorology and in Gopher Canyon they began experiments with various mixtures of chemicals. In April of 1902 the two boys, with Charles as the leader, placed a batch of their latest chemical mixture atop a windmill platform and performed a rite which to the end they kept secret. A fog drifted in and the slight precipitation which followed was not conclusive as to the experiment's success. The same circumstance occurred the following month. Testing was put off until July, when fog and rain generally are almost entirely absent, and Charles Hatfield has insisted over the years that a cloudless sky was converted into a stormy one and .65 of an inch of rain resulted.

Though Charles Hatfield was earning his living as a sewing machine salesman, his experiments attracted the attention of the Los Angeles Chamber of Commerce in 1904 and he was offered $1000 to produce rain. In four months Los Angeles had eighteen inches of rain and the Hatfields were launched on a rainmaking career. They made no claims as to "creating" rain and said they merely persuaded nature to release vast stores of moisture always present in the air even in desert areas. Newspaper clippings saved

Paul A. Hatfield

Making Rain to Order

The man who astonished parched California by producing 18 inches of floods

A GLORIOUS wet winter and spring, following years of harrowing drought, have made Charles M. Hatfield, the rainmaker, the sensation of Southern California.

The population is divided as to whether he is a genius, worthy to be placed with the inventor of X-rays, or merely a toy of Fortune, who, when she is tired of flirting, will turn him adrift to be the laughing stock of half a nation.

The indisputable fact is that Hatfield went into the hills nineteen times to bring on a rain, and nineteen times it rained when he promised.

Last December a reward of $1000 was offered him, half a joke, on condition that he make it rain eighteen inches in Southern California between December 15 and May 1. He has collected that reward.

Long before he undertook to produce rain in San Diego Charles Hatfield had made a reputation that had reached as far as Denver, as this drawing and feature article in the DENVER POST *of 1905 illustrate.*

by the Hatfields over the next dozen years describe rainfalls coincident with their efforts. There were no clippings of failure.

Braving a barrage of ridicule, but figuring they had nothing to lose, a Council majority of Otto M. Schmidt, C. W. Fox, Percy J. Benbough and Walter P. Moore, over the objections of Councilman Herbert R. Fay, who said it was all a lot of nonsense, voted to accept the offer to fill Morena Reservoir and instructed City Attorney T. B. Cosgrove to prepare a contract, which, however, was never signed. As it already was late in the season, Hatfield immediately began moving his equipment by wagon to the area of Morena Reservoir. The lake, sixty miles from San Diego, lies in the lower elevations of the Laguna Mountains at about 3000 feet. A quarter of a mile east of the dam he erected a tower with a platform about twelve feet across. Nothing happened for a while and the name of Hatfield disappeared from the local news.

The exposition began its second year and with money left over

This was a typical Hatfield rain-making operation, though only one tower was used at San Diego, where, however, he mixed what he said was a specially potent brew of chemicals.

from exhibits at San Francisco, the United States Government took over the former Sacramento Counties Building and the Bureau of Fisheries erected its own building in another area. Canada, France, Brazil, Russia and Germany became major participants. A horse racing track opened in Tijuana, at a location just a few hundred feet across the border, on January 1, 1916. The track had been under construction for six months by the Lower California Jockey Club headed by James W. Coffroth.

Charles Hatfield never disclosed the chemicals which he used in his rain-making activities, though he claimed they were the results of many laboratory experiments which began when he was yet a youth.

Out over the Pacific Ocean, the "Pacific High," a high pressure area extending over a vast area of the sea, began to move southward. As it did it opened a path for storms from the North Pacific to swing down the length of California. In San Diego County the sky had clouded up and some scattered rain had fallen. No one was particularly interested in what the Hatfields were doing up in the dry hills around Morena Reservoir. An estimated crowd of 10,000 persons attended a day of racing which raised the little border town to an important tourist attraction.

Those who visited the site of the Hatfield experiments saw little to impress them and their curiosity was not encouraged. There were no sounds of explosions nor clouds of fumes from the square basin atop the platform into which the Hatfields poured their chemicals and dissipated them into the sky. On Friday, January 14, a steady rain began to fall and continued for the following two days, and on Sunday, January 16, began to reach torrential proportions. The town suddenly remembered the Hatfields. Cosgrove was quoted as saying that while it obviously was raining and runoff was pouring into Morena Reservoir no money should be paid until it was ascertained that this was the direct result of Hatfield's efforts.

A half century later Dr. Don I. Eidemiller of San Diego State College made a study of weather maps compiled by the United States Army during the World War to aid in predicting battle conditions. The Army's data included weather studies of January, 1916. They indicated that at that time the low pressure area over Southern California sucked in four separate air masses. As these masses were pulled together, air of different temperatures was brought together along their edges, or fronts, creating a "pinwheel" figure on weather maps, a condition which causes heavy rains.

By morning, the 17th, the situation was serious. The San Diego River was rising rapidly and there were reports of bridges being washed out in interior valleys, of the drowning of cattle, of delays in Santa Fe trains, of wires that were down and roads made impassable. One resident of Mission Valley who was rescued by row boat wiped the rain from his brow and said "let's pay Hatfield $100,000 to quit." At Morena, where the Hatfields were working their mysteries, the rainfall in four days was 12.73 inches. Using the telephone line from Morena Reservoir, Charles Hatfield called the City Hall and was quoted as saying:

I just wanted to tell you that it is only sprinkling now. So far we have encountered only a couple of showers. Within the next few days I expect to make it rain right...just hold your horses until I show you a real rain.

United States Weatherman E. H. Nimmo was unimpressed and said the storm was very widely distributed. "It may rain some more," he said, "and then it may not. Lack of telegraphic reports from the north makes it impossible for this office to issue a report." Each day the headlines in the newspapers got blacker. The race track at Tijuana closed down. By January 20 it was still raining and the Sweetwater Reservoir was filled to overflowing. A Santa Fe train was stalled near Oceanside for forty hours and attempts were made to get provisions to the passengers by ocean-going launch. The railroad bridge across the San Dieguito River near Del Mar was carried away. Much of the Little Landers Colony in the Tia Juana River Valley where the river crosses into the United States before reaching the sea, disappeared, leaving 100 families homeless.

The bridge at Old Town was bolstered with a sand bag jetty. Then the storm began to let up. Though intermittent rain continued, San Diegans consoled themselves that the worst was over. Communications were gradually restored, a relief fund of several thousand dollars was collected for the Little Landers people. Though the city's reservoirs had impounded about twenty-one billion gallons of water, there was an estimated loss of $300,000 in bridges alone.

The rainfall in the lower areas, for example at Lower Otay Reservoir at an elevation of 500 feet, was 5.60 inches from January 15 to 20. In the higher elevations, it was much greater. Cuyamaca Reservoir at 4766 feet recorded 17.96 inches from January 14 to January 19. By then the ground was thoroughly saturated. The Hatfields were trying to make good on their promise and could present no claim for payment until the rainfall or the storage in Morena Reservoir met the stipulated conditions. There had been nothing like thirty inches of rain even in the wettest mountain areas. They remained at their tower and as far as anybody knew were sending their chemical vapors into the atmosphere. Most of the rainy season was still ahead of them.

Meteorological conditions similar to those of January 17 reappeared on January 24 and heavy rain began to fall again in an area extending from the sea edge of San Diego County north to the Canadian border and in another interior area covering most of Arizona, New Mexico, Utah and Colorado.

The ground could hold no more water. The rainfall swept down the sides of the mountains and hills, was gathered up in swollen

Flood waters rise menacingly in the San Diego River, swelling up out of the main channel and spreading across the valley, picking up houses and barns on the way to both bays.

streams and poured down the canyons into the river beds which snaked through the wide coastal valleys. The rivers again jumped their banks and spread from bank to bank. The coast road to Los Angeles was impassable though the inland route by way of Escondido was kept open. Teams were on hand to pull autos out of the roaring waters in Bernardo Valley. The San Diego River reached a crest six feet higher than in the previous storm. The city's concrete bridge across the river at Old Town was the first to go. Then the Santa Fe Railroad bridge was washed away, even though it had been weighed down with loaded freight cars. High winds swept boats from their moorings and whipped water onto bay front streets. Telephone communications with Point Loma went out. The forecaster Nimmo predicted still more rain.

On January 26 the city dynamited the dam in Switzer Canyon in the south portion of Balboa Park, as it had been cracked and weakened over the years, and two houses were overturned on Sixteenth Street as the water rushed down to the bay. THE SAN DIEGO UNION reported on the morning of January 27:

The memory of the famous storm of 1884 was put to shame yesterday and last night by the presence of the most serious weather conditions which have been felt in this part of the country for half a century...San Diego's wind records were shattered at 4:30 yesterday morning when a velocity of fifty-four miles an hour was recorded for a period of five minutes. For one minute the wind blew at the rate of sixty-two miles an hour.

The level of Lower Otay Reservoir rose more than twenty-seven feet in ten days. Morena rose seventeen and a half feet in the same period. Upper Otay filled in three days. Water was going over the top of the Sweetwater Dam more than three and a half feet deep. The north abutment wing dam washed away, leaving a gap ninety feet wide, as did the auxiliary dam on the south rim. A deputy United States marshall, W. C. Carse, rode out to warn Otay Valley ranchers that the Lower Otay Dam might be in danger. As he dashed across the Sweetwater River, the bridge went out behind him. In a telephone call to THE SAN DIEGO UNION he said conditions were beyond description. Then the telephone line was severed.

A break in the wings of the Sweetwater dam sent millions of gallons of water rushing down the Sweetwater Valley, destroying bridges and railroad embankments.

Lower Otay Lake was one of two reservoirs lying at the foot of the junction of the Jamul and San Ysidro Mountains. The two ranges swing near the coast at this point, not far from the international border, and the waters of the several creeks come together to form the Otay River which cuts along the edge of Otay mesa and empties into the southern portion of San Diego Bay. The dam had been started as a masonry structure in 1887, but work had been stopped until 1894, when the Southern California Mountain Water Company resumed construction and changed it to an earth and rock fill dam with a central wall of steel plates. It was 134 feet high and 565 feet wide along its crest and held 42,000 acre feet of water. There were many engineers who were aware that its spillway was entirely inadequate. When the water went over the top of the dam itself it washed away supporting fill at the base of the structure.

Soon after 6 o'clock on the evening of Thursday, January 27, the steel diaphram tore from top to bottom as if it were a piece of paper and the dam opened like a gate. A wall of water slammed against the side of a mountain just below the dam, where the canyon swings sharply to the right, and then plunged down Salt Canyon for a mile and spread out across the valley floor and rushed for the sea. Emanuelle Daneri was ascending the steps of his wine cellar in his winery and through a window saw a wave of water. He cried out to his wife and they ran for their lives. In a few minutes an aged couple who had lived and worked on that location for thirty-seven years were homeless and penniless.

Only the anchoring sections were left when the Otay Dam went out in the flood of 1916. Many lives were lost as the water rushed toward the bay, sweeping everything before it.

It required two and a half hours for the dam to empty itself of thirteen billion gallons of water, and the water on its seven-mile course to the bay swept nearly everything before it. Nothing remained of the neat ranches, the citrus groves and chicken farms. The land was left "like a gravel bed." Of twenty-four houses, only one was left standing. Near the mouth of the valley the San Diego & Arizona Railway had built an embankment for its tracks 3000 feet long. Over the main river channel was a bridge. The channel was choked with debris trapped by bridge supports and in a few seconds or minutes the entire embankment gave way under the pressure of the mounting waters. An express car was carried a mile down stream to the edge of the bay. C. Killingsworth of Palm City who watched from a few feet away described the destruction of the railroad embankment:

The terrible wave came almost without warning. I heard a great roar that cannot be described in words. There was a crash, a boom, a mighty swish and before I could realize what was happening, the water was upon me. The seething wave, bearing before it spars of wood, roofs of houses, trees and rubbish, hit the railroad embankment with a smash. The waters towered what seemed to me a hundred feet in the air. Folks living in the valley were running for their lives…The water couldn't have paused more than a few seconds for the embankment. It just seemed to me that it hesitated there, that was all.

It was never determined for certain how many persons lost their lives; probably not more than fourteen or fifteen. Some of them had ignored warnings or had failed to receive them. The loss of human life in the entire county reached perhaps eighteen or twenty. Property losses in the Lakeside-Foster area, from flooding waters of the San Diego River emerging from narrow mountain gorges, were almost as great as in the Otay Valley. J. A. Pierce, an auto dealer, came into town and said refugees were living in the few remaining homes or in the Lakeside Inn and as for the topsoil, "you might as well try to farm on a cement sidewalk as on what is left."

Pipe lines from reservoirs were broken and some sections swept out to sea. Mail was being sent north on naval vessels. Mail and supplies were being taken by boat between San Diego and Chula Vista. The Tia Juana River Valley was swept clear of the last of the bottom land homes and farms of the Little Landers. United States Marines were detailed to prevent looting.

In the five days from January 25 to 30 at Lower Otay there had been 5.60 inches of rain upon an already soaked earth. At Cuyamaca Lake the rainfall was reported as 14.38 inches from January 23rd to the 29th. At Morena the two-storm total was more than thirty-five inches. Hatfield let it be known he was going to stay on the job. Water had risen to within eighteen inches of the top of the parapet wall, or eighteen inches above the crest of the dam, but debris accumulating behind trash racks had choked the expected flow through the spillway to a trickle and, incidentally, created a dangerous situation.

Other areas of California also suffered heavily. The Southern Pacific lines were severely damaged and train service to Southern California was discontinued. Flat lands in the San Pedro area were flooded and Long Beach was reported to be an island. The Los Angeles River caused considerable damage in low-lying areas.

(Opposite page) Glowering clouds forecast that the worst was yet to come. Soon after the picture shown at top was taken the auto and wagon bridge over the San Diego River went out. The railroad bridge, weighed down with loaded freight cars, was still standing — but it didn't for very long.

212

213

As the storms subsided relief and repair work got under way. Emergency water lines were installed. A goal of $150,000 to aid sufferers was set by the Chamber of Commerce.

On February 4 THE SAN DIEGO UNION reported that Charles Hatfield had come out of the hills and in later years his brother Paul acknowledged that they had denied their identity to angry persons they met on the trail down from their abandoned tower. They used the name of Benson. Their friend Binney was quoted as saying that anyone who had in mind shooting the rainmaker had better be quick on the draw, as Hatfield had been practicing slipping a gun from his hip pocket ever since he had "turned on the water and thrown away the key."

The next morning reporters cornered Hatfield in Binney's real estate office and reported that his demeanor was "that of the proverbial conquering hero, home from the fray and awaiting the laurel wreath." He disclaimed all responsibility for the damage and loss of lives. Later that same day he appeared at the city attorney's office to begin proceedings to collect the $10,000 he said was due him. He said that while there would have been considerable rainfall at Morena anyway he had doubled it and that he could produce still more rain if desired but he didn't believe the Council would want any more at the moment. He was asked how he accounted for the heavy rains all over the state, and he replied:

I expected that question...You will remember that it often rains as hard around Los Angeles as it did this year, but that San Diego gets only a small part of the rainfall...my tests at Morena were the most potent I ever made. I used 300 percent stronger forces than ever before. Up at Morena they told me that it frequently clouded up like rain, but that the clouds passed away without shedding a drop. None of them got away while I was there, I can tell you.

His claim for $10,000 was based upon filling Morena Reservoir. Water had gone over the spillway. Two days later he filed a formal

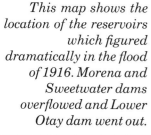

This map shows the location of the reservoirs which figured dramatically in the flood of 1916. Morena and Sweetwater dams overflowed and Lower Otay dam went out.

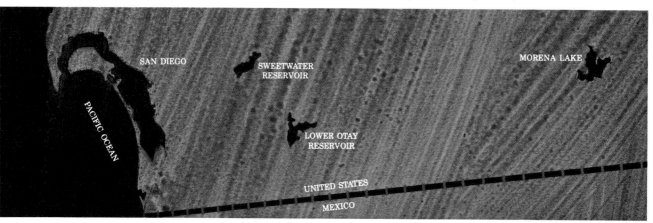

demand with the Council, contending that he was responsible for twelve inches of rainfall and until he was paid he was the owner of four billion gallons of water in Morena Reservoir which at ten cents a thousand gallons were worth $400,000. His demand was referred to the city attorney but as far as Cosgrove was concerned there had been no contract and the city owned him nothing. Hatfield was not easily turned away and at the same time was prophetic in warning:

I wish to draw to your attention that during my operations throughout January you had only three days of sunshine...as soon as I ceased you have had continual bright sunshine, with your usual morning fog...the time is coming, at no great distance when drought will overtake this portion of the state...your population has increased to such a size that with a series of two, three or four dry years, you would suffer, especially in the backcountry. It will be then that you will call for my services again.

F. A. Binney

The city had more to contend with than Hatfield at the moment. Roads had to be opened, temporary bridges constructed, and emergency lines laid down to bring water to the townspeople. It wasn't until February 18 that the first Santa Fe train was able to reach San Diego.

In San Diego City the January rain total was 7.56 inches, about three times the normal of 2.2. But the records of time showed that the storms were widespread. Oregon had the heaviest snowfall in many years; Arizona had the wettest month of records going back to 1892; Nevada had its stormiest month in twenty-six years; and Idaho reported the heaviest snowfall it had ever recorded.

When the city failed to respond to his claim for payment, Hatfield filed suit on December 2, 1916. Six months later he offered to settle for $1800, a sum which he said was less than the expenses he incurred in setting up his operation at Morena. The city offered to settle if he assumed responsibility for settling law suits amounting to $3,500,000 which had been filed against the city for the failure of Lower Otay Dam and the hiring of a rainmaker. No more was heard from him. In time, most of the suits were settled by the city and the two that went to trial in August, 1919, resulted in a verdict that the flood and collapse of the dam had been an "act of God." The Hatfield suit remained in court files until 1938, when it was dismissed as a dead issue. Meanwhile the Hatfields went about their trade of rainmaking up and down California and even to Central America, and of amassing newspaper clippings of successful rainfall.

The floods had been severe blows to the community and attendance at the exposition in the first two months of 1916 was discouraging. In March a rededication ceremony was conducted at noon in Plaza de Panama and all records for attendance were broken, with 22,741 persons entering the grounds before 3 o'clock in the afternoon. President Wilson was represented by Secretary of the Interior Franklin Lane and in Washington Secretary of the Navy Josephus Daniels pressed an electric button which set exposition bells ringing. By May 4 it appeared that the decision to maintain the exposition for a second year had been a wise one. The attendance had passed 400,000, which was 9564 more than in the same period of the previous year.

The year of 1915 had been a good one, agriculturally and industrially. The Escondido area shipped about 100 carloads of grapes and raisins, 238 of oranges, 182 of lemons and twenty of honey, and 2500 head of cattle. El Cajon Valley shipped fifty carloads of grapes and Chula Vista 800 carloads of lemons. In the South Bay the Western Salt Company shipped 30,000 tons of salt from its beds in the lower bay.

The population of the county-wide metropolitan area was estimated at 109,195 and had almost doubled in four years. There were 200 factories, twice as many as four years before, employing 2500 persons. The municipal pier and the 2675 feet of bayfront bulkheading were nearing completion and ten steamship lines now were making San Diego their southern terminus.

A change in the management of the Southern Pacific Railroad was bringing new officers closer to Spreckels and the possibility of settling their long financial dispute over the building of the San Diego & Arizona Railway. Spreckels had abandoned plans to erect six more six-story buildings along the south side of D Street, from Third to the waterfront, and he announced that he might close Tent City in Coronado, because of continuing operating losses. He said he had maintained it largely as an advertising measure for the summer climate of San Diego. Hotel del Coronado had made money only in one year, 1915. He also disposed of some of the area of Mission Beach, where he had once planned a little "Venice," and J. M. Asher put up a small resort of thirty tents.

Then there was the unexpected burden of the flood damage to the San Diego & Arizona. Its tracks were expected to reach Campo by February, and from the east end, tracks had been laid as far as Carrizo Gorge, making a total of ninety-seven miles of which fifty-nine were in use. The final thirty-six miles, however, represented one of the most difficult railroad projects to be under-

The troubled San Diego & Arizona Railway saw bridges and roadbeds disappear in the flood. The financial loss was a serious blow to John D. Spreckels.

taken in America, with eleven miles through the gorge itself and four and a half miles of tunneling through solid rock.

Threats of a recall action against Mayor Capps were heard, particularly from a group claiming the support of organized labor, as the result of an incident involving a $5000 check. E. W. Scripps had written the check for the relief fund for the Little Landers, but for an unexplained reason it never was turned over to the fund. When pressed about the matter, Capps produced the check and indignantly tore it up. Scripps refused to write another. Capps withheld comment except to say that he did not fear any recall proceedings.

During the floods the city had relied on water service from the Cuyamaca flume and La Mesa Reservoir owned by the Cuyamaca Water Company. The flume had been repaired and a storage reservoir, later named Murray Dam, was built to serve the steadily growing population of East San Diego, La Mesa, El Cajon and Spring Valley. James A. Murray and Fletcher offered the system to the city at a price to be agreed upon by the State Railroad Commission. At one time the system had been offered to the city for $300,000; the commission now set a value of $778,000. Again, as with the previous offer, according to Fletcher's memoirs, Spreckels induced the city to reject the purchase.

The war in Europe was on all people's minds and it was becoming apparent too that the United States would soon be involved.

With conditions still unsettled in Mexico, and fearing Germany's fishing in its troubled waters, the United States Army established Camp Hearn at Imperial Beach. During a Preparedness Day parade in San Francisco, a bomb exploded and killed six persons, fatally wounded four others and injured forty more. Tom Mooney, for ten years an associate of I.W.W.'s, was arrested along with a friend, Warren K. Billings, and accused of murder. Mooney was sentenced to be hanged and Billings to life imprisonment, and their cases became a center of controversy for years.

In the national election that year, with the Progressives now weakened in influence and membership, Gov. Johnson had taken full control of the Republican machinery and became a candidate for the United States Senate. Charles Evans Hughes was the Republican candidate for President against Woodrow Wilson. Johnson gave little support to Hughes' campaign in California, and ignored the conservatives who were supporting him, and Wilson carried the state, though only by a majority of less than 4000 votes. The loss of California cost Hughes the presidency and altered the course of history at one of the world's most perilous moments. San Diego County turned Republican again, but only by a small margin, with 16,894 votes for Hughes and 16,784 for Wilson. The Spreckels interests fought the Johnson candidacy with bitterness. He was assailed as "Holy Hiram." But in the county he was an easy winner over Democrat George S. Patton.

The exposition and an era drew to a close. A half century had passed since Father Horton had laid out a town that had thought it could challenge its great rival cities to the north. All of the results from the exposition were not yet in. The attendance in the second year, after a brief period in which it went beyond expectations, slowly dropped off, for a 1916 total of 1,697,886 as compared with 2,050,030 for 1915. The two-year total was 3,747,916. On the formal closing day of the fair the troops of the First Battalion of the Twenty-first Infantry staged a mock battle demonstrating the fighting in the trenches of France and Germany. Later there were fireworks and formal dinners. At 10 o'clock in the evening all of the exhibits were closed. At 11:59, taps were sounded from the balconies of Plaza de Panama. At midnight the organ began AULD LANG SYNE and Madame Schumann-Heink began to sing. Tears filled her eyes. As the song ended, the lights went out. Atop the Organ Pavilion San Diego presented in a "moving picture of fire" what was described as a message to the future: "World's Peace, 1917." Tommasino's band played the STAR SPANGLED BANNER as fireworks exploded to form the flags of all nations.

Twelve

The Military Appreciated What the Natives Did Not

Rooftops were crowded with people as the Army staged a mass air review over San Diego at the end of World War I. The Air Age had arrived.

CHAPTER XII

The time had come again to pose the question of the future development of Southern California. Los Angeles had passed San Francisco in population and its industries which largely had supplied only local markets were expanding outward, in oil and canning and clothing manufacturing and motion pictures. A few weeks before the exposition formally closed its gates at San Diego, a decision was reached to preserve as many of the buildings as possible, as had been urged by Theodore Roosevelt. The San Diego Zoological Society acquired possession of the animal exhibit and the Board of Park Commissioners agreed to provide a site for a permanent zoo.

Still basking in the glow of the praise for the exposition, the officers vowed that "a veritable enchanted city...will open its gates to every San Diego visitor and to the citizenry for a time beyond present estimate." The plan to preserve the temporary buildings drew strong protests from the exposition's principal architect, Bertram Goodhue, who believed they were mostly stage scenery and their features playful and meaningless while the bridge and California quadrangle had been designed to ex-

221

press and insure permanence in the manner of the great monuments of the past.

Though it had closed with all operating expenses paid, for the first three months of 1917 a small charge was made for admission to the grounds in order to help defray the cost of moving exhibits and restoring the gardens. The glow, however, soon faded. The number of tourists dropped alarmingly and war approached. In late 1916 voters had failed to approve a bond issue for rebuilding Lower Otay Dam, but in February of 1917, with private construction work slowing down, a $682,200 bond issue carried by a safe majority, though a contract for the work could not be awarded until the Fall.

The same voters, however, in 1916 approved the transfer of 500

Bertram Goodhue, who designed the permanent buildings of the Panama-California Exposition, also drew this concept of the Marine Base at San Diego for which he was consulting architect.

acres of submerged land to the Navy Department for the proposed Marine base. The vote was 40,288 to 305. The Navy Department also agreed to purchase 232 adjoining acres from private interests for $250,000 and was persuaded to retain the architect Goodhue, who had created the exposition buildings, to design the base.

The efforts of Congressman Kettner to bring more military operations into San Diego ran into a generally unfavorable report of the Helm Commission. The commission of five ranking naval officers appointed by the President was to study the defense of the Pacific Coast from Point Arguello to the Mexican border and specially recommend a site for a submarine base. It found that San Diego was suitable for flying and training, because of its climate, but it was of no commercial importance, as its railroad and steamship service was inferior and it was not at the time a natural outlet for any large interior territory; it lacked adequate harbor defenses and its proximity to the border was a distinct disadvantage, and the bay itself lacked sufficient deepwater anchorages. The Los Angeles-San Pedro area, the commission said, was far superior as a location of a submarine base.

By Spring San Diego was in economic trouble. This precipitated the most vigorous campaign for mayor in the history of the city. The voters were told that they had to decide between smokestacks and geraniums. For the second time George Marston became a candidate for mayor, upon the urging of most of the community's leading citizens who included nearly all of those who had participated in the exposition and in development of the park. He was opposed in the primary by the banker Louis J. Wilde and Charles H. Bartholomew, a former postmaster.

The campaign was only a few days old when William Clayton, manager of the Spreckels interests, was shot in the abdomen by a former employe who had been crippled in a street car accident. Clayton was just entering his auto parked in front of the Union Building when Lorenzo Bellomo stepped up and fired two shots, because "he is rich and I am poor." Clayton recovered. Bellomo, whose hospital bills had been paid by the company and who had been given other jobs which he failed to perform, was sent to prison.

The result of the primary election in March was a surprise. Wilde led with 8749 votes. Marston had 7582 and Bartholomew, 2295. Wilde and Marston went into their final campaign. Wilde's supporters charged that Marston was holding out "a beautiful figment of the imagination for the tourist and the pensioner" while Wilde offered the working man and the permanent resident a true opportunity for prosperity. In support of Wilde, James E. Wadham, the former mayor, stated:

George W. Marston has been in San Diego for nearly half a century, and in that length of time has established one business. Louis J. Wilde has been in San Diego for fourteen years, and has identified himself with twenty permanent and flourishing institutions.

The accusation that Marston was against industrial development, and thus not concerned with employment opportunities, was refuted time and again, by Marston himself as well as his supporters. In his talks, Marston stated:

I feel the development of the city's beauty and civic welfare can

George White Marston in exposition years

These were cartoons typical of the times. San Diegans were asked which they preferred: Climate or Prosperity.

go along with the industrial development...I am in favor of all things that make for commerce, manufacturing, for all business activity...It is absurd to say that I am not in favor of industrial development. I believe in a Greater San Diego—everything that makes for a bigger city. Let us build a great city on a good foundation. Let us have our industries as large as possible. Let us build a complete city.

Whether the exposition would have the beneficial effects promised or expected, either in the short or long range growth of the community, produced arguments from both sides. Speaking for Wilde in a rally in the Hippodrome Theater, Charles Sumner said:

For twelve years we have been banqueting, making speeches and resolutions; it is time now we are doing something...Now the exposition is closed and the days of entertaining are over and we need to have a city that produces something. We need not merely the idle rich, but the working man and woman.

Those who had supported the exposition had not lost confidence that it had advertised the beauty, climate and possibilities of San Diego to an extent that in time the city was bound to experience new growth and prosperity. Marston told the Wide Awake Improvement Club that:

What we need most of all is harmony...we stand at present on the threshold of the greatest prosperity San Diego ever dreamed—unless we have war—and to take full advantage of it we all must have a properly qualified man for the office of mayor. What have so-called smokestacks to do with the qualifications for mayor?

A newspaper advertisement in the closing days of the campaign, on behalf of Marston, posed the issue and for the first time used the words "smokestacks" and "geraniums" together, and it stated:

Mr. Wilde's campaign managers refer to Marston as Geranium George...They are terrified at the thought that the aroma of flowers may destroy the fumes from the smoke emanating from ten thousand smokestacks...They cry aloud in terror to the citizens to vote for him who is called the Smokestack candidate and save the city from Beautification...voters of San Diego, be consistent...vote for Marston, a man who is not ashamed to be for flowers for all times.

Though he was strongly supported by both the Spreckels and Scripps newspapers, Marston was badly defeated in the general election early in April. He received 9167 votes and Wilde 12,918.

The election barely had come to a close when Congress declared war on Germany on April 6, 1917. San Diego was severely shak-

Even before the United States entered World War I steps were taken to protect its shores and these mortars were rolled out to Fort Rosecrans to be ready for the Kaiser.

en and its economy dipped even further. There was no use arguing over smokestacks now. Marston and Wilde shook hands beneath a large American flag at a patriotic dinner at which $3922 was collected to be used to help influence the erecting of additional defenses for San Diego. Exposition buildings were offered for military training purposes and 300 San Diegans offered their automobiles to the government.

The emergency nature of the times also overruled the objections to San Diego as listed in the Helm Commission report. While Memorial Day on May 30 was being observed with a parade and speeches, the Secretary of the Navy recommended that aviation and submarine bases be established at San Diego and that $500,000 be set aside for development of North Island. This was an opportunity San Diego could not afford to miss. If it couldn't have smokestacks, it could have ships and airplanes.

Immediate construction work on all of the projects was not in sight. The seriousness of San Diego's economic condition led Kettner into an inter-city struggle to obtain the U. S. Army training cantonment which the War Department planned to locate somewhere in the Southwest. San Diego once again was ranged against Los Angeles and San Francisco. The rivalry became so bitter, particularly between San Diego and Los Angeles, that the War Department eliminated Southern California from consideration.

In June, representatives of the chambers of commerce of San Diego and Los Angeles met and as a result Los Angeles abandoned its claim and supported that of San Diego. The War Department reconsidered its rejection of Southern California, as the result of a study made of comparative costs of training camps on the Atlantic seaboard and near ports of embarkation, but with adverse weather conditions, as against those which might be placed on the southern Pacific Coast, where year-round outdoor training was possible. In the long run, despite the geographical disadvantages, it was found that camps in Southern California would prove to be less expensive. A site was leased in San Diego on Linda Vista mesa and the camp named in honor of Gen. Stephen Watts Kearny, who had led the American expeditionary force to California in the War with Mexico. It contained 3254 acres within the city limits and 9466 adjoining acres in the county.

The finding on weather versus geography had an important bearing on the location of additional military camps, especially

Mechanization had not taken over as yet in World War I and these soldiers training at Camp Kearny wheel their mounted gun into action.

of flying schools, on the southern Pacific Coast.

For a number of years the Army had sought to obtain North Island, where the Signal Corps had established its flying school, but had found the Spreckels companies uninterested in selling. Now with war in progress, a bill was introduced in Congress to take over the property and let the courts decide on the price. Kettner, with the support of San Diego's civic and political leaders, helped to carry the fight on the floor of the House of Representatives and after various amendments had been offered, it was passed by both houses of Congress and signed into law by the President on July 30, 1917. It was named Rockwell Field.

Before the year was out, on November 8, 1917, a total of 524 acres were transferred to the Navy for use by the Naval Air Service. Four years passed, however, before a final court settlement of $6,098,333, which included interest from 1912, was made.

Another proposal to move the Pacific Coast Naval Training Station from San Francisco to San Diego, as had been suggested by Franklin D. Roosevelt, was experiencing slow progress, and meanwhile the Navy leased exposition buildings in the park for immediate recruit training and hospital purposes. The Marine Corps also moved into exposition buildings and set up a temporary recruit training camp and built a rifle range between

Camp Kearny and La Jolla. By September construction of Camp Kearny was well under way, at a cost rate of about $17,000 a day. It was predicted that the camp would cost in all about $3,500,000. Here were trained the men from California, Arizona, Nevada, New Mexico and Utah who made up the 40th Division. When the 40th was dispatched overseas, it was replaced by the 16th Division.

Just as it appeared that San Diego was emerging from its troubles, the Wilson Administration took over management of the railways and all railroad building was halted. The San Diego & Arizona, beset these many years with financial and con-

This is the second plank road across the sand hills of Imperial County. It proved that the hills were stable enough for a road, or even a canal.

struction problems, seemed destined to be left in an unfinished state; for how long, nobody knew. This blow came just as John D. Spreckels and the Southern Pacific had reached an agreement to share the cost of completing the line through the Carrizo Gorge to the desert. San Diego's only direct connection with Imperial Valley and the East still was by the rough road carved out of the steep mountain sides and which at the east side of the valley crossed the sand dunes on a makeshift bed of planks. The original plank road of parallel wooden tracks on crossties had been replaced in 1916 with one made of solid crossties coated with asphalt and sand.

Spreckels and representatives of the Southern Pacific went to Washington and appealed to William Gibbs McAdoo, the new railroad czar and a friend of San Diego as the result of his visit to the exposition. They insisted that completion of the road was necessary because of its route along the international border and for supplying the new military bases contemplated for San Diego and Southern California. The San Diego & Arizona was exempted from the order and work continued, though money and materials were scarce and progress continued to be agonizingly slow.

With the cooperation of Congressman Kettner San Diego managed to wrest from Los Angeles a government-subsidized shipyard which was established late in the war by the Pacific Marine and Construction Company, on the bayfront between Twenty-eighth Street and the boundary of National City. It eventually produced two concrete tankers of 7500 tons.

Though the federal government was committed to the spending of approximately $19,000,000 on military establishments in the San Diego area, and business was being stabilized, population slowly declined and by the end of 1917, as far as can be determined, the city had about 4000 less residents than in 1915. Developers who looked more to agriculture and residential opportunities were not discouraged. With the financial backing of the Santa Fe Railroad, the San Dieguito Mutual Water Company organized by William G. Henshaw and Ed Fletcher was building Hodges Dam on the San Dieguito River, to serve the railroad lands in Rancho Santa Fe and the new frost-free irrigation districts and towns on the north coast.

T. B. Cosgrove

The city of San Diego, so long influenced by the Spreckels interests, at last became alarmed when Fletcher and the Cuyamaca Water Company began to exercise claims to ownership of all the water of the San Diego River. Several dams were proposed, one

of them a large one at a site known as El Capitan, and its reservoir would flood the Capitan Indian Reservation. The city came into possession of a filing on the river which had been made secretly by a discharged employe of the Cuyamaca Water Company, and went before Congress asking on its behalf permission to flood the Indian lands by the building of a dam and reservoir at the El Capitan site.

However, the testimony before a Congressional committee by City Attorney Cosgrove indicated that the city was more interested in conserving any surplus waters of the San Diego River, and preventing flood damage below the Cuyamaca system, than in asserting ownership of water being diverted to East San Diego, La Mesa and El Cajon. It was acknowledged that the development of the surrounding backcountry by the Cuyamaca Water Company could only contribute to the general prosperity of the community. As its rights to most, if not to all of the water,

The wartime boom was still evident when this picture was taken. Soldiers and sailors stroll the streets of San Diego, drawn by some civic event for which the main street was blocked off.

229

were not being directly challenged, the Cuyamaca Water Company withdrew objections to the city's proposal to build El Capitan Dam, but made it clear it was going ahead with a large diverting dam above its intakes higher up the river. Congress granted the city permission to flood the Indian lands, with compensation to the Indians for the loss of their homes and lands. However, James A. Murray, the Montana financier who was backing private development of the river, continued to move cautiously.

Murray made a million dollars available to the Cuyamaca Water Company for the construction of the diverting dam on the upper river on the understanding the Common Council by reso-

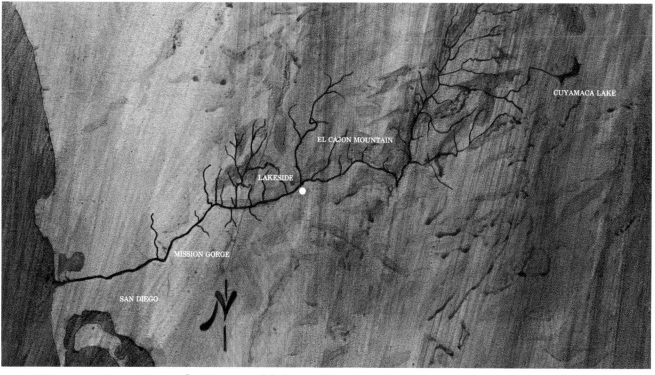

This map shows the San Diego River system, over which raged a struggle for water rights. In dry periods water disappeared in the sands; in wet periods, there were floods.

lution would formally state it had no objections. At the last minute this assurance was not forthcoming. The proposed dam was abandoned. It was becoming all too clear that Cosgrove and the city were playing for time. They no longer were interested in preventing flood damage, but in taking possession of the entire river. Cosgrove had become convinced that the city had slept for a century on its historic rights.

With the approach of the Fall of 1918 the nation felt the second and most deadly wave of a world-wide influenza epidemic. In late September there were eleven cases under observation at Camp Kearny, though they were described as only of the "common garden variety." By October 20 there were a total of 329 reported cases in the city, with seventy-seven new cases and eleven deaths being reported to health authorities in one day. Gauze face masks had been ordered for all persons in positions of public contact and all public gatherings were discontinued. Fifty-five new cases and four deaths were recorded on October 27 and a supply of anti-influenza vaccine was due to arrive the next day. The Board of Health appealed to all persons to wear gauze masks. By November the situation had eased and the general quarantine was lifted on the 17th. Churches, theaters and other public halls reopened though schools were to remain closed until December.

The disease had not run its course, however. By early December it was necessary to close all stores for three days, from December 6 to 9, and face masks became mandatory. This phase of the epidemic began to recede, and for good, though schools remained closed until January 6, 1919. In the city in 1918, in all, there were 4392 cases and 324 deaths in a population of perhaps 70,000; in 1919, 648 cases and 44 deaths. The epidemic was compared in its severity with the Black Death. More than a half million persons died in the United States, four times the number of Americans who met death in Europe, and 20,000,000 throughout the world.

The war had come to an end and San Diego was never to be the same again. It was now a military city and would so remain. And for the country an era was drawing to a close and the Roaring Twenties were not far away. On November 27, nine days after the Armistice had been signed, 212 airplanes from Rockwell and other nearby Southern California military aviation fields flew in massed formation over the city. Aviation was coming of age and was to profoundly change not only San Diego but the world. With the close of the war Rockwell Field had 101 officers and 381 enlisted men and 497 planes of all types. The Navy had spent almost $2,000,000 on its Naval Air Station on the same island and was providing for forty officers, 110 student officers and 800 enlisted men.

Rear Adm. J. S. McKean was named to head a new commission appointed by the Secretary of the Navy to study future naval operations on the West Coast. McKean had been enthusiastic about San Diego ever since he had been able to maneuver his battleship division into San Diego Harbor to take on coal, even though the Helm Commission had stressed the lack of deep water. The McKean Commission agreed with the Helm report that San Diego was ideal for expanded naval aviation training, but

Rufus Choate

went further and said that fleet operations would require additional facilities at San Diego consisting of a large supply base, a repair base for all but capital ships, and a large addition to the fuel supply depot. However, the war already had taken care of some of these recommendations and the Navy was beginning to look upon San Diego as "home."

The access to quiet water appealed to the Navy as well as the mild climate which the Army had found so advantageous, and the Navy acknowledged interest in transferring the Naval Training Station from San Francisco to San Diego, as had been suggested by Franklin D. Roosevelt. The San Diego Chamber of Commerce sent Rufus Choate to Washington to lend assistance to Kettner and the House Naval Affairs Committee was invited to visit San Diego, at the chamber's expense, to check the progress of the Marine Base, then under construction, and the proposed site for a Naval Training Station. This site adjoined the Marine lands on the north in the area known as Loma Portal. Melville Klauber, president of the Chamber of Commerce, banker Frank J. Belcher Jr., Mayor Wilde and George Burnham organized a two-week campaign to raise $250,000 to purchase 135 acres owned by private interests and the Council agreed to donate seventy-nine acres of submerged land on the bay. Kettner told business men, "raise this money and I'll assure you the finest harbor in the United States." They responded again with contributions as they did in assuring the completion of the U.S. Grant Hotel and in financing the exposition. With Spreckels donating $15,000 and Marston $10,000, a sum of $280,000 was raised. The land was accepted by the Navy.

In August of 1919 Adm. Hugh Rodman brought all of the Pacific Fleet units into the harbor except the battleships which were anchored as customary in the Coronado Roadstead. With the fleet was Secretary of the Navy Josephus Daniels. In an interview upon arriving at Hotel del Coronado on August 7, he cautioned against allowing the Navy to deteriorate as had happened after the Civil War, and envisioned the day when a larger Navy would be just as much at home in the Pacific as the Atlantic. The next day he told a huge throng of San Diegans at the Spreckels Organ Pavilion that he would not be satisfied until Congress had appropriated sufficient money to make San Diego Bay one of the great harbors of the world. San Diego Harbor became an operating base for squadrons of the Pacific Fleet, and home port for mine and aircraft detachments and torpedo boat destroyers with their tenders, tugs and other auxiliary craft.

Capt. H. C. Curl, in command of the temporary war-time hospital in the park, favored San Diego as a site for a permanent hospital. A sum of $500,000 already was available in the Navy Department for construction work and an additional appropriation of $1,975,000 came from Congress. Again there was a gift of a site, this time in Balboa Park, in 1919, of about eighteen acres.

A San Diego quite different from the one foreseen by the early settlers was emerging. The pioneers who had placed all their faith in a transcontinental railroad terminus were largely gone from the scene. Those who had seen the future in terms of new factories had met frustration. But commercial fishing had grown almost unnoticed into a sizable industry. Fish canning in nine years had grown from one to ten canneries in San Diego for a total of twelve in the area. Albacore had become the principal fish for canning, and had risen in price from $20 to as high as $200 a ton. Sardine canning was also on the increase. The ten San Diego canneries employed 1500 persons, and more at season peaks, and employed 150 boats. In the deep sea as well as fresh market fishing there were now more than 600 fishermen and the Portuguese who early in the Century had moved into the fishing shacks of the Chinese at La Playa now were exceeded in numbers by Japanese and Italians. By 1920 there were 368 fishing boats, 188 of them registered at San Diego and 180 elsewhere.

After the passing of all the years the olives that were so important to the mission and Spanish days still constituted a sizable industry. In 1919 the local canners packed 60,000 cases of olives and 10,000 cases of olive oil. The gold mines which once had promised so much were almost forgotten, but not the gem

An olive industry dating back to the days of the missions was important in Southern California. This is the plant once situated in historic Old Town.

mines. Sporadic mining continued and it was John Ware, a watch maker turned jeweler, who found in the pegmatites of Aguanga Mountain surprising pockets of blue topaz and Nile-green tourmaline crystals. One blue topaz weighing seventeen carats was cut in a pear shape to bring out its full brilliance and later it was exhibited in the Smithsonian Institution in Washington, D.C.

Though times still were hard, population was slowly rising again, as it always had done. Spalding, one of the numerous wealthy Eastern and Midwestern people who had been attracted to San Diego by its climate, had died. The war had taken E. W. Scripps away from San Diego and then a stroke forced him to abandon much of his activity and he took to the sea. Lyman J. Gage and William R. Timken continued to maintain their interest in San Diego. Timken was a member of a St. Louis family which had founded a carriage making company and then invented the roller bearing so important to the mechanical age. When he first came to Southern California, he settled on a ranch in Escondido. E. S. Babcock, who had been a partner in the building of Hotel del Coronado and in early water development projects, and had come to the end of the road with Spreckels, was almost bankrupt. He never recovered from the losses sustained by his salt works in the South Bay and by his La Jolla Railway in the flood of 1916.

Lyman J. Gage

Babcock's misfortunes were not peculiar to this frontier region. Horton, the founder of New San Diego, and his partner in so many enterprises, Ephraim W. Morse, and the Kimball Brothers who founded National City and once estimated their worth in the millions, all had died poor, victims of the "booms and busts" of the early rush to the West.

The exposition had an influence totally unexpected. Throughout California appeared a new style of architecture in homes, the Spanish-Colonial. Rows of bungalows, as well as gasoline stations and mortuaries, sprang up with white or pink plastered walls and red tile roofs. The exposition buildings designed by Goodhue got the credit — or the blame. Irving Gill and his simplified style passed out of favor before the rush of people to attain, however so flimsily, a bit of life different from that they had known on the plains and in the drab cities of the East and Midwest.

Mission San Diego

Interest in restoring the old Spanish missions also revived. By 1919 Protestants as well as Catholics of San Diego, under the leadership of Marston, and with the encouragement of the Right

234

Rev. John J. Cantwell, Bishop of Monterey and Los Angeles, raised $6,000 to begin the restoration of Mission San Diego that had been talked about for so long. The restoration of Mission San Luis Rey, which had been begun and carried on slowly by Fr. Joseph O'Keefe, O.F.M., was continued under impetus of the Franciscans after his departure in 1912.

The decline of the Theosophical Society of Point Loma was well advanced by the end of the first two decades. The war had cut off revenue from overseas, and other lodges in this country had been starved of funds by the demands at Point Loma. As a result membership and support were falling away. The legacies on which Madame Tingley had counted, from the estates of the wealthy people whom she had attracted to San Diego, had proved disappointing and those that she did receive were often tied up in will contests. The Spalding estate had yielded nothing, though she was able to borrow $125,000 from Spalding's widow by mortgaging the Isis Theater. To the end she hoped for financial assistance of some kind from Gage as well, but had been disappointed. In addition Mrs. Tingley was beset by other embarrassing and trying legal troubles, including a $100,000 alienation of affections suit which dragged on for years, and which she eventually lost.

The change in efforts and goals tempered the old civic quarrels and produced new ones. Wilde ran for re-election and was accused of having attended only eighty-five of the 179 meetings of the Common Council in the two years he had been mayor, and of having allowed vice to run rampant. In his defense Wilde contended that he had been unable to fire the chief of police, Stewart P. McMullen, because of Council resistance, and as for his original promises to assure industry for San Diego, an advertisement in his support stated:

If he had been let alone, or given any support whatever in the past two years, San Diego would now have two big permanent shipyards, the Otay dam finished...good roads completed, a new city hall occupied, a sensible and workable charter and a lower tax rate.

Stewart P. McMullen

There was no reference to any choice between "smokestacks and geraniums." His opponent in the general election, A. P. Johnson, promised to clean up the town and declared that "I want smokestacks—with smoke coming out of them." Wilde won easily, by a margin of 2047 votes. The smokestack issue had lost its appeal.

On the national scene President Woodrow Wilson was fighting

Guarded by the Secret Service, President Woodrow Wilson waves to a capacity crowd in San Diego's stadium as he arrives to plead for United States participation in the League of Nations.

a losing battle for United States participation in the League of Nations. On September 19, 1919, he spoke in the city stadium which was filled for the first time with an overflow crowd estimated at 50,000 and which heard him over a new electric voice amplification system. He waved aloft a copy of the League of Nations covenant and declared "the heart of humanity beats in this document" and that it would be a "death warrant" to the children of the country should League participation be rejected.

Though it seemed that at last the San Diego & Arizona Railway was conquering the mountains, California was fast becoming a state on wheels. Voters in the state in 1919 approved a $40,000,000 bond issue for highway improvements and voters in San Diego County a bond issue of $2,300,000 to pave roads leading to county towns. The federal government was aiding in improving the road over the Tecate Divide while the state was paving twenty-six miles of mountain roads between San Diego and El Centro, and planned to lay a paved road across the sand hills.

San Diego was suggested as the terminus for two transcontinental highways. One was the Bankhead National Highway running from Washington, D. C., and through the Central States southwest to El Paso and west to Yuma, which was advocated by the Bankhead Highway Association. The other was the Dixie Overland Highway which would traverse eight Southern states as an all-weather route and which had been advocated by the Dixie Overland Highway Association. Fletcher, as president of the Dixie Association and vice president of the Bankhead Association, warned that 100 to 150 autos a day were entering Southern California and Los Angeles by way of the Needles gateway on the Colorado River, along the route followed by the Santa Fe Railroad:

I don't blame Eastern people for stopping at Los Angeles and saying "this is good enough for me," after driving across 400 miles of desert waste from Ash Fork (Arizona) to Barstow to San Bernardino.

With transcontinental travel increasing at the rate of fifty percent a year, Fletcher urged that pressure be brought for construction of the highway between El Centro and Yuma and said that when it was completed through Arizona it would mean the diversion to San Diego of all the traffic of the Dixie and Bankhead Highways and fully half of the travel then going to Southern California by way of Needles.

Much of the thinking on the future was returning to envisioning San Diego as a point of transshipment, of the heart of a trading empire, a conception consistent with the ambitions of Spreckels who knew the history of San Francisco and whose family wealth had been built by the importing of sugar. The war had interfered with commercial shipping before the value of the Panama Canal to San Diego and the West Coast had been fully demonstrated. Whatever it might mean to San Diego was expected to depend to a large extent on the San Diego & Arizona Railway. Cotton from Imperial Valley and cattle from California, Arizona and Baja California, for the markets of the Pacific, would, or so it appeared, call for more piers and for stockyards, packing plants and refrigerated ships. And the potentials of fruit and vegetable packing with the expanding agricultural development in Imperial Valley could not even be guessed at.

The people of Imperial Valley had lived for a decade with the threat of disaster from Colorado River floods and the vulnerability of the canal running through foreign territory. For years Mark Rose, a pioneer developer, had been advocating a new canal on the valley side of the border and through the sand hills in order to obtain water for land on the 200,000-acre east mesa. While the mesa is west of the sand hills it is higher in elevation than the valley proper and could not be watered by gravity flow of the Imperial Canal. Rose proposed to get government permission to reclaim and sell mesa land to finance a separate canal. He contended that the plank road had demonstrated that the sand hills were not as unstable as had been believed.

Becoming apprehensive of Rose's plans to draw off water before it reached the valley, and perhaps acquire prior rights, the Imperial Irrigation District sent its young attorney, Phil D. Swing, to Washington to suggest a comprehensive plan for development of river resources. If an All-American canal was to be built, the district proposed to do it. The chief of the U.S. Reclamation Service, Arthur Powell Davis, agreed that there should be a new canal but pointed out that to reclaim the east mesa would require a storage reservoir higher on the river, which would not only conserve the water but also remove the threat of floods. Rose fell in with this plan and the Reclamation Service recommended to Congress the building of a dam in Boulder Canyon and construction of the All-American Canal. Long years of struggle against almost overwhelming political and financial odds lay ahead.

The railroad that would link all this together—the wealth of the interior with the service of the port—had crept as far as Jacumba Hot Springs by July 18, 1919. Forty-four miles of its tracks had passed through the territory of a foreign country, under the name of a Mexican division, and still it had not reached the peak of the mountain barrier which was more than sixty miles thick.

Thirty-six miles out of San Diego ten miles of bow knots and horseshoe curves had lifted the line up out of Redondo Valley, 766 feet in elevation. Soon after leaving the little Baja California settlement of Tecate, at an elevation of 1685 feet, and already fifty-two miles from San Diego on its rambling journey, it had begun to climb again and crossed the international border through a tunnel to reappear in the United States. This was not far from Campo, sixty-five miles from San Diego and a thousand feet above Tecate. From there it crossed Campo Creek on a spectacular trestle, 600 feet long and 180 feet high, bridging Stony Canyon and reached its highest elevation, the Tecate Divide at Hipass, and eighty-two miles from San Diego at 3660 feet. From there it was downhill ten miles to Jacumba at 2835 feet. Jacumba was about seventy-four miles from San Diego by highway but by the San Diego & Arizona it was ninety-two miles. Ahead was the sharp descent to the desert. To go east where it wanted to go the line had to go north and turn down the great gorge.

Thirteen

Southern California and the Gold Nobody Noticed

Heat, rocks and dirt—that is the Carrizo Gorge. Nothing crawled over this land except the San Diego & Arizona Railway. Here the first train clings to its tiny ledge as it fights its way up a great mountain barrier.

CHAPTER XIII

The goal for which several generations of pioneers had worked finally appeared to be at hand. The Utah Construction Company began laying railroad tracks from both ends of Carrizo Gorge to accomplish what so many had considered impossible. But to do it, the San Diego & Arizona virtually had to make its own mountain pass.

Jacumba Valley is on the dry side of the mountains and the storms have surrendered much of their rain before reaching it. From there the country dries out rapidly to the harshness of the desert. The approach to the gorge from Jacumba rounds a conical black lava hill and follows the green bed of Carrizo Creek, passing Arsenic Spring, Lone Tiger Spring and Camp Sizzle Spring.

At its entrance the gorge falls away sharply into a deep and striking V-shaped trench at places a thousand feet deep and over which hangs a primitive silence. Along its bottom is a hairline of green and a few native palm trees growing out of gravel swirled and rounded by the violence of the flash floods of the desert country. There is little else except rocks. It is like a great dumping ground for Nature's building materials. One has never seen so many rocks — piles upon piles left over from one age seem to await another.

The war and the scarcity of materials were given as the reason for the abandonment of the original engineering plans to make the descent through three long straight-line tunnels, which would have provided a much easier gateway to San Diego, and there were always those who wondered about that. Instead, the track was laid on a narrow bench cut out of the steep and sharply curving walls of the gorge, at one place 900 feet above the bottom and here and there supported by sidehill trestles where one rail rested on solid earth and the other on wooden supports. Wood was used instead of steel because of the problem of the summer heat. Work went on during the summer of 1919 and the heavy sunlight seemed to reverberate between the mountain sides.

Even though the plans for the straight-line tunnels had been

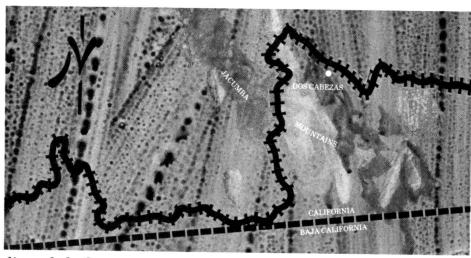

This map shows the twisting course of the San Diego & Arizona from Jacumba through Carrizo Gorge on its journey down to the high desert.

discarded, there was no way around some of the almost vertical shoulders of rock hills and seventeen tunnels of various lengths had to be dug in eleven miles of a snake-like course. The shortest was 287 feet and the longest, 2604. Tunnel No. 8 was 2500 feet long and for a time it seemed it would never be bored. Most of it had to be cut through solid rock and time and again loose rock and gravel choked it up, causing one death and weeks of lost time. At one time engineers considered giving up and constructing a by-pass.

(Opposite page) Seemingly flimsy wooden trestles propped up the tracks of the San Diego & Arizona across the canyons of the gorge.

From the crest of the divide at Hipass to the entrance of the gorge it was a drop of 1300 feet. Another 700 feet was lost through Carrizo Gorge to Dos Cabezas, or Two Heads, in the high desert country where the elevation was about 1600 feet. From there the rails straightened out across the Colorado Desert and when they reached El Centro, thirty-nine miles away and 148

miles from San Diego, they were fifty feet below sea level. The average grade on the west slope of the mountains was 1.4 percent and on the east slope, 2.2 percent. Though the drop in the gorge was only 1.4 percent, the curves of as much as twenty degrees meant a slow and cautious pull and continual oiling of the wheel flanges and sanding of the rails.

Tracks were never laid beyond Seeley. From Seeley the trains used the tracks originally built by the Holton-Interurban Railway which were later taken over by the Southern Pacific and leased to the San Diego & Arizona. El Centro was the end of the line. It was still a long way across the desert and the sand hills to the Yuma crossing of the Colorado River. From El Centro railroad tracks reached like arms of pincers around the ends of the sand hills. The rails of the Southern Pacific subsidiary, the Inter-California Railway, ran north from El Centro to Niland, 127 feet below sea level, to meet the main line near the eastern side of the Salton Sea and above the north end of the sand hills. To the

In the days of the immigrant wagon trains the mountain barrier in the distance diverted settlers to Los Angeles. The mountains finally were conquered by iron rails—or so it seemed.

south they ran to the sea-level border towns of Calexico and Mexicali and then through fifty miles of Mexican territory, following in part the line of the Imperial Canal, to round the bottom of the sand hills and reach Yuma.

This was not the transcontinental line that pioneers had envisioned so long before. The San Diego & Arizona was only a short haul line servicing the main Southern Pacific route from New Orleans to Los Angeles and San Francisco. But it had shut the last door of the port of San Diego to any other railroads, as Harriman had known it would do when he secretly entered into the arrangements for Spreckels to appear as the builder.

These facts were small things at the moment. From Spreckels there was no hint that circumstances and the mountains had defeated him, nor that the line would never realize all that had been hoped for it.

On Saturday, November 15, 1919, at Carrizo Gorge Station, Spreckels drove the symbolic golden spike that marked the com-

John D. Spreckels drives the golden spike completing the San Diego & Arizona Railway. He had promised San Diego a railroad, and he delivered one, at a cost of twelve years of work and $18,000,000.

pletion of the San Diego & Arizona. It had taken twelve years and $18,000,000. The section through the gorge alone had cost $4,000,000 which was near the original estimate of the cost of a road all the way to Yuma. A thousand persons were on hand to witness the event. In paying tribute to Spreckels, Mayor Wilde said:

You have often heard the remark that San Diego is a one-man town. Personally I feel proud to live in San Diego when it is referred to as a one-man town...this afternoon you can't give our great leader enough glory.

Sixteen days later, on December 1, the first train pulled by Southern Pacific engines arrived at San Diego as the climax of a week-long celebration. Spreckels was cheered by crowds lining the streets when he led a military and fraternal procession to the Santa Fe Station which was to be used by both lines and was renamed the Union Depot. There were some who could recall a similar day in 1885 when the first transcontinental train arrived over the Santa Fe line. The Santa Fe had headed west from New Mexico and crossing the Colorado River at Needles reached Southern California by the Cajon Pass and skirting San Diego's mountain barrier entered the county from the northeast through Temecula Canyon. Floods washed out the line in the canyon and the Santa Fe abandoned San Diego as a terminus in favor of Los Angeles. San Diego was left at the end of a branch line. It had been a long struggle since that time and no one knew it better than Spreckels. At a banquet that evening in Hotel del Coronado, Spreckels said:

It is fortunate that in undertakings of this kind men do not see all the difficulties and obstacles that will arise when they begin enterprises of such magnitude as the San Diego & Arizona Railway. If we could see all of the obstacles we had to surmount before we could reach the completion of the enterprise, then surely there would be many undertakings that would never begin.

He said it had been his principal aim in life for a number of years to make San Diego a city of the first class and he had never lost his faith in its future:

Our climate, our harbor and our backcountry, supported by Imperial Valley, one of the most remarkable and prolific producers of nearly everything that can be grown on land with the aid of sunshine and water, must mean prosperity for San Diego...and this railroad opens up a wide field for enterprise...in Arizona, New Mexico and through the Middle West to the Atlantic Coast.

Southern Californians could be forgiven if they did not fully appreciate the advantages of their climate and foresee their place in the age of flight. The names of later years meant nothing then. Charles A. Lindbergh was an unnoticed college freshman in Wisconsin who already had failed as a farmer. The man who was to create the basic design of the airplane which Lindbergh flew alone across the Atlantic Ocean, T. Claude Ryan, was studying engineering at Oregon State College but was to give it up to take pilot training at March Field.

Death already had taken the man who built the first airplane in San Diego County. He was Charles F. Walsh, who had been born in Mission Valley in 1877. He had become fascinated by the daring feats of the pioneers of flight and put together two airplanes, only one of which flew. He abandoned manufacturing in favor of barnstorming and crashed to his death in Princeton, New Jersey, while on a practice flight in the airplane in which he was scheduled to take president-elect Woodrow Wilson on a sightseeing flight.

During World War I, Reuben Fleet, a former real estate salesman and legislator in the State of Washington, served at North Island and became a major in charge of flight training for the Army Signal Corps. He witnessed so many unnecessary crashes he vowed that when peace came he would build a safe airplane.

Population was approaching the 74,000 of the exposition days though few new homes were being built, and those who were arriving had visited or heard of the exposition and were more interested in climate than in industry or warehouses or railroad shipments. Attempts to attract industry to Southern California cities by advertising in the East had not been productive but Oscar Cotton, the land developer, recalled his experience in the early 1900's in trying to sell lots by advertising the glories of San Diego in national magazines. He didn't sell any lots but received many requests for information about San Diego. They wanted to know about San Diego as a place in which to reside or to retire. Perhaps the emphasis had been misplaced all these years and it just wasn't a problem of trying to attract factories and occasional tourists. Perhaps the military had come to San Diego for reasons not fully appreciated.

It was Cotton who suggested that an organization be formed to advertise San Diego as a place to live. Even the geranium growers wanted factories, he told San Diegans at a mass meeting in the Isis Theater, though most of them would prefer to see them located where they would not be objectionable, but it was obvious factories would not come until there was more capital in the area, as they followed money and people. He said:

The outstanding opportunity that San Diego has to offer today is the opportunity to the man who has earned his pleasure and ease. To him we offer at minimum cost, the greatest abundance of riches, the most charming place to live, of any city in the United States...it is then to the man or woman of established income that we shall appeal; to the man or woman who wants a home. The states from which the great bulk of our homesteaders have come in the past...(are) the great Middle West states because they lack the things we have to sell.

Thus was formed the San Diego-California Club, the forerunner of all California community advertising organizations. In San Diego the geranium growers were winning out after all. A wealth that barely had been tapped, in attracting settlers of established means as well as seasonal visitors, and supplemented with a newer generation in search of opportunities in a more open and kinder land, were to enrich California beyond the most extravagant forecasts. In the 1920's more than 2,000,000 people were to move into California in another one of history's great migrations, and nearly three quarters of them were to find homes and gardens and fruit trees in Southern California. The first great wave to California in 1849 had torn at the mountains in search for gold. In Southern California there was gold in the sun.

HERITAGE OF AN EXPOSITION

How the architecture of the Panama-California
Exposition, which influenced the appearance of
all California, flowed from designs of famed
buildings in historic Spain, Mexico and Italy

World-traveled people who first walked across the bridge to enter the Panama-California Exposition at San Diego were reminded of the approach to the ancient brown city of Toledo in central Spain, famous for centuries for its finely tempered steel. There were the same long bridge, the guarding gate and the mounting mass of buildings.

Toledo lies in a loop of Rio Tajo and the photo below shows the west approach over the old San Martín bridge which dates from the 13th and 14th Centuries. Above it rises the monastery of San Juan de los Reyes commissioned in 1476, an architectural mixture of Gothic and Mudéjar, or post-Moorish, styles. It bears the coat of arms of Ferdinand and Isabella who financed Columbus' voyage of discovery of America.

From the east approach over the Alcántara bridge one sees high on the hill the famed Alcázar.

Salamanca in northwest central Spain became a center of culture and education as early as the 13th Century. By the 15th Century the wealthy Spaniards who sent their sons to its university built palaces for them to live in.

One of these was the Palace of Monterey. The design of its noted tower, shown below, was borrowed for a number of the towers of the exposition.

Above is the one on the building which stood on the northeast corner of the central Plaza de Panama.

A similar tower, though more ornate, crowned the building across the Prado and which became known as the House of Hospitality.

Cool archways are typical of much of Latin America and Spain. The heavy arches of Genoa in Italy and Salamanca in Spain and Celaya in Mexico, and yes, those of the Franciscan Missions of California, were repeated in the exposition. The mission atmosphere was reflected in the arcades of Plaza de California with their slanting wooden beams. In the top photo is a quiet and shaded passage once along the north side of the Prado.

In Celaya in central Mexico, which was founded in 1570, the town plaza is enclosed on four sides by buildings lined with arches, as is the central plaza of Salamanca in Spain. The view below, however, was taken through the shaded arches of the Church of Carmen in Celaya.

One of the most important examples of the Franciscan style is the Basílica de Guadalupe in Guadalajara, Mexico.

The Franciscan fathers were the first missionaries into that section of Mexico, long before they were assigned to the unknown territory of Upper California.

Instead of towers the basílica has belfries, as shown in the photo below. The same influence is found in many of the missions of early California.

Above, in the exposition the facade and entrance were adapted to the east front of a building on the southwest corner of Plaza de Panama, and which, though considered temporary, continued in use over the years. It was designed by Carleton M. Winslow and the sculpture was the work of H. L. Schmohl.

An inspiration for a
building even came from
Italy. In its early
centuries Verona in
northern Italy, which
likes to point out to
tourists the supposed
balcony and tomb of
Juliet, had an obsession
for arches and vaults.
For the exposition Frank
P. Allen Jr. created one
of its most beautiful
buildings by borrowing
from Verona the high
arches of its municipal
buildings, the
picturesqueness of the
Venetian style as
represented by a jewel
of the Renaissance, the
Loggia del Consiglio,
shown in the photo below,
and overlaid it all with
Spanish-Colonial
ornamentation.
The exposition building,
shown above, stood on the
north side of Plaza de
Panama, and was
replaced by the Fine
Arts Gallery.

254

The California Tower, a landmark of San Diego, at top left, owes its origin to the praying towers of the Arab world, and its ornamentation to the art of the Moors and the Spanish Renaissance.

It has been likened to the tower of the Cathedral of Cordova in southern Spain, shown below left, which once was a Moorish mosque.

Cordova was the first Roman colony in Spain and later under the Moors became one of the great capitals of the Mohammedan world.

In Seville, not far away, is the Giralda, shown below right.

The original Moorish edifice was completed in 1176 and then when Spain was reconquered by the Christians the ornate belfry was superimposed on it.

Seville is the heart of Andalusia from where came so many of the early Spanish settlers of California.

In Palma de Majorca, the capital of the Spanish Balearic Islands, where some of the olive trees are said to be a thousand years old, is a building known as the Casa Consistorial, or town hall, shown below. It is distinguished by the extraordinary projection of its roof, which extends nine feet and is supported by carved buttresses and caryatids whose colors are dimmed by time. The carved upper figures of women, dimmed by age and barely visible from in front, appear to droop with their timeless burden of weight. The concept of this building was carried to San Diego, in the creation of the richly carved frieze of one of the exposition's largest buildings, shown above, on the south side of the Prado and at its east end. A half century ago a writer described how drummers announced decisions of the ayuntamiento from the front of Palma's town hall.

The clustering of the domes on the California Building in Balboa Park often have reminded visitors of the Cathedral of Oaxaca, Mexico, which has fourteen domes.

However, the large blue dome of the building, shown above, without doubt had its origin with the one on the parish church of Santa Prisca in the silver town of Taxco, southwest of Mexico City.

This sparkling blue dome, shown below, can be seen from any point of the town and surrounding mountains.

The church was built by Don José de la Borda, who made a fortune in silver mining, between 1751 and 1758.

Around the base of the dome is the message of his gift.

Around the base of the California Building dome is written from the Vulgate of St. Jerome: "A land of wheat and barley; of vines and fig-trees and pomegranates; a land of oil olives, and honey." Unsung is the pottery expert, Walter Nordhoff, who produced the colorful ceramic tiles in his plant in National City.

Fr. Junípero Serra was well-acquainted with the Mexican town of Queretaro which lay on the edge of the Sierra Gorda where he spent so many years before being assigned to establish the missions of California. A town with buildings and streets of pink blocks, it is known for its patios with double arcades. At lower right is the patio of what once was the Convent of San Augustine, later converted to government use. The same double arcades appeared in the patio of the exposition's Southern California Counties Building, shown at upper right, and again between the flanking entrance pavilions, upper left, of the large building along the north side of the Prado.

Adjoining the great
Cathedral of Mexico in
Mexico City is the
Sanctuary with its two
flanking chapels, as
shown in an old sketch.

Its facade is considered
one of the best examples
of the Spanish-Colonial
Churrigueresque style
which Bertram Grosvenor
Goodhue adapted to his
California Building.

The facade of the
California Building,
shown at upper left, is set
with the sculptured
figures of San Diego's
early history, the work
of the Piccirilli brothers.

The design of the little
chapels became the
inspiration for the east
entrance to the largest of
the exposition buildings,
shown at upper right,
facing along the road to
the amusement area,
later the zoo.

It was in Puebla that the use of color reached its height in Colonial Mexico.
Native craftsmen created the rich tiles which made Puebla a city of glistening domes and towers.
Tile even was carried to the facade of churches, as in the Church of San Francisco, shown below, which was completed in about 1570.
Its red main portal is spotted with colorful tiles. It was the design of this portal which inspired the east frontispiece of the large building on the north side of the Prado between the California Tower and Plaza de Panama. It is shown in the upper photo, as adapted to conform with its surrounding architecture.
In the Church of San Francisco is buried the friar, Sebastián de Aparicio, who is credited with building the first roads in the new world.

The elegance of life in the old colonial capital of Mexico is reflected in the town houses built by the Dons and some of which still survive in Mexico City.

The House of the Counts of Heras, of faded red color and with chipped ornamentation, shown below, was suggested in the design of the exposition building, above, which also was crowned by the tower inspired by the Palace of Monterey.

While the House of the Counts of Heras has been preserved by the Mexican government, many other of the gracious town houses, with their inner courtyards, have vanished.

The countryside of Mexico is dotted with ruined and deserted haciendas, victims of revolution.

Gone, too, though before time and change, is the building in the park which recalled this past.

A distinct characteristic
of the exposition were the
many little and colorfully
tiled domes, towers and
turrets, some completely
Moorish in style, which
rose against the sky above
so many of the
buildings.
The top photo shows a
typical tower of the
building facing on the
main Plaza, on the
southwest corner, and
which was in use a half
century later, even
though the tower long
since had vanished.
Below is a similar tower
of Puebla, Mexico, on the
Church of the Nuns, St.
Catherine. Its yellow,
green and blue tiles have
excited anyone who ever
visited Puebla.
The dome, it has been
written, was the obsession
and also the masterwork
of the Puebla architect.

CHRONOLOGY

1900 C. P. Huntington, last of the "Big Four" of railroad fame, dies.

1900 George Chaffey begins irrigation of the Colorado Desert.

1900 John D. Spreckels opens Tent City at Coronado.

1901 First water turned into Imperial Valley canals.

1901 San Diego purchases water systems within city limits.

1901 President William McKinley shot by anarchist, Sept. 6; Theodore Roosevelt becomes President.

1902 Congress passes Spooner Act to build Panama Canal.

1902 Samuel Parsons Jr. designs plan for City Park.

1902 Katherine Tingley brings Cuban children to Theosophical Homestead on Point Loma.

1903 O. W. Cotton advertises San Diego nationally.

1903 Wright brothers fly first powered airplane.

1904 Mexican cut in Colorado River made to divert additional water to Imperial Valley.

1904 Theodore Roosevelt re-elected President.

1905 Gem mining in San Diego County reaches peak; tourmaline shipped to China.

1905 Floods on Colorado River bring disaster to Imperial Valley farmers and create the Salton Sea.

1905 First California auto registration law.

1905 New charter reduces City Council from 27 to 9 members.

1905 Horton House torn down.

1905 U.S.S. *Bennington's* boiler explodes in San Diego Harbor, July 21.

1906 Construction of U.S. Grant Hotel begun.

1906 Southern Pacific Railway spends $2,000,000 in attempt to control flood waters of Colorado River.

1906 John D. Spreckels announces he will build railroad to Yuma, Dec.

1907 Imperial Valley floods controlled, Feb.

1907 Imperial County formed; San Diego County is decreased by 4089 square miles, Aug. 6.

1908 Nolen Plan for city development presented.

1908 First traffic ordinance passed by City Council.

1908 Great White Fleet arrives off Coronado, Dec. 5.

1909 Alonzo E. Horton, "Father of San Diego," dies, Jan. 7.

1909 Little Landers Colony begun by William E. Smythe.

1909 Charter amendment reduces councilmen from 9 to 5 members.

1909 State legislature plans 3000-mile highway system.

1909 Panama-California Exposition planned to celebrate completion of Panama Canal.

1909 City Park renamed Balboa Park.

1910 City population reaches nearly 40,000 in national census.

1910 U.S. Grant Hotel dedicated, Oct. 15.

1911 Glenn Curtiss flying school established on North Island.

1911 Naval aviation history made as Curtiss hydroplane taken aboard U.S.S. *Pennsylvania,* Jan. 26.

1911 Baja California revolution begins in Mexicali, Jan. 29.

1911 Tijuana taken over by rebels, May; retaken by Federal forces, June.

1911 State Legislature grants city control of tidelands, May.

1911 Exposition groundbreaking, July 19.

1911 Bonds voted to build D Street pier violate Nolan Plan.

1912 I.W.W. "free speech" riots, Jan. to May, climaxed with expulsion of Emma Goldman.

1912 San Diego vies with Los Angeles for transcontinental auto route connection with Phoenix.

1912 Woodrow Wilson elected President; William Kettner elected to Congress, Nov.

1913 Southern California Mountain Water Company purchased by city.

1913 Mountain Springs Road dedicated, May.

1913 Representative Kettner influential in obtaining Senate appropriations for naval coaling and radio stations.

1914 Archduke Ferdinand shot at Sarajevo, starting World War I, June 28.

1914 Panama Canal opens and first private craft through the canal arrives at San Diego, Sept. 6.

1915 Panama-California Exposition opens, Jan. 1.

1915 First plank road laid in Imperial Valley.

1915 Decision made to continue exposition for another year.

1916 "Rainmaker" Charles Hatfield commissioned to fill Morena Reservoir, Jan.

1916 Heavy floods in county; Lower Otay Dam washed out.

1916 Tijuana racetrack opens.

1916 Second Plank road constructed in Imperial Valley.

1916 Woodrow Wilson re-elected President, Nov.

1917 Formal closing of Panama-California Exposition, Jan. 1.

1917 Louis J. Wilde defeats George Marston in "smokestacks vs. geraniums" mayoralty race, April.

1917 United States declares war on Germany, April 6.

1917 Camp Kearny established; Marine Base and Naval Hospital approved; Rockwell Field and Naval Aviation Station set up on North Island.

1918 Influenza epidemics strike; more than 300 deaths in San Diego.

1918 Armistice signed in Europe, Nov. 11.

1919 Groundbreaking for Marine Base.

1919 All-American Canal proposed in Congress.

1919 Pacific Fleet enters harbor; naval era begins.

1919 Woodrow Wilson speaks at San Diego Stadium, Sept. 19.

1919 Spreckels drives golden spike in San Diego & Arizona Railway, Nov. 15.

POPULATION

	1900	1910	1920
SAN FRANCISCO	342,782	416,912	506,676
LOS ANGELES	102,479	319,198	576,673
SAN DIEGO	17,700	39,578	74,683
SAN DIEGO COUNTY	35,090	61,655	112,248
IMPERIAL COUNTY	–	13,591	43,453
SOUTHERN CALIFORNIA	304,211	751,310	1,347,050
CALIFORNIA	1,485,053	2,377,549	3,426,861

MAYORS OF SAN DIEGO

1899-1901	Edwin M. Capps
1901-1905	Frank P. Frary
1905-1907	John L. Sehon
1907-1909	John F. Forward, Sr.
1909-1911	Grant Conard
1911-1913	James E. Wadham
1913-1915	Charles F. O'Neall
1915-1917	Edwin M. Capps
1917-1921	Louis J. Wilde

GOVERNORS OF CALIFORNIA

1899-1903	Henry T. Gage (Rep.)
1903-1907	George C. Pardee (Rep.)
1907-1911	James N. Gillett (Rep.)
1911-1915	Hiram W. Johnson (Prog.)
1915-1917	Hiram W. Johnson (Rep.)
1917-1919	William D. Stephens (Rep.)

ACKNOWLEDGEMENTS

The Bancroft Library of the University of California and head of public services, John Barr Tompkins; Henry E. Huntington Library and Art Gallery at San Marino and librarian, Robert Dougan; Southwest Museum of Los Angeles and director, Carl S. Dentzel; University of California Library at Los Angeles and assistant head of special collections, James V. Mink; California Historical Society of San Francisco and director, Donald C. Biggs; Junípero Serra Museum at San Diego and director, Ray Brandes; San Diego Historical Society and secretary, Wilmer Shields; San Diego State College History Department and professors Abraham Nasatir and Lionel U. Ridout; San Diego State College Library and library assistant, Mrs. Mildred LeCompte; San Diego Public Library and director of the California Room, Mrs. Zelma Locker; San Diego County Department of Agriculture and specialist for natural resources and statistics, Roy M. Kepner Jr.; New York Public Library; Boston, Massachusetts, Public Library; United States Naval Academy Museum, Annapolis, Maryland; and Library of Congress, Washington, D.C.

PERMISSION CREDITS

Alfred A. Knopf: Quotation from *Living My Life*, by Emma Goldman, 1931

Archbishop of Los Angeles, Cardinal McIntyre: Quotation from *Documents of California Catholic History*, by Francis J. Weber, 1965.

The Bancroft Library: Documents of the District Court of the United States concerning the suit of the Southern Pacific Company vs. John D. and A. B. Spreckels, 1913 and 1916; San Francisco Labor Council Special Investigating Committee Report entitled *San Diego Free Speech Controversy*, 1912; Report to the governor entitled *Disturbances in the City of San Diego and the County of San Diego, California*, by Harris Weinstock, 1912.

California Historical Society Quarterly: Quotations from *An Autobiography* by Julius Wangenheim, Vol. XXXV, No. 2, 1956 through Vol. XXXVI, No. 2, June 1957.

Exposition Press Inc.: Quotations from *The Good Old Days*, by Oscar W. Cotton, 1962.

National Archives and Record Service: House of Representatives hearing before the Committee on House Joint Resolution No. 99, concerning the *Panama-California Exposition*, 1911; House of Representatives hearing before the Committee on Public Lands on H.R. 4037, entitled *The Conservation of Storage of Water, San Diego, California*, 1918; Senate Executive Document No. 212, 59th Congress, 2nd Session, address entitled *Imperial Valley*, by Theodore Roosevelt, 1907.

San Diego & Arizona Eastern Railway Co.: Quotation from *Memoirs of Conductor W. G. McCormick*, 1948.

San Diego Historical Society: Quotation from the correspondence of George White Marston.

University of California Library, Los Angeles: Quotations from the correspondence and papers of William Clayton.

BIBLIOGRAPHY

Adams, H. Austin
The Man John D. Spreckels (San Diego: Frye & Smith, Ltd., 1924)
The Story of Water in San Diego (Chula Vista: Denrich Press, n.d.)

Adams, Hepsy A.
Pilgrims from Portugal (Westways, May 1953)

Alexander, J. A.
The Life of George Chaffey (London: Macmillan & Co., Ltd., 1928)

Aronson, Arthur (ed.)
Military and Naval Personnel in San Diego During the Exposition (Army and Navy Review, Panama-California Edition, 1915)

Aubury, Lewis E.
Register of Mines and Minerals (Sacramento: California State Mining Bureau, 1902)

Baur, John E.
Health Seekers of Southern California (San Marino: Huntington Library, 1959)

Baxter, Sylvester
Spanish Colonial Architecture in Mexico (New York: Architectural Publishing Co., 1902)

Beckler, Marion F.
Palomar Mountain: Past and Present (Palm Desert: Desert Magazine Press, 1958)

Bellon, Walter and Lane, Fred T.
A Condensed History of San Diego County Park System (San Diego: Board of Supervisors, 1944)

Biographical Files, 1900-1920
(Collection: San Diego Historical Society, Junipero Serra Museum)

Birkett, Charles V.
The Fiftieth Year: El Cajon and La Mesa (San Diego Historical Society Quarterly, Vol. VIII, No. 4, Oct. 1961)

Bishop, Joseph Bucklin
Theodore Roosevelt and His Time (New York: Charles Scribner's Sons, 1920)

Black, Samuel F.
History of San Diego County, California (Chicago: S. J. Clarke Publishing Co., 1913)

Blaisdell, Lowell L.
The Desert Revolution: Baja California 1911 (Madison: University of Wisconsin Press, 1962)

Bohme, Frederick G.
The Portuguese in California (California Historical Society Quarterly, Vol. 35, No. 3, Sept. 1956)

Bowles, Helen Margaret
The Automobile is Here to Stay (San Diego Historical Society Quarterly, Vol. IV, No. 2, April 1958)

Brennan, Joe
Interview, San Diego, 1957 *(Collection: San Diego Historical Society,* Junipero Serra Museum)

Bright, Tom (ed.)
What is DMV? (Sacramento: State of California Department of Motor Vehicles, 1964)

Brissenden, Paul F.
The I.W.W., a Study of American Syndicalism (New York: Russell and Russell, 1957)

Britt, Albert
Ellen Browning Scripps: Journalist and Idealist (Great Britain: Oxford University Press, 1960)

Broell, Percy C.
Presidio Park and Old San Diego: 1905-1937 Typescript, n.d. (Collection: San Diego Historical Society, Junipero Serra Museum)

Brown, Christian N.
Hey-Day of the N.C. & O. (San Diego Historical Society Quarterly, Vol. IV, No. 2, April 1958)

Caidin, Martin
Golden Wings: History of the U.S. Navy and Marine Corps in the Air (New York: Random House, Inc., 1960)

California Department of Natural Resources, Division of Beaches and Parks
Torrey Pines State Park (Sacramento: California State Printing Office)

California Department of Public Works, Division of Water Resources
San Diego County Investigation Bulletin No. 48 (Sacramento: California State Printing Office, 1935)

California Garden
The Kate Sessions Issue (Vol. 44, No. 2, 1953; San Diego Floral Association)

Carpenter, Ford A.
The Climate and Weather of San Diego, California (San Diego Chamber of Commerce, 1913)

Carroll, Leo
The San Diego & Arizona Eastern Railway Typescript, 1947 (Collection: San Diego & Arizona Eastern Railway Company)

Caughey, John Walton
California (Englewood Cliffs, N.J.: Prentice-Hall, Inc., 1953)

Choate, Rufus
Interview, San Diego, 1957 (Collection: San Diego Historical Society, Junipero Serra Museum)

Clark, A. W.
The Little Landers: Social Survey of San Ysidro, California, the Mother Colony (San Francisco: Modern Homestead Association, 1914)

Clarkson, Edward Dessau
Ellen Browning Scripps, a Biography Thesis, 1958 (San Diego State College)

Clayton, William
Correspondence and Papers: 1900-1920 (Collection: University of California Library, Los Angeles)

Cleland, Robert Glass
A History of California: The American Period (New York: The Macmillan Co., 1926)
California in Our Time: 1900-1940 (New York: Alfred A. Knopf, 1947)
California Pageant: The Story of Four Centuries (New York: Alfred A. Knopf, 1955)

Cleveland, Daniel
San Diego's Pueblo Lands: How the City Acquired Title (The San Diego Union, March 14, 1926)

Cook, S. F.
Population Trends Among the California Mission Indians (Berkeley and Los Angeles: University of California Press, 1940)

Cory, H. T.
Imperial Valley and the Salton Sink (San Francisco, John J. Newbegin, 1915)

Cotton, Oscar W.
The Good Old Days (New York: Exposition Press Inc., 1962)

Crane, W. B.
The History of the Salton Sea (Historical Society of Southern California Quarterly, Vol. IX, Part 3, 1914)

Cross, Ira B.
A History of the Labor Movement in California (Berkeley: University of California Press, 1935)

Crouch, Herbert
  Diaries: 1868-1917 (Collection: Henry E. Huntington Library, San Marino)

Darnell, William Irvin
  The Imperial Valley, Its Physical and Cultural Geography Thesis, 1960 (San Diego State College)

Davis, Edward J. P.
  Historical San Diego: Beginnings to the Present Day (San Diego: Pioneer Printers, 1953)
  The United States Navy and U.S. Marine Corps at San Diego (San Diego: Pioneer Printers, 1955)

District Court of the United States
  Southern Pacific Company, Plaintiff, Vs: J. D. Spreckels and A. B. Spreckels, Defendants, 1913 and 1916 (Collection: The Bancroft Library, Berkeley)

Dixon, Ben F.
  Don Diego's Old School Days (San Diego County Historical Days Association, 1956)

Dodge, Richard V.
  San Diego's 'Impossible' Railroad (Dispatcher, No. 6, June 1956; Railway Historical Society of San Diego)
  Rails of the Silver Gate: The Spreckels San Diego Empire (Pacific Railway Journal, 1960)

Drinnon, Richard
  Rebel in Paradise: A Biography of Emma Goldman (Chicago: Chicago University Press, 1961)

Du Bois, Constance G.
  The Condition of the Mission Indians of Southern California (Philadelphia: Indian Rights Association, 1901)

Eckenrode, H. J.
  E. H. Harriman, The Little Giant of Wall Street (New York: Greenberg & Co., 1933)

El Centro Progress
  San Diego & Arizona Railway Edition (El Centro: Otis B. Tout, 1919)

Evenson, O. J.
  Benson Log Raft Typescript, KGB Historical Series, 1962 (Collection: San Diego Historical Society, Junípero Serra Museum)

Exposition News
  Panama-California Exposition (Vol. 1, No. 1, Dec. 1911; San Diego Exposition News Publishing Co.)

Farr, F. C.
  The History of Imperial County (Berkeley: Elms and Frank, 1918)

Federal Writers' Project
  California, a Guide to the Golden State (New York: Hastings House, 1939)

Fenton, Laura
  Henry Fenton: Typical American (Private Printing, n.d.)

First National Trust & Savings Bank of San Diego
  1883-1943: Sixty Years in the Service of San Diego (San Diego: Raymert Press, 1943)

Fletcher, Ed
  Memoirs of Ed Fletcher (San Diego: Pioneer Printers, 1952)

Forward, Frank G.
  Recollections of a Native Son: 1898 Typescript (Collection: San Diego Historical Society, Junípero Serra Museum)

Fowler, Lloyd Charles
  A History of the Dams and Water Supply of Western San Diego County Thesis, 1953 (University of California, Los Angeles

Gaebel, Arthur H. (ed.)
  Makers of San Diego Panama-California Exposition 1915 (San Diego: Arthur H. Gaebel, 1915)

Gardner, Gilson
  Lusty Scripps: The Life of E. W. Scripps (New York: The Vanguard Press, 1932)

Geiger, Louise Jarratt (ed.)
  Where We Live: Our Spanish-named Communities and Streets of San Diego County (San Diego: Myra Bedel Cockran, 1965)

Glasscock, Carl Burgess
  The Gasoline Age (New York: The Bobbs-Merrill Co., 1937)

Goldberg, Alfred (ed.)
  A History of the United States Air Force (Princeton, N.J.: D. Van Nostrand Company, Inc., 1957)

Goldman, Emma
  Anarchism and Other Essays (New York: Mother Earth Publishing Association, 1910)
  Living My Life (New York: Alfred A. Knopf, 1931)

Goodhue, Bertram G.
  Mexican Memories (New York: Alley-Allen Press, 1892)
  A Book of Architecture and Decorative Drawings (New York: Architectural Book Publishing Co., 1914)

The Architecture and the Gardens of the San Diego Exposition (San Francisco: Paul Elder and Co., 1916)

Grant, U. S., Jr.
  A Sojourn in Baja California (Southern California Quarterly, Vol. XLV, No. 2, June 1963)
  Correspondence (Collection: Henry E. Huntington Library, San Marino)

Greenwalt, Emmett A.
  The Point Loma Community in California (Berkeley and Los Angeles: University of California Press, 1955)

Gudde, Erwin G.
  1000 California Place Names: Their Origin and Meaning (Berkeley and Los Angeles: University of California Press, 1962)

Guinn, James M.
  A History of California and an Extended History of Its Southern Coast Counties (Los Angeles: Historic Record Co., 1907)

Hansen, Esther (ed.)
  The Official Guide and Descriptive Book of the Panama-California Exposition (San Diego: 20th Century Press, 1916)

Hanson, Virgil Raymon
  Mission Valley, San Diego County: A Study in Changing Land Use, 1769-1960 Thesis, 1960 (University of California, Los Angeles)

Harper, Franklin (ed.)
  Who's Who on the Pacific Coast (Los Angeles: Harper Publishing Co., 1913)

Harraden, Beatrice
  Some Impressions of Southern California (Blackwood's Edinburgh Magazine, CL XI, 1897)

Hatfield, Charles M.
  Claim: Statement of Conditions and Arrangements with City Council to Fill Morena Reservoir Doc. 97054 (San Diego: Office of the City Clerk, 1916)
  Claim: Compromise Proposition for Settlement of Claim Against City for Filling Morena Reservoir (San Diego: Office of the City Clerk, 1917)

Hatfield, Paul A.
  Scrapbook (Collection: P. A. Hatfield, Pearblossom, Calif.)
  Interview, Pearblossom, 1965 (Collection: Union-Tribune Publishing Co., San Diego)

Hawes, William T.
  The Pioneer Development of Aviation

in San Diego Thesis, 1953 (San Diego State College)

Hazard, Roscoe
Interview, San Diego, 1953 (Collection: San Diego Historical Society, Junípero Serra Museum)

Hebert, Edgar Weldon
The San Diego Naval Militia: 1891-1920 Thesis, 1956 (San Diego State College)
San Diego's Naval Militia (San Diego Historical Society Quarterly, Vol. IX, No. 2, April 1963)
The Last of the Padres (San Diego Historical Society Quarterly, Vol. X, No. 2, April 1964)

Heilbron, Carl H.
History of San Diego County (San Diego: San Diego Press Club, 1936)

Hensley, Herbert C.
The Little Landers of San Ysidro Typescript (Collection: Wilmer Shields, San Diego)

Hevener, Harold Guy
The Pueblo Lands of The City of San Diego: 1769-1950 Thesis, 1950 (San Diego State College)

Hewett, Edgar Lee and Johnson, W. Templeton
Architecture of the Exposition (Santa Fe: Papers of the School of American Archeology, Archeological Institute of America, No. 32, 1916)

Higgins, C. A.
To California Over the Santa Fe Trail (Chicago: Atchison, Topeka & Santa Fe Railway System, 1910)

Higgins, Shelley J.
This Fantastic City, San Diego (City of San Diego, 1956)

Hill, Joseph J.
History of Warner's Ranch and Its Environs (Los Angeles: Young & McCallister, 1927)

Hilliard, Mrs. J. L.
Chronicles of Point Loma Typescript, n.d. (Collection: San Diego Historical Society, Junípero Serra Museum)

Holt, L. M.
The Unfriendly Attitude of the United States Government Towards the Imperial Valley (Imperial Daily Standard, 1907)

Hopkins, Harry C.
History of San Diego: Its Pueblo Lands and Water (San Diego: City Printing Co., 1929)

House of Representatives, United States
Panama-California Exposition: Hearing Before the Committee on Industrial Arts and Expositions on House Joint Resolution No. 99 (Washington: Government Printing Office, 1911)
Conservation of Storage of Water, San Diego, California: Hearings Before the Committee on Public Lands on H.R. 4037 (Washington: Government Printing Office, 1918)

Howe, Edgar F. and Hall, Wilbur J.
The Story of the First Decade in Imperial Valley, California (Imperial: Private printing, 1910)

Hunt, Rockwell D.
Fifteen Decisive Events of California History (Los Angeles: Historical Society of California, 1959)

Imperial Irrigation District
Historic Salton Sea (El Centro: 1965)

Imperial Press
Vol. I, 1901-1902

Imperial Standard
Vols. I and II, 1904-1905

Imperial Valley Farm Lands Association
Broadside to Members 1915 (Collection: Henry E. Huntington Library, San Marino)

Indian Sentinel
Files, 1910

Jahns, Richard H.
The Gem Deposits of Southern California (Engineering and Science Monthly, Vol. XI, No. 2, Feb. 1948)

Jahns, Richard H. and Wright, Lauren A.
Gem- and Lithium-bearing Pegmatites of the Pala District, San Diego County Special Report 7-A (San Francisco: California Division of Mines, 1951)

James, George Wharton
Wonders of the Colorado Desert (Boston: Little Brown, 1906)
Exposition Memories (Pasadena: Radiant Life Press, 1917)

Jansen, A. E.
Keno Wilson — A Lawman's Lawman (San Diego Historical Society Quarterly, Vol. VIII, No. 4, Oct. 1961)

Jensen, Joan M.
Irving Gill: San Diego's Progressive Architect Lecture, San Diego County Historical Convention, 1965 (Collection: San Diego Historical Society, Junípero Serra Museum)

Jessop, Alonzo
Interview, San Diego, 1960 (Collection: San Diego Historical Society, Junípero Serra Museum)

Kennan, George
The Salton Sea: An Account of Harriman's Fight with the Colorado River (New York: Macmillan, 1917)
E. H. Harriman, A Biography (New York: Houghton, 2 vols., 1922)

Kettner, William
Why It Was Done and How (San Diego: Frye & Smith, 1923)

Klauber, Allan S.
The Story of Klauber Wangenheim Co. (San Diego Historical Society Quarterly, Vol. V, No. 3, July 1959)

Klauber, Laurence M.
Interview, San Diego, 1960 (Collection: San Diego Historical Society, Junípero Serra Museum)
A Store at Campo in 1899 (San Diego Historical Society Quarterly, Vol. VI, No. 3, July 1960)

Kornbluh, Joyce L. (ed.)
Rebel Voices: An I.W.W. Anthology (Ann Arbor: University of Michigan Press, 1964)

Kreizinger, Marcella C.
History of the Portuguese in San Diego Typescript (Collection: San Diego Historical Society, Junípero Serra Museum)

Kroeber, A. L.
Handbook of the Indians of California (Berkeley: California Book Company, Ltd., 1953)

Kunz, George F.
The Gem Mining of California Bulletin 37 (Sacramento: California State Mining Bureau, 1905)

Layne, J. Gregg
The Lincoln-Roosevelt League: Its Origin and Accomplishments (Historical Society of Southern California Quarterly, Vol. XXV, No. 3, Sept. 1943)

Little Landers Colony, San Ysidro
Scrapbook (Collection: Wilmer Shields, San Diego)

Los Angeles County Museum
Irving Gill: Los Angeles County Museum and La Jolla Art Center (Los Angeles: 1958)

McCormick, W. G.
Memoirs of Conductor W. G. McCormick Concerning the Mexican Insur-

rection of 1911 Typescript, 1948 (Collection: San Diego & Arizona Eastern Railway Company)

McCoy, Esther
Five California Architects (New York: Reinhold Publishing Corporation, 1960)

McGrew, Clarence Alan
San Diego and San Diego County (Chicago and New York: The American Historical Society, 2 vols., 1922)

McWilliams, Carey
Southern California Country (New York: Duell, Sloan and Pearce, 1946)

Maas, John
The Gingerbread Age (New York: Bramhall House, 1957)

Manasse, Simon
Interview, San Diego, 1957 (Collection: San Diego Historical Society, Junípero Serra Museum)

Marquis, Albert Nelson (ed.)
Who's Who in America: 1922-1923 (Chicago: A. N. Marquis & Co., 1923)

Marston, George White
Biographical File and Correspondence (Collection: San Diego Historical Society, Junípero Serra Museum)

Marston, Mary Gilman
George White Marston: A Family Chronicle (Los Angeles: Ward Ritchie Press, 2 vols., 1956)

Martinez, Pablo
A History of Lower California (Mexico City: 1960)

Meadows, Don
Baja California, 1553-1950 (Los Angeles: The Plantin Press, 1951)

Meixner, G. Donald
Historical Development of Water Utilization Typescript; Study prepared for the California State Water Resources Board, 1952 (Collection: San Diego Historical Society, Junípero Serra Museum)

Melendy, H. Brett
California's Cross-filing Nightmare: The 1918 Gubernatorial Election (Pacific Historical Review, Vol. 33, No. 3, Aug. 1964)

Merrill, Frederick J. H.
Geology and Mineral Resources: Part V, The Counties of San Diego, Imperial 14th Report (San Francisco: California State Mining Bureau, 1914)

Middlebrook, R. P.

The Chinese at Sorrento (San Diego Historical Society Quarterly, Vol. X, No. 1, Jan. 1964)

Millikan, Frank M.
Commercial Banking in San Diego County Thesis, 1960 (San Diego State College)

Miller, William C.
When the Rainmaker Came to San Diego (Westways, Vol. 57, No. 3, March 1965)

Mills, James
Comes the Revolution! San Diego, 1912 (San Diego Magazine, Vol. 11, No. 12, Oct. 1959 and Vol. 12, No. 1, Nov. 1959)
Historical Landmarks of San Diego County (San Diego Historical Society Quarterly, Vol. V, No. 1, Jan. 1959)

Mills, John S.
The Banner County of the Golden State (San Diego Board of Supervisors, 1907)
San Diego, California: A Country Rich in Resources with Superior Attractions for People Who Want the Best (San Diego Chamber of Commerce, 1915)

Moore, Bertram B.
History of San Diego Roads and Stages Typescript (Collection: San Diego Historical Society, Junípero Serra Museum)
The Santa Ana Winds (San Diego Historical Society Quarterly, Vol. IV, No. 1, Jan. 1958)

Moore, Floyd Roscoe
San Diego Airport Development Thesis, 1960 (San Diego State College)

Morgan, H. Wayne
William McKinley and His America (Syracuse: Syracuse University Press, 1963)

Mowry, George Edwin
The California Progressives (Berkeley and Los Angeles: University of California Press, 1951)

Mullineaux, Mrs. Myrtle
Interview, San Diego, 1965 (Collection: Union-Tribune Publishing Co., San Diego)

Mury, Maude (ed.)
The Tuna Industry of San Diego (San Diego Works Progress Administration, 1936)

Nadeau, Remi A.
The Water Seekers (Garden City:

Doubleday & Co., 1950)
Los Angeles from Mission to Modern City (New York: Longmans, Green and Company, 1960)

Nelson, Herbert J.
The Port of San Diego Thesis, 1956 (San Diego State College)

Neuhaus, Eugen
San Diego Garden Fair: The Art of the Exposition (San Francisco: Paul Elder, 1916)

Newell, F. H.
The Salton Sea Annual Report of the Smithsonian Institution, 1907 (U. S. Reclamation Service)

Nolen, John
San Diego, a Comprehensive Plan for Its Improvement (Boston: G. H. Ellis Co., 1908)

Panama-California Exposition
Picture Album (San Diego: The Pictorial Publishing Co., 1915)

Parker, Carleton
The I.W.W. (Atlantic Monthly, CXX, 1917)

Parker, Horace
Anza-Borrego Desert Guide Book: Southern California's Last Frontier (Palm Desert: Desert Magazine Press, 1957)

Parsons, Samuel
The Art of Landscape Architecture (1915)
Memories (New York and London: G. P. Putnam's Sons, 1926)

Peavey, Newell Jacob
Interview, San Diego, 1960 (Collection: San Diego Historical Society, Junípero Serra Museum)

Peterson, J. Harold
The Coronado Story (Coronado: Coronado Federal Savings and Loan Association, 1954)

Porterfield, Lottie G.
Interview, San Diego, 1959 (Collection: San Diego Historical Society, Junípero Serra Museum)

Portuguese in San Diego
Miscellaneous File (Collection: San Diego Historical Society, Junípero Serra Museum)

Pourade, Richard F.
The History of San Diego: Vol. I, *The Explorers;* Vol. II, *Time of the Bells;* Vol. III, *The Silver Dons;* Vol. IV, *The Glory Years* Commissioned by James S. Copley (San Diego: The

Union-Tribune Publishing Co., 1960, 1961, 1963 and 1964, respectively)

Powers, Edward
War and the Weather in the Artificial Production of Rain (1871)

Randolph, Howard S. F.
La Jolla Year by Year (La Jolla: The La Jolla Library Association, 1955)

Raymenton, H. K.
San Diego's Expositions Typescript (Collection: San Diego Historical Society, Junípero Serra Museum)
History of the San Diego Museum Association (San Diego: Museum of Man, 1962)

Reading, James E.
The San Diego and Escondido Stage (*San Diego Historical Society Quarterly*, Vol. III, No. 3, July 1957)
Historical Background of Transit in San Diego Typescript, 1962 (Collection: San Diego Historical Society, Junípero Serra Museum)

Rhodes, Fred A.
Interview, San Diego, 1957 (Collection: San Diego Historical Society, Junípero Serra Museum)

Rider, A. F.
Rider's California, A Guidebook For Travelers (New York: The Macmillan Co., 1925)

Rockwood, Charles Robinson
Born of the Desert (*Calexico Chronicle*, 1909; reprinted in Tout's History of Imperial Valley)

Rolle, Andrew F.
California: A History (New York: Thomas Y. Crowell Co., 1963)

Roosevelt, Theodore
Imperial Valley Senate Executive Document No. 212, 59th Congress, 2nd Session, Jan. 12, 1907 (Washington: National Archives and Record Service)

Ruhlen, George
San Diego Barracks (*San Diego Historical Society Quarterly*, Vol. I, No. 2, April 1955)
Fort Rosecrans (*San Diego Historical Society Quarterly*, Vol. V, No. 4, Oct. 1959)
Interview, San Diego, 1961 (Collection: San Diego Historical Society, Junípero Serra Museum)
Early Military Forts and Camps in the San Diego Area Typescript, 1962 (Collection: San Diego Historical Society, Junípero Serra Museum)

Rush, Philip S.

History of the Californias (San Diego: P. S. Rush, 1958)

Ryan, Frederick L.
A History of the San Diego Labor Movement: Problems from 1887 to 1957 Report, 1959 (San Diego State College, Bureau of Business and Economic Research)

Sanborn, Kate
A Truthful Woman in Southern California (New York: D. Appleton and Co., 1902)

San Diego Board of Education
100 Years of Public Education in San Diego: 1854-1954 (San Diego Unified School District, 1954)

San Diego California Club
Pertinent Facts Concerning San Diego, California: City and County (San Diego County Board of Supervisors, 1923)

San Diego Chamber of Commerce
Minute Books: 1900-1920 (San Diego Public Library)
San Diego, California: Cool in Summer, Warm in Winter (San Diego Board of Supervisors, 1910)
San Diego, California (San Diego Board of Supervisors, 1913)
San Diego Survey and Exposition News (weekly journal, 1913)

San Diego-Eastern Railway Committee
Prospectus of the San Diego-Eastern Railroad (San Diego Chamber of Commerce, 1902)

San Diego Federal Writers' Project
San Diego, A California City (San Diego Historical Society, 1937)

San Diego Evening Tribune
General Files 1900-1920

San Diego Herald
U. S. Grant Hotel (Souvenir Edition, Oct. 13, 1910) General Files 1906-1920

San Diego Sun
General Files 1900-1920

San Diego Union
General Files 1900-1920

San Francisco Labor Council
San Diego Free Speech Controversy Report by Special Investigating Committee, 1912 (Collection: The Bancroft Library, Berkeley)

Sawday, Mrs. George
Interview, Witch Creek, 1957 (Col-

lection: San Diego Historical Society, Junípero Serra Museum)

Schmid, Dorothy Clark
Pioneering in Dulzura (San Diego: Robert R. Knapp, 1963)

Scripps College Bulletin
Ellen Browning Scripps: Woman of Vision (Clairemont: Scripps College, 1959)

Scripps, E. W.
Damned Old Crank: a Self-Portrait of E. W. Scripps from His Unpublished Writings (New York: Harper & Brothers Publishers, 1951)

Scripps Family
Biographical Files (Collection: San Diego Historical Society, Junípero Serra Museum)

Sessions, Kate
Scrapbook (Collection: San Diego Historical Society, Junípero Serra Museum)

Smythe, William E.
The Conquest of Arid America (New York: The Macmillan Company, 1905)
History of San Diego (San Diego: The History Company, 1908)

Soares, Celestino
California and the Portuguese (Lisbon: S.P.N. Books, 1939)

Spreckels Family
Scrapbook (Collection: San Diego Historical Society, Junípero Serra Museum)

Steere, Collis H.
Imperial and Coachella Valleys: An Illustrated Guide (Stanford: Stanford University Press, 1952)

Steffens, Lincoln
Shame of Cities (New York: McClure, Phillips & Co., 1904)

Stevens, Edward D.
They Used to Call It 'Wireless' (*San Diego Historical Society Quarterly*, Vol. IX, No. 1, Jan. 1963)

Stewart, Don
Memoirs of Don Stewart (San Diego, 1965)

Stone, Adolf (ed.)
California, Information Almanac (Lakewood: California Almanac Co., 1963)

Stuart, Gordon
When the Sands of the Desert Grew Gold (Pacific Palisades: Private printing, ca. 1961)

Title Topics, Title Insurance & Trust Co., San Diego
San Diego's Beach Communities (Jul-Aug 1950); *Point Loma* (Jul-Aug 1951); *Buried Treasure, San Diego County's Mining Industry* (Nov-Dec 1951); *Aviation in San Diego: 1883-1952* (Mar-Apr 1952); *Balboa Park* (May-Jun 1954); *Freeways* (Jul-Aug 1959)

Todd, Frank Morton
The Story of the Exposition: Official History of the San Francisco International Exposition (New York: G. P. Putnam's Sons; 5 vols., 1921)

Tout, Otis B.
The First Thirty Years in Imperial Valley, California: 1901-1931 San Diego: Arts & Crafts Press, 1931)

Transit Topics
Transportation Progress (Vol. 6, No. 7, Apr-May 1949)

Volger, William H.
Silk, Iron, and Oil in San Diego County: 1900-1910 Thesis, 1953 (San Diego State College)

Walker, Franklin
A Literary History of Southern California (Berkeley and Los Angeles: University of California Press, 1950)

Wangenheim, Julius
An Autobiography (California Historical Society Quarterly, Vol. XXXV, No. 2, June 1956 through Vol. XXXVI, No. 2, June 1957)

Waterman, Waldo Dean
Interview, San Diego, 1958 (Collection: San Diego Historical Society, Junípero Serra Museum)

Waters, Frank
The Colorado (New York and Toronto: Rinehart & Company, 1946)

Weber, F. Harold, Jr.
Mines and Mineral Resources of San Diego County, California County Report III (Sacramento: California Division of Mines and Geology, 1964)

Weber, Francis J.
Documents of California Catholic History (Los Angeles: Dawson's Book Shop, 1965)

Wegeforth, Harry Milton and Morgan, Neil
It Began With a Roar: Story of the San Diego Zoo (San Diego: Pioneer Printers, 1953)

Weinstock, Harris
Disturbances in the City of San Diego and the County of San Diego, California Report to His Excellency Hiram W. Johnson, Governor of California (Sacramento: 1912)

Weintraub, Hyman
The I.W.W. in California: 1905-1931 Thesis, 1947 (University of California, Los Angeles)

Wenzel, Paul and Krakow, Maurice
A Book of Architecture and Drawings of Goodhue (New York: Architectural Book Publishing Co.)

Whitaker, Charles Harris (ed.)
Bertram Grosvenor Goodhue: Architect and Master of Many Arts (New York: American Institute of Architects, 1925)

Whitaker, Thomas W. (ed.)
Torrey Pines State Reserve (La Jolla: The Torrey Pines Association, 1964)

Willis, Purl
Interview, La Cresta, 1957 (Collection: San Diego Historical Society, Junípero Serra Museum)

Women's Regional Planning Club
Historical Series for Broadcast (San Diego: KGB Radio Station, 1961-1963)

Wood, H. P.
Homeland: The Port of San Diego (San Diego Chamber of Commerce, 1902)

Woodbury, David O.
The Colorado Conquest (New York: Dodd, Mead & Company, 1941)

Wright, Harold Bell
The Winning of Barbara Worth (Chicago: The Book Supply Company, 1911)

Wright, Lauren A.
Mineral Commodities of California Bulletin 176 (San Francisco: California State Division of Mines, 1957)

Wueste, Rudolph
The Last Pack Train (San Diego Historical Society Quarterly, Vol, I, No. 3, July 1955)

ART SOURCES AND CREDITS

Acknowledgement for providing pictorial materials is made to the following institutions and individual collections, which are indicated in the Index to Illustrations by key initials:

American Institute of Architects, Washington, D.C. (AIA); The Bancroft Library, University of California, Berkeley (B); Grolier Society, New York (G); Henry E. Huntington Library and Art Museum, San Marino (H); Image, Art Division of Frye & Smith, Ltd., San Diego (I); Imperial Irrigation District, El Centro (IID); Leo Hetzel Historic File, Imperial County Board of Trade, El Centro (LH); The Metropolitan Museum of Art, George A. Hearn Fund, 1914, New York (M); Naval Academy Museum, Annapolis (NA); National Cyclopedia of American Biography, New York (NC); Paul Hatfield Collection, Pearblossom (PH); San Diego Historical Society, Junipero Serra Museum, San Diego (SDHS); Southwest Museum, Los Angeles (SM); Title Insurance & Trust Company, San Diego (T); U.S. Geological Survey, Department of Agriculture, San Diego (USGS); Wilmer Shields Collection, San Diego (WS).

INDEX TO ILLUSTRATIONS

INDEX

This fifth volume of the History of San Diego was designed by Jim Millard, Art Director for Image, the Art Division of Frye & Smith, Ltd. Lithography by Frye & Smith, Ltd., on Hamilton Louvain 80 pound text. Typography by Linotron, the Typesetting Division of Frye & Smith, Ltd., using Mergenthaler's Linofilm system. The type face used in this book is Century Schoolbook. Binding is by Cardoza Bookbinding Co.